Contents

THE RULES AND SYLLABUSES

Rules for the Sergeants' and Inspectors' Exams

ON STUDYING

CONTENTS

About the authors

Born in Glasgow in 1945, Tom Barron joined the army, aged 15, as a boy soldier. He subsequently saw service in Germany, Cyprus (United Nations), Singapore, Malaya and in Borneo where he saw active service with the Royal Corps Of Transport (Air Despatch).

He joined the Police Service in 1969 where he served for 27 years in many operational and training roles. Two years were spent teaching crammer courses for officials taking the sergeants' and inspectors' exams, followed by prosecuting in magistrates' courts in the West Country. He was also in charge of The Avon & Somerset Interview Technique training unit.

Tom has had a number of articles published, most notably in the *Daily Telegraph,* and an exclusive in the *Daily Mail.* He enjoys lecturing in colleges and universities on his subject, The Anatomy of a Lie. He is the author of The Special Constable's Manual.

Julianna Mitchell LLB(Hons), BCL (Oxon) is a barrister practising from chambers in The Temple, London and a contributing author of *Halsbury's Laws of England.*

To Isobel

The rules and syllabuses

Rules for the Sergeants' and Inspectors' Exams

1. Admission to the Sergeants' exam is currently restricted to regular constables who, by 30th November of the calendar year in which they take the exam, will have completed not less than 2 years service; been confirmed in their appointment, and have not previously obtained a pass in a Sergeants' promotion exam. Admission to the Inspectors' exam is currently restricted to Sergeants who, on 1st July of the calendar year in which they take their exam, will have attained the substantive rank and have not previously obtained a pass in an Inspectors' promotion exam.

2. Part I consists of a single multiple choice paper of 3 hours duration, which is normally held in March for Sergeants and September for Inspectors. The exam will comprise 150 questions.

3. There is now a set pass mark for each exam. This is 55% for the Sergeants' exam and 65% for the Inspectors'.

Notes

There have been extensive changes to both the rules and the syllabus for the 2005 exams. All candidates are advised therefore to obtain a copy of the official rules booklet, or visit www.lg-employers.gov.uk/ skills/ospre/rules.html to familiarise themselves with the details. Note in particular that whilst the exams are based on material contained in the 2005 Blackstone's Police Manuals (and it is therefore recommended that candidates make reference to those books during their studies), there are a number of subjects within those Manuals which have now been removed from the exam syllabus and which will not therefore appear on the exams. Take care to revise the correct material!

Sergeants' and Inspectors' syllabus

[a summary]

Part 1 – General Police Duties
Police
Police Powers
Powers of Entry, Search and Seizure
Human Rights
Public Order and Terrorism
Harassment and Anti-Social Behaviour
Offences involving communications
Firearms
Weapons
Nuisance
Offences Relating to Premises
Licensed Premises
Disputes
Offences involving information and data
Equal Opportunities and Discrimination

Part 2 – Crime
State of Mind
Criminal Conduct
Incomplete Offences
Defences
Homicide
Misuse of Drugs
Offences Against the Person
Miscellaneous Offences Against the Person
Sexual Offences
Offences Against Children etc
Theft
Deception and Fraud

Criminal Damage
Offences Against the Administration of Justice and the Public Interest
Immigration Offences

Part 3 – Road Traffic
Definitions
Standards of Driving
Notice of Intended Prosecution
Accidents
Drink, Drugs and Driving
Insurance
Safety Measures
Construction and Use Regulations
Driving Licensing
The Fixed Penalty System
Forgery and Falsification of Documents

Part 4 – Evidence and Procedure
Sources of Law
The Courts
Parties to Criminal Cases
Summonses and Warrants
Bail
Witnesses
Youth Justice
Evidence
Similar Fact Evidence
Exclusion of Evidence
Disclosure
Police Station Procedure
Identification
Interviews

On studying...

THE NEED TO KNOW PRINCIPLE

The need to know principle is summed up thus:

'If you don't need to know it, don't study it!'

This book is designed to help you pass the Sergeants' and Inspectors' exams at the first attempt.

It is a 'no nonsense - no frills' book aimed at people who want to get as much as possible from their time spent studying, with all the verbiage thrown overboard together with everything else that seems to cloud the issues with facts, leaving only the bare bones of what you **need to know** to pass the exam. The bare bones are laid out in manageable bite-size portions which you can digest with relative ease and regurgitate when necessary. Why read the whole of the Bible if you can achieve a pass mark with a good knowledge only of the 10 Commandments? There are no semantic somersaults or linguistic limbo dancing in this book – just what you **need to know.**

MEMORY IS REPETITION

I know a three-year-old who can speak Chinese. Surprised? You shouldn't be, he lives in China.

We are all born with a blank sheet [our brain where we keep our memory]. That sheet has things imprinted on it, language say, and we learn the most difficult things possible, with apparent ease - how come? By repetition. By hearing the same thing over and over again we memorise something as difficult as a language. Police Officers fail exams, not because they have misunderstood a section of legislation when they **read it,** but because they did not **learn it.** Reading and learning are two different things. Learning takes place when you can remember or write down what you have read. By constant repetition, information is memorised and when memorised it is learned. Why do you have to write down other people's telephone numbers but not your own? Repetition has caused you to memorise your number and therefore it is learned. Read this book over and over again until you reach a point whereby you know what is on the next page. When you reach that point

ON STUDYING...

you have learned it. The enormity of what you have to learn seems daunting. It actually begs the question 'How do you eat an elephant?'

Any elephant eater will tell you, one piece at a time. Learn 10 pages and have your partner test your knowledge. He or she needs no police knowledge in that the pages are set as questions and answers. Once you have satisfactorily mastered the first 10 pages, go on to the next. Remember, one piece at a time. Stick to basic facts, don't allow anything to cloud the issue with facts.

Do not stray from the concept of **KISS** - Keep It Simple **Stupid!**
And remember the elephant.

Tom Barron
Cannington
Somerset

Part 1 - General Police Duties

POLICE

Q What is the jurisdiction of a Police Officer?

A He has all the powers and privileges of a constable throughout England & Wales and the adjacent United Kingdom waters.

S. 30 POLICE ACT 1996

Q What is the jurisdiction of a Special Constable?

A He has all the powers and privileges of a constable:

[a] in his own force area, and where there is a coast, the adjacent UK waters;
[b] in forces contiguous [next to] his own force area, and
[c] in other forces where he is sent as part of a mutual aid scheme,

and in the case of The City of London Police

[a] in the City of London;
[b] the Metropolitan Police District, and
[c] in forces next to the Metropolitan Police District.

S. 30(2) POLICE ACT 1996

Q What is meant by Vicarious Liability of Chief Officer of Police?

A The Chief Officer of Police is legally responsible for the actions of his/her officers when acting in the course of their duties. He may have to pay any damages arising out of civil claims against such officers for any unlawful conduct, but not officers seconded to central services, e.g. National Crime Squad [where liability rests with the Home Office or relevant Director].

S. 88 POLICE ACT 1996

Q Can a Police Officer be a member of a Trade Union?

A **No.** However, where he was a member before joining the police, the chief officer of police may consent to him remaining a member. Any police officer may be a member of the Police Federation.

S. 64 POLICE ACT 1996

Q   What is meant by a Best Value Authority?

A   Best value authorities (which includes police authorities) are those which are under a duty to make arrangements to secure *continuous improvement* in the way in which their functions are exercised, having regard to a combination of *economy, efficiency* and *effectiveness.*

SS. 1, 3 LOCAL GOVERNMENT ACT 1999

Unsatisfactory Performance

The Police (Efficiency) Regulations 1999 apply as follows:

Apply to	*Do not apply to*
Constables	Cadets
Sergeants	Probationers
Inspectors	Chief Superintendent and above
Chief Inspectors	Civilian staff
Superintendents	

Q   What is the Purpose of the Regulations?

A   To deal with matters of poor performance.

Q   Who are the players?

A   [a]   The *member:* the officer subject to complaint.
[b]   *Reporting officer:* the line manager [police or civilian] or person with immediate supervisory responsibility for the member e.g. their Sergeant. Where the reporting officer is a civilian he shall liaise with a Police Officer.
[c]   *Countersigning officer:* Inspector, Chief Inspector or Superintendent.
[d]   *Representative:* fellow Police Officer or member of staff association.

Q   Unsatisfactory Performance – what happens first?

A   1.   Evidence of unsatisfactory work is:
[a]   noted in the workplace, or
[b]   arises from a complaint by a member of the public.

2.   In the event of a single or occasional act, advice may be given.

3.   If there is a pattern of poor performance, formal action may be required.

4.   The officer is given time and help to remedy the problem.

5.   [a] If performance is improved - NFA (No Further Action),
     [b] If performance is not improved it shall be recorded and formal procedures started.

The Formal Procedures
The 1st Interview - notice

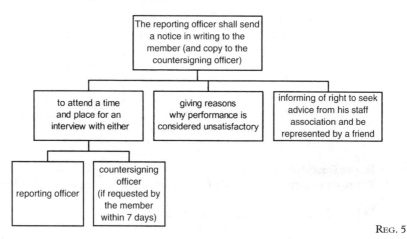

The reporting officer shall send a notice in writing to the member (and copy to the countersigning officer)

to attend a time and place for an interview with either

giving reasons why performance is considered unsatisfactory

informing of right to seek advice from his staff association and be represented by a friend

reporting officer

countersigning officer (if requested by the member within 7 days)

REG. 5

Q   What if the reporting officer is a civilian?

A   Where the member is a constable and his line manager is a civilian, a police officer with supervisory responsibility for the member must be identified, and should consult with the civilian.

Q   Reporting officer or countersigning officer - whose choice?

A   The member may, within seven days of receipt of the notice of first Interview, request in writing that the interview be conducted by the countersigning officer.

Q Who is the 'friend' and what is their function?

A An officer of any rank can take the role of representative or friend as long as they are not involved in the procedures. Their job is to advise and assist including speaking on the officer's behalf. They can call and question witnesses, produce witness statements, documentation or exhibits. They are on duty when attending meetings and may wear civilian clothes at a hearing.

The 1st Interview

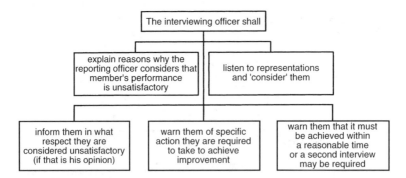

REG.6

Representations
Representations can be made by the member or by their friend or both.

Q What if they have a good explanation?

A Where appropriate, NFA may be agreed.

Q What is a reasonable time for improvement?

A Normally between three and six months.

Recommendations
The interviewing officer may make recommendations that the member seek assistance with health or welfare.

Record
Within seven days the interviewing officer shall make a record of the interview and send a copy to the member.

REG. 7.

Member's Response
Within seven days he/she may submit written comments or make no comment.

Duration
The record shall be expunged from the member's personal record after two years since the last action was taken.

Q What are the interviewing officer's responsibilities concerning copies of the interview?

A They must send copies of the interview and comments by the member to:
[a] the senior manager, and
[b] the personnel officer.

Q What if the interview was conducted by the reporting officer?

A A copy must be sent to the countersigning officer [generally a chief inspector or superintendent].

Q What if the interview was conducted by the countersigning officer?

A A copy must be sent to the reporting officer.

Q What is meant by [a] the senior manager and [b] the personnel officer?

[a] the supervisor of the countersigning officer (generally a Chief Inspector or Superintendent)

[b] the police officer or civilian responsible for personnel.

The Decision to hold a 2nd Interview
Where the Reporting Officer opines that the member who was warned has not made sufficient improvement by the end of a reasonable period they *may* refer the matter to the Countersigning Officer. The countersigning officer may, after consulting the personnel officer, order a 2nd interview.

REG. 8

POLICE

2nd Interview - notice

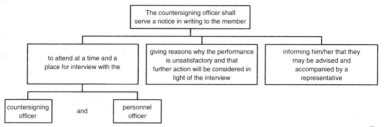

REG. 9

On whom must copy notices be served ?

- reporting officer
- personnel officer
- senior manager

The 2nd Interview

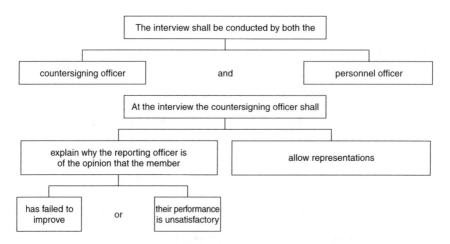

then...

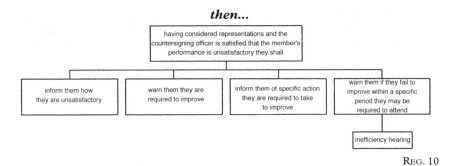

REG. 10

Note. Within 7 days of the 2nd interview a written record must be prepared.

REG. 11

Q   Who makes a copy of the record of interview?

A   It shall be made by the countersigning officer and the personnel officer.

Q   Who receives a copy?

A   The member and their representative together with a notice.

Q   What does the notice contain?

A   It confirms the warning and informs the member that they can [within seven days] submit written comments or indicate that they have no comments to make.

Q   Who else receives copies?

A   The countersigning officer shall send a copy of the record and written comments by the member to:
● the reporting officer
● personnel officer, and
● senior manager.

Assessment of Performance
Within 14 days of the specified period given for improvement [normally 3-6 months] the countersigning officer in consultation with the reporting officer shall assess the performance of the member and they shall inform the member in writing whether or not there has been a sufficient improvement in performance.   REG. 12

If the countersigning officer opines that there has been insufficient improvement the member must be informed that they may be required to attend an *inefficiency hearing* [not sooner than 21 or later than 56 days from notification]. The countersigning officer shall inform the senior manager who may direct that an inefficiency hearing be arranged.

The Inefficiency Hearing

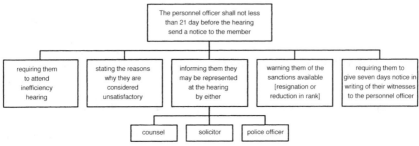

REG.13

Q   Who conducts the Hearing?

A   City of London Police   Commander + 2
                                  Superintendents

     Metropolitan Police   Commander + 2
                                  Superintendents

     Provincial Forces (or NCS) ACC + 2 Superintendents

The hearing must be in private unless the chairman and member agree to it being in public.

REG.14

Documents to be made available

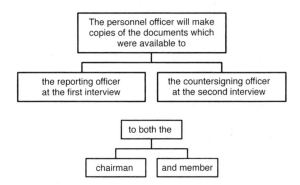

Postponement and Adjournment

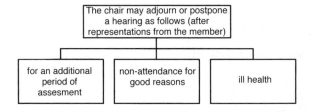

The Finding

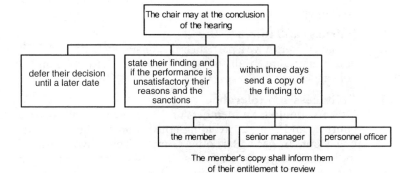

The Sanctions

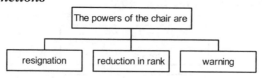

REG. 17

Resignation
This means one month after receipt of the decision or a specified later date. Where they refuse to resign they shall be dismissed.

Reduction in rank and Warning
This takes effect immediately, and they shall be issued a written warning that unless a sufficient improvement in their performance is made within a specified time they will face a first interview (i.e. the procedure will begin again).

Review
The member is entitled to request a Review of the finding or sanction, or both. The Review will be conducted by the member's Chief Officer (or Assistant Commissioner in the Metropolitan Police).

REG. 19

Misconduct and Discipline

The Code of Conduct

1. **Honesty and integrity**

   It is of paramount importance that the public has faith in the honesty and integrity of police officers. Officers should therefore be open and truthful in their dealings; avoid being improperly beholden to any person or institution, and discharge their duties with integrity.

2. **Fairness and impartiality**

   Police Officers have a particular responsibility to act with fairness and impartiality in all their dealings with the public and their colleagues.

3. **Politeness and tolerance**

   Officers should treat members of the public and colleagues with courtesy and respect, avoiding abusive or deriding attitudes or behaviour. In particular, officers must avoid: favouritism of an individual or group; all forms of harassment, victimisation or unreasonable discrimination; and overbearing conduct to a colleague, particularly to one junior in rank or service.

4. **Use of force and abuse of authority**

   Officers must never knowingly use more force than is reasonable, nor should they abuse their authority.

5. **Performance of duties**

   Officers should be conscientious and diligent in the performance of their duties. Officers should attend work promptly when rostered for duty. If absent through sickness or injury, they should avoid activities likely to retard their return to duty.

6. **Lawful orders**

   The police service is a disciplined body. Unless there is good and sufficient cause to do otherwise, officers must obey all lawful orders and abide by the provisions of Police Regulations. Officers should support their colleagues in the execution of their lawful duties, and oppose any improper behaviour, reporting it where appropriate.

7. **Confidentiality**

   Information which comes into the possession of the police should be treated as confidential. It should not be used for personal benefit and nor should it be divulged to other parties except in the proper course of police duty. Similarly, officers should respect, as confidential, information about force policy and operations unless authorised to disclose it in the course of their duties.

8. **Criminal offences**

   Officers must report any proceedings for a criminal offence taken against them. Conviction of a criminal offence may of itself result in further action being taken.

9. **Property**

   Officers must exercise reasonable care to prevent loss or damage to property (excluding their own property but including police property).

10. **Sobriety**

    Whilst on duty officers must be sober. Officers should not consume alcohol when on duty unless specifically authorised to do so or it becomes necessary for the proper discharge of police duty.

11. **Appearance**
Unless on duties which dictate otherwise, officers should always be well turned out, clean and tidy whilst on duty in uniform or in plain clothes.

12. **General conduct**
Whether on or off duty, police officers should not behave in a way which is likely to bring discredit upon the police service.

POLICE (CONDUCT) REGULATIONS 2004, SCH 1

Sobriety
The superintendent who has had too much to drink: Home Office guidance suggests that superintendents will be classed as being 'on duty' where they were formerly 'on call'. But for the purposes of Rule 10 they will not be on duty by reason only of their general 24-hour responsibility for their own area of command. The guidance further provides that an officer who is unexpectedly called out for duty should be able, at no risk of discredit, to say that he has had too much to drink.

Q To whom does the Code of Conduct apply?

A All police officers including ACPO rank officers, and special constables.

Q What happens when there has been an allegation of Misconduct?

A Where 'the appropriate authority' receives a complaint or allegation that the conduct of a police officer does not meet the appropriate standard, and it appears to the authority that the officer concerned ought to be suspended from his office as constable and membership of a force, the authority may suspend that officer provided the authority is satisfied

[a] that the effective investigation of the matter may be prejudiced without suspension, or
[b] that the public interest requires suspension.

POLICE (CONDUCT) REGS 2004 REG. 4

Q   What is the effect of suspension?

A   The officer concerned continues to be a 'member' of his force for the purposes of the Police Regulations 2004, but ceases to enjoy the powers and privileges of the office of constable. (And he will not be able to sit any promotion exams without express permission!)

Q   Who is the 'appropriate authority'?

A   Generally the officer's own chief officer (who may delegate this function to an officer of at least ACC/Commander rank). In the case of chief officers it is the police authority.

Q   What Sanctions can be imposed at Disciplinary Hearings?

A   [a]   Dismissal;
[b]   requirement to resign (as an alternative to dismissal);
[c]   reduction in rank;
[d]   fine;
[e]   in the case of special constables only, suspension from operational duties for up to 3 months;
[f]   reprimand;
[g]   caution.

REG. 31

Public Complaints

Q   What is a 'complaint'?

A   A complaint (for the purposes of Part of the Police Reform Act 2002) is any complaint about the conduct of a person serving with the police i.e. a sworn constable, an employee under the direction or control of a chief officer or a special constable. It will amount to a Part 2 complaint when it is made, in writing or otherwise, by any of the following:

[a]   a member of the public who claims to be the person in relation to whom the conduct took place; or

[b] a member of the public who claims to have been adversely affected by the conduct or to have witnessed the conduct (in such a way that they could be a competent witness capable of giving or producing admsssible evidence about the incident in criminal proceedings); or

[c] any person acting on behalf of any of the above (with their written consent).

Q   What are 'conduct matters'?

A   Any matter which is not and has not been the subject of a complaint but where there is an indication that a person serving with the police may have committed a criminal offence or behaved in a manner which would justify criminal proceedings. 'Recordable conduct matters' are those requiring to be recorded by the appropriate authority (under the relevant regulations).

Other Regulations
Restrictions on Private Lives
A member of a police force:
1. shall at all times abstain from any activity which is likely to interfere with the impartial discharge of his/her duties or which is likely to give rise to the impression amongst members of the public that it may so interfere, and in particular a member of a police force shall not take any active part in politics. [They may however be a school governor];
2. shall not reside at premises not approved by the chief officer of police;
3. shall not, without the previous consent of the chief officer of police, take in a lodger in a house or quarters with which they are provided by the police authority, or sub-let any part of the house or quarters;
4. shall not, unless they have given written notice to the chief officer of police, take in a lodger in a house in which they reside and in respect of which they receive rent allowance, or sub-let any part of such a house; and
5. shall not wilfully refuse or neglect to discharge lawful debts.

POLICE REGS 2004, SCH 1

Business Interests

If [a] a police officer, or [b] a relative,

proposes to have, or has, a 'business interest', the officer shall give written notice to the chief officer of police, [unless they did so when appointed]. The chief officer of police shall determine whether the interest is compatible with the officer remaining a police officer and shall notify them in writing. The officer has a right of appeal to the Police Authority against any finding of incompatibility.

REG. 7

A 'business interest' is where a police officer or relative:

1. holds any office or employment for hire or carries on any business;
2. a shop [or like business] is kept or carried on by the officer's spouse (not being separated) in the police area, or by a relative living with them; or
3. the officer, their spouse (not being separated) or relative living with them has a pecuniary interest in any licence or permit granted in relation to:
    a) liquor licensing
    b) refreshment houses
    c) betting or gaming
    d) regulating places of entertainment

'Relative' includes spouse, parent, son, daughter, brother or sister.

POLICE

Offences

Q   What is the offence concerning Constables on Licensed Premises?

A

If the holder of a Justices licence		
knowingly suffers a constable to be on the premises whilst on duty otherwise than in the execution of his duty	supplies liquor or refreshments to a constable without a senior officer's authority	bribes or attempts to bribe a constable
	he commits an offence	

S. 178 LICENSING ACT 1964

The meaning of 'knowingly suffering'
The landlord's knowledge relates to him both [1] knowing they are a constable and [2] knowing that they are on duty.

Who is guilty? (Beware of aiding and abetting!)
Where a constable and sergeant visit licensed premises and accept a cup of coffee from the licensee, the PC commits no offence because they have a senior officer's authority [the Sergeant]. The Sergeant however commits the offence because they have no such authority!

Q   What is the offence of Impersonating a Police Officer?

A

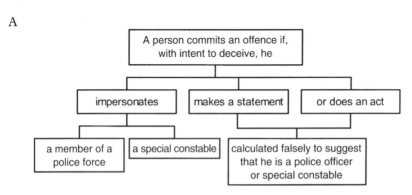

A person commits an offence if, with intent to deceive, he		
impersonates	makes a statement	or does an act
a member of a police force / a special constable	calculated falsely to suggest that he is a police officer or special constable	

S. 90(1) POLICE ACT 1996

Q What is the offence of Wearing or Possessing Uniform?

A

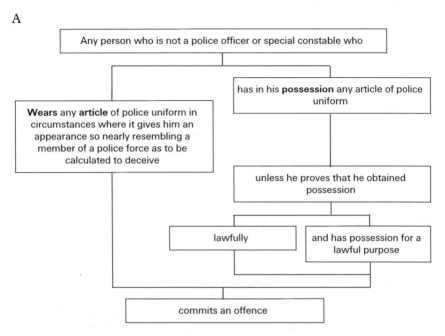

Any person who is not a police officer or special constable who

has in his **possession** any article of police uniform

Wears any **article** of police uniform in circumstances where it gives him an appearance so nearly resembling a member of a police force as to be calculated to deceive

unless he proves that he obtained possession

lawfully

and has possession for a lawful purpose

commits an offence

S. 90 Police Act 1996

Q What is an 'article'?

A An article of police uniforms means:

- uniform
- a distinctive badge or mark, or
- documents of identification.

Q What is the offence of Impersonating a Designated/ Accredited Person?

A Any person who, with intent to deceive,

[a] impersonates a designated or accredited person,
[b] makes any statement or does any act calculated falsely to suggest he is such a person, or
[c] makes any statement or does any act calculated falsely to suggest that he has powers as a designated or accredited person that exceed the powers he actually has

is guilty of an offence.

S. 46(3) POLICE REFORM ACT 2002

Q What is the offence of Causing Disaffection?

A It is an offence to:

[a] cause [or attempt], or do an act calculated to cause disaffection amongst the members of any police force, or
[b] induce [or attempt] or do any act calculated to induce any member of a police force to withhold their services.

S. 91 POLICE ACT 1996

Q What is the offence of Misconduct in a Public Office?

A It is an offence at common law for the holder of a public office to do anything that amounts to a malfeasance or a culpable misfeasance *(R v Wyatt (1705))*. **Mal**feasance requires action with a wrongful motive or intention (bad faith), whilst a wilful (deliberate) neglect of duty would be a culpable **mis**feasance.

Arrest. Arrestable offence.

Purpose. Essentially to deal with cases of abuse of public power in bad faith (rather than, for example, the misbehaviour of public officials whilst 'off-duty').

POLICE POWERS

Q **What is the primary purpose of stop and search powers?**

A To enable police officers to allay or confirm any suspicions about individuals without exercising their powers of arrest.

Q **What principles govern the use of stop and search?**

A Powers to stop and search must be used fairly, responsibly, with respect for people being searched and without unlawful discrimination. The Race Relations (Amendment) Act 2000 makes it unlawful for police officers to discriminate on the grounds of race, colour, ethnic origin, nationality or national origins when using their powers. The intrusion on the liberty of the person stopped or searched must be brief and detention for the purposes of a search must take place at or near the location of the stop.

CODE A PARA 1.1-1.2

Q **Where there is no power to search, may an officer conduct a search if the person consents to it?**

A No. This should not be done, notwithstanding the person's agreement to it. Para 1.5 Code A states that an officer must not search a person, even with his/her consent, where no power to search is applicable. The only exception, where an officer does not require a specific power, applies to searches of persons entering sports grounds or other premises carried out with their consent given as a condition of entry.

Q **What are your powers to stop and search under S. 1 PACE 1984?**

A

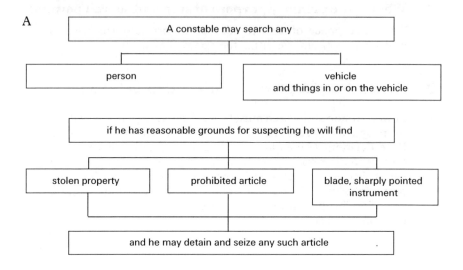

A constable may search any

| person | vehicle and things in or on the vehicle |

if he has reasonable grounds for suspecting he will find

| stolen property | prohibited article | blade, sharply pointed instrument |

and he may detain and seize any such article .

Q   What is meant by a 'prohibited article'?

A

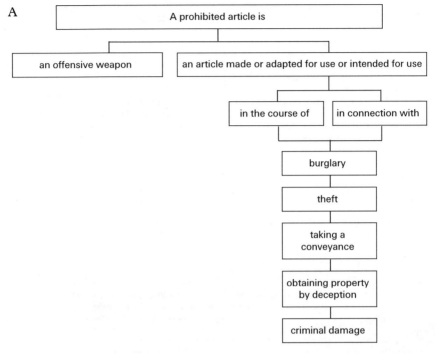

A prohibited article is

an offensive weapon

an article made or adapted for use or intended for use

in the course of

in connection with

burglary

theft

taking a conveyance

obtaining property by deception

criminal damage

S. 1(7) PACE ACT 1984

Q   What is meant by an 'offensive weapon'?

A   Offensive weapon means any article:

[a]   made or adapted for use for causing injury to any person, or
[b]   intended for such use by the person having it with him or another.

S. 1(9) PACE ACT 1984

POLICE POWERS

Q Where can the powers to Stop and Search be exercised?

A

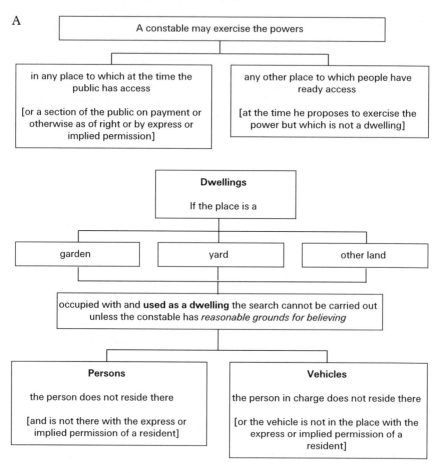

A constable may exercise the powers

in any place to which at the time the public has access

[or a section of the public on payment or otherwise as of right or by express or implied permission]

any other place to which people have ready access

[at the time he proposes to exercise the power but which is not a dwelling]

Dwellings

If the place is a

garden

yard

other land

occupied with and **used as a dwelling** the search cannot be carried out unless the constable has *reasonable grounds for believing*

Persons

the person does not reside there

[and is not there with the express or implied permission of a resident]

Vehicles

the person in charge does not reside there

[or the vehicle is not in the place with the express or implied permission of a resident]

S. 1(4) PACE Act 1984

Q   What must be done before a search is carried out?

A

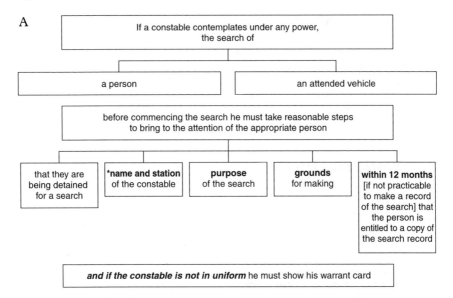

If a constable contemplates under any power,
the search of

a person

an attended vehicle

before commencing the search he must take reasonable steps
to bring to the attention of the appropriate person

| that they are being detained for a search | *name and station of the constable | purpose of the search | grounds for making | within 12 months [if not practicable to make a record of the search] that the person is entitled to a copy of the search record |

and if the constable is not in uniform he must show his warrant card

*Note. In terrorism cases the requirement to provide his/her name is removed: Code A para 3.8

S. 2/3 PACE ACT 1984

Q   What is meant by the 'Appropriate Person'?

A   [a]   Where a person is searched, that person.
     [b]   Where a vehicle is searched [or anything in or on it] the person in
            charge of the vehicle.

S. 2(5) PACE ACT 1984

Q   What if the Person does not appear to understand?

A   Under para 3.11 Code A if the person to be searched, or in charge of a
     vehicle to be searched, does not appear to understand what is being
     said, or there is any doubt about the person's ability to understand
     English, the officer must take reasonable steps to bring information
     regarding the person's rights and any relevant code provisions to his/
     her attention. If the person is deaf or cannot understand English and is
     accompanied by someone, then the officer must try to establish
     whether that person can interpret or otherwise help the officer to give
     the required information.

Q What should be left on a Searched Unattended Vehicle?

A   A notice stating:

[a]   the vehicle has been searched;
[b]   the police station to which the officer is attached [not his name];
[c]   an application for compensation for damage to the vehicle which can be made at [b], and
[d]   the owner and person in charge of the vehicle are entitled to a copy of the search record for up to 12 months.

S. 2(6) PACE ACT 1984

Q Where should the Notice be left?

A   Inside the vehicle (unless it is not reasonably practicable to do so without damaging the vehicle).

S. 2(7) PACE ACT 1984

Q What does 'Vehicle' include?

A   Vessels, aircraft and hovercraft.

S. 2(10) PACE ACT 1984

Q What clothing can be removed *in public* for the purpose of a Person Check?

A   Outer coat, jacket and gloves. (This restriction does not apply to searches elsewhere.) The Terrorism Act 2000 also allows for removal of footwear and headgear.

S. 2(9) PACE ACT 1984

Q How long can a person be detained for the purposes of a search?

A   Such time as is reasonable to carry out the search at the scene or nearby.

S. 2(8) PACE ACT 1984

Q   What shall a search record contain?

A

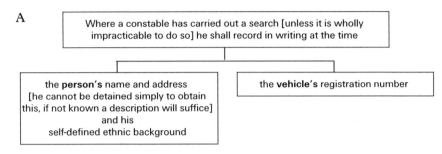

Where a constable has carried out a search [unless it is wholly impracticable to do so] he shall record in writing at the time

the **person's** name and address [he cannot be detained simply to obtain this, if not known a description will suffice] and his self-defined ethnic background

the **vehicle's** registration number

and

[a]   the object of the search;
[b]   the grounds for making it;
[c]   the date and time it was made;
[d]   the place it was made;
[e]   what was found, if anything;
[f]   any injury or damage caused; and
[g]   the identity of the constable

S. 3 PACE Act 1984

Q   When might it be 'wholly impracticable' to make a search record at the time?

A   In circumstances where there was realistically no real opportunity for the officer to make the record eg. in situations of public disorder or where his presence was urgently required elsewhere. In such cases the officer must make the search record as soon as practicable after the search has been completed.

S. 3(2) PACE Act 1984 & Code A para 4.1

Q   What record has to be kept when searching people entering Football Grounds?

A   None. Records are required to be made only when searches are carried out in the exercise of any power to which the Codes apply. Nothing in the Codes affects the routine searching of persons entering sports grounds or other premises where their consent is a condition of entry.

Q   What is a Road Check?

A

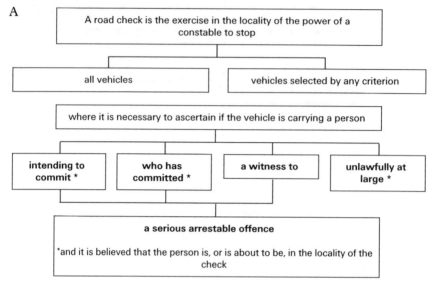

A road check is the exercise in the locality of the power of a constable to stop

all vehicles

vehicles selected by any criterion

where it is necessary to ascertain if the vehicle is carrying a person

intending to commit *

who has committed *

a witness to

unlawfully at large *

a serious arrestable offence

*and it is believed that the person is, or is about to be, in the locality of the check

S. 4 PACE Act 1984

Q   Give an example of vehicles selected by any criterion

A   Stopping all yellow Escorts carrying three youths ... all blue VWs ... all white vans etc.

Q   Who may authorise a road check?

A   A **superintendent** (or above), in writing. Or an officer of **any rank in the case of urgency**, in which case he must, as soon as possible, make a written record of the time at which the authorisation is given and cause a superintendent (or above) to be informed.

S. 4(5)-(7) PACE Act 1984

Q **Can a superintendent discontinue the road check when reported to him?**

A Yes, he may
[a] authorise it to continue, in writing, or
[b] discontinue the check and record in writing:

[i] the fact that it took place, and
[ii] its purpose.

Q **What are the time limits on non-urgent road checks?**

A **7 days,** which can be renewed (in writing) if it appears to the superintendent that it ought to continue. The check may be:

[a] continuous, or be
[b] conducted at specified times.

S. 4(11) PACE ACT 1984

Q **What shall the written authorisation of a road check state?**

A [a] The name of the authorising officer;
[b] the purpose of the road check; and
[c] the locality in which the vehicles are stopped.

S. 4(13) PACE ACT 1984

Q **What entitlement have persons who are stopped at road checks?**

A A person in charge of a vehicle stopped at a road check shall be entitled to a written statement of the purpose of the check if he applies for it not later than **12 months** from the date of being stopped.

S. 4(15) PACE ACT 1984

Q **What is not a road check?**

A Stopping vehicles for road traffic offences, excise offences, or the stopping of vehicles for any purpose other than those mentioned in Section 4.

Q   What stop powers are there under the Criminal Justice & Public Order Act 1994?

A

> Where an **inspector (or above)** reasonably believes [a] incidents involving **serious violence** may take place in a locality in his area and it is expedient to prevent their occurrence, or [b] that persons are carrying dangerous instruments or offensive weapons in any locality in his area without good reason, he may give authorisation in writing to

stop	search

persons	vehicles, drivers and passengers

for

offensive weapons	dangerous instruments

S. 60 CJ & PO Act 1994

Q   How long does the authorisation last?

A   For no longer than appears reasonably necessary to prevent, or seek to prevent incidents of serious violence, or to deal with the problem of carrying weapons/instruments and in any event for no longer than 24 hours.

Q   Can this period be extended?

A   Yes, by a superintendent (or above) if

[a]   violence or the carrying of instruments/weapons has occurred, or is suspected to have occurred, and
[b]   the continued use of the powers is considered necessary to prevent or deal with further such activity.

The extension can be for a further 24 hours, and must be in writing.

Q **Does the officer stopping and searching need reasonable suspicion to act?**

A No. The authorisation to search is enough. The officer must be in uniform.

Q **What are 'dangerous instruments'?**

A Bladed or sharply pointed instruments.

Q **Who is entitled to a statement?**

A The driver of any vehicle stopped under S. 60 is entitled to demand a written statement that the vehicle was stopped (not of 'the purpose of the check' – compare S. 4(15) PACE re road checks) provided s/he applies for one within 12 months of the day on which the vehicle was stopped. Additionally any person searched is entitled to a statement stating that s/he was searched if they apply within 12 months.

Q **What are the powers to require removal of disguises?**

A Where any S. 60 authorisation is in force in any locality, or if an inspector or above reasonably believes (a) that activities may take place in any locality in his area that are likely to involve the commission of offences, and (b) that it is expedient in order to control or prevent the activities, he may authorise any constable in uniform:

[i]   to require any person to remove any item which the constable reasonably believes is being worn to conceal his identity;

[ii] to seize any such item.   S. 60AA CJ & PO ACT 1994

Q **For how long can the authorisation last?**

A For no longer than appears reasonably necessary to prevent, or seek to prevent the commission of offences and in any event for no longer than 24 hours. If an inspector gives an authorisation s/he must inform a superintendent or above as soon as reasonably practicable, and this officer may direct an extension of the authorisation for a further 24 hours if crimes have been committed or suspected, and the continued use of the power is considered necessary to prevent further such activity.

Q **What is the offence of failing to comply with a requirement to remove items?**

A   It is an arrestable offence for a person to fail to remove an item worn by him when required to do so by a constable exercising his S. 60 powers.

S. 60AA CJ & PO Act 1994

Q **What is the power to set up a cordon under the Terrorism Act 2000?**

A   A superintendent or above may authorise the setting up of a cordon if it is considered expedient to do so for the purpose of a terrorist investigation. In cases of urgency, an officer below that rank may make the designation, but he/she must make a written record of the time at which it was made and ensure that a superintendent or above is informed as soon as reasonably practicable.

S. 33/34 Terrorism Act 2000

Q **What directions may be given when a cordon is in place?**

A   A constable in uniform (including a PCSO) may

[a]   order a person in a cordoned area to leave it immediately, or
[b]   order a person immediately to leave premises in or adjacent to a cordoned area, or
[c]   order a driver or person in charge of a vehicle in a cordoned area to immediately move it, or
[d]   arrange for the removal of a vehicle from a cordoned area, or
[e]   arrange for the movement of a vehicle within a cordoned area, or
[f]   prohibit or restrict access to a cordoned area by pedestrians/ vehicles.

S. 36 Terrorism Act 2000

Q **What is the power of arrest for an arrestable offence?**

A   **Any person** may arrest without warrant

[a]   anyone **who is in the act** of committing an arrestable offence;
[b]   anyone whom he has reasonable grounds for suspecting **to be committing** an arrestable offence.

Where an arrestable offence **has been committed** any person may arrest without warrant:

[a] anyone **who is guilty** of the offence;
[b] anyone who he has reasonable grounds **for suspecting to be guilty** of it.

A constable may arrest without warrant:

[a] where he has reasonable grounds for **suspecting** that an arrestable offence has been committed, any person whom he has reasonable grounds **for suspecting** to be guilty of the offence; and
[b] anyone who is **about to commit** an arrestable offence; and
[c] anyone who he has reasonable grounds **for suspecting to be about to commit** an arrestable offence.

S. 24 PACE Act 1984

Q What information must be given on arrest?

A [a] That the person is under arrest and
[b] the grounds for arrest

However, the above does not apply if is impracticable to inform him by reason of his having escaped arrest before the information could be given.

S. 28 PACE Act 1984

Q What did *Christie v Leachinsky (1947)* decide?

A The reason given for the arrest must be the **real reason** in the officer's mind at the time, and they must clearly indicate the reason for arrest at the time of the arrest.

Q What does Article 5(2) of the European Convention on Human Rights add?

A That everyone who is arrested shall be informed promptly, *in a language which he understands*, of the reasons for his arrest and of any charge against him.

POLICE POWERS

Q What is an arrestable offence?

A

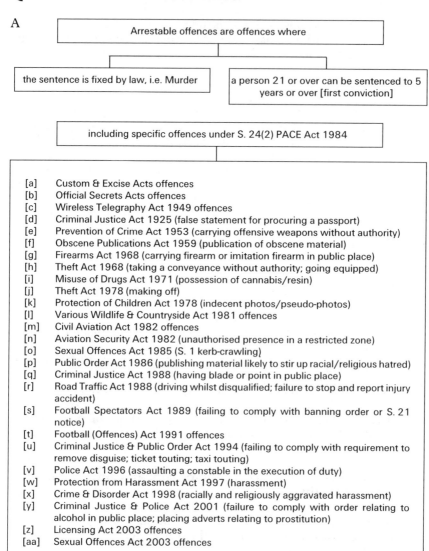

Arrestable offences are offences where

the sentence is fixed by law, i.e. Murder

a person 21 or over can be sentenced to 5 years or over [first conviction]

including specific offences under S. 24(2) PACE Act 1984

[a] Custom & Excise Acts offences
[b] Official Secrets Acts offences
[c] Wireless Telegraphy Act 1949 offences
[d] Criminal Justice Act 1925 (false statement for procuring a passport)
[e] Prevention of Crime Act 1953 (carrying offensive weapons without authority)
[f] Obscene Publications Act 1959 (publication of obscene material)
[g] Firearms Act 1968 (carrying firearm or imitation firearm in public place)
[h] Theft Act 1968 (taking a conveyance without authority; going equipped)
[i] Misuse of Drugs Act 1971 (possession of cannabis/resin)
[j] Theft Act 1978 (making off)
[k] Protection of Children Act 1978 (indecent photos/pseudo-photos)
[l] Various Wildlife & Countryside Act 1981 offences
[m] Civil Aviation Act 1982 offences
[n] Aviation Security Act 1982 (unauthorised presence in a restricted zone)
[o] Sexual Offences Act 1985 (S. 1 kerb-crawling)
[p] Public Order Act 1986 (publishing material likely to stir up racial/religious hatred)
[q] Criminal Justice Act 1988 (having blade or point in public place)
[r] Road Traffic Act 1988 (driving whilst disqualified; failure to stop and report injury accident)
[s] Football Spectators Act 1989 (failing to comply with banning order or S. 21 notice)
[t] Football (Offences) Act 1991 offences
[u] Criminal Justice & Public Order Act 1994 (failing to comply with requirement to remove disguise; ticket touting; taxi touting)
[v] Police Act 1996 (assaulting a constable in the execution of duty)
[w] Protection from Harassment Act 1997 (harassment)
[x] Crime & Disorder Act 1998 (racially and religiously aggravated harassment)
[y] Criminal Justice & Police Act 2001 (failure to comply with order relating to alcohol in public place; placing adverts relating to prostitution)
[z] Licensing Act 2003 offences
[aa] Sexual Offences Act 2003 offences

Q When does an Arrestable Offence become a Serious Arrestable Offence?

A Any arrestable offence will be serious if the commission would lead to, or is intended to lead to:

[a] serious harm to the security of the state or public order;

[b] serious interference with the administration of justice or with the investigation of offences;

[c] the death of any person;

[d] serious injury to any person;

[e] substantial financial gain to any person; and

[f] serious financial loss to any person.

S. 116(6) PACE ACT 1984

Q What is meant by 'serious financial loss'?

A This is based on the victim's circumstances; the test is subjective, i.e. 'is it serious for the person who suffers it?'

Q What are the general arrest conditions?

A

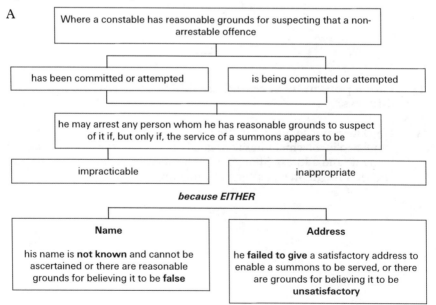

S. 25 PACE Act 1984

POLICE POWERS

Note

An address is satisfactory if:

[a] that person will be at the address long enough for the service of a summons; or
[b] that some other person specified will accept the summons on his behalf

OR

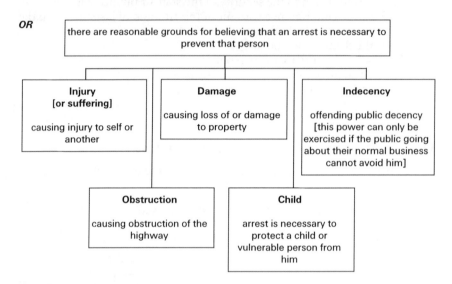

there are reasonable grounds for believing that an arrest is necessary to prevent that person

Injury [or suffering]	Damage	Indecency
causing injury to self or another	causing loss of or damage to property	offending public decency [this power can only be exercised if the public going about their normal business cannot avoid him]

Obstruction	Child
causing obstruction of the highway	arrest is necessary to protect a child or vulnerable person from him

Q Can a person be arrested for failing to furnish a name or address?

A   No. This is not an offence in itself. However, he may be arrested for his suspected involvement in the original offence together with the fact of no name and address (though not if his name and address are already known through previous contact with him).

Q **What power of arrest exists for absentees and deserters from HM Forces?**

A Where a constable has reasonable cause to suspect that a person is an absentee or deserter from HM Forces he may arrest without warrant. The person must be taken directly to a Magistrates' court and the service informed. The court may remand in custody until a service escort can be arranged. The court must issue a certificate which must be given to the service escort.

S. 186 ARMY ACT 1955 AND AIR FORCE ACT 1955
S. 105 NAVAL DISCIPLINE ACT 1957

Q **What power of arrest exists for failure to answer police bail?**

A Persons who are in breach of a duty to surrender to police bail may be arrested and taken to the original bailing police station where they will be treated as if arrested for the original offence.

S. 46A PACE ACT 1984

Q **Explain cross-border arrest without warrant.**

A

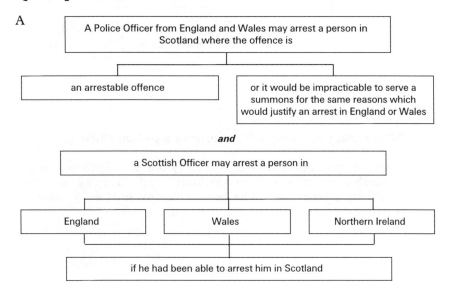

A Police Officer from England and Wales may arrest a person in Scotland where the offence is

an arrestable offence

or it would be impracticable to serve a summons for the same reasons which would justify an arrest in England or Wales

and

a Scottish Officer may arrest a person in

England   Wales   Northern Ireland

if he had been able to arrest him in Scotland

S. 137 CRIMINAL JUSTICE AND PUBLIC ORDER ACT 1994

Q   **What are the rules concerning voluntary attendance at a police station?**

A   Where a person voluntarily attends a police station [or anywhere where a constable is present] and is assisting with an investigation and is not under arrest he shall be:

[a]   entitled to leave at will, and

[b]   informed at once that he is under arrest if a decision has been made to prevent him from leaving, and

[c]   if he is under arrest at a police station and it appears that if he were released from that arrest, he would be liable to arrest for another offence, he shall be arrested for that other offence.

SS. 29, 31 PACE ACT 1984

Q   **After arrest, where shall a person be taken?**

A

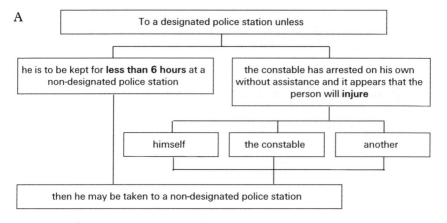

Q   **When can you delay taking him to a police station?**

A   When his presence is necessary to carry out investigations that are reasonable to carry out **immediately**, e.g. checking an alibi, recovering property etc. The reason for any such delay must be recorded upon arrival at the police station.

S. 30 PACE ACT 1984

POWERS OF ENTRY, SEARCH & SEIZURE

Q   What is the procedure for applying for a search warrant?

A   The application must be made with the written authority of an **inspector** unless he is not readily available and the case is **urgent** when the senior officer on duty may make the application and he must state:

[a]   the grounds for the application;
[b]   the Act under which it would be issued;
[c]   the premises to be entered and searched;
[d]   the identity of the articles/persons sought;

The application must be supported by written information.

SS. 15 & 16 PACE ACT 1984 & CODE B, PARA.2

Q   What if the application is refused?

A   Then no further application may be made unless it is supported by additional grounds.

Q   How often can a search warrant be executed?

A   Once only, within one month of issue.

Q   What shall the warrant specify?

A   [a]   The name of the person applying for it;
[b]   the date of issue;
[c]   the Act under which it is issued;
[d]   the premises to be searched, and
[e]   identify the articles/persons sought [if possible].

Q   What is the procedure for executing a search warrant?

A   It shall be executed by a constable at a reasonable hour unless that would frustrate its purpose.

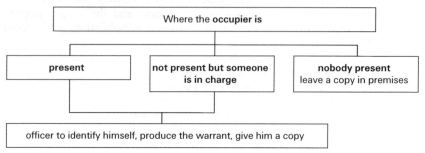

S. 16 PACE Act 1984

Q   What shall be endorsed on the warrant after execution?

A   [a]   Whether the articles or persons sought were found; and
[b]   apart from what was sought, whether anything else was seized.

Q   If a warrant is wrongly addressed can it be executed?

A   No.

Q   What is the procedure for applying for a search warrant for a serious arrestable offence?

A   The constable must satisfy a JP that there are reasonable grounds for believing:

[a]   a serious arrestable offence has been committed; and
[b]   there is material on the premises likely to be of substantial value to the investigation of the offence; and
[c]   it is likely to be relevant evidence [ie. admissible at trial]; and
[d]   that it does not consist of:

[i]   items subject to legal privilege;
[ii]   excluded material; or
[iii]   special procedural material, and
[iv]   a condition at [e] below applies

[e]   [i]   it is not practicable to communicate with any person entitled to grant **entry to the premises;**

[ii] a person at [i] can be found but it is not practicable to communicate with any person entitled to grant **access to the evidence;**

[iii] entry will not be granted unless a warrant is produced;

[iv] the search may be frustrated or seriously prejudiced unless the constable arriving at the premises can **secure immediate entry.**

If so satisfied, the JP may grant a search warrant.

S. 8 PACE ACT 1984

Q   What is meant by an S. 18 PACE [Inspectors] authority to search?

A   This is a power to search premises following arrest for an arrestable offence:

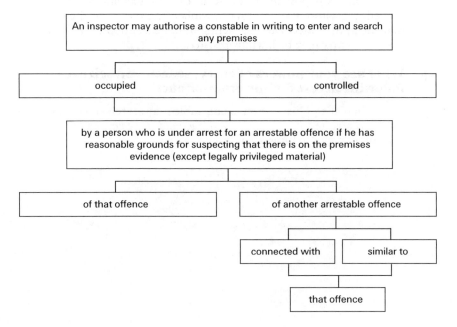

Q   Can a constable conduct an S. 18 search without authorisation?

A   Yes. A constable can conduct the search before taking the person to the police station if his presence is necessary for the effective investigation of the offence. He must inform an inspector as soon as practicable after the search.

Q   What must be recorded in writing regarding the search authority?

A   The grounds for the search and the nature of the evidence sought. If the occupier/controller of the premises searched is in police custody at the time the record is made it shall form part of his/her custody record.

Q   Must the occupier be informed of the reason for the search?

A   Yes, so far as is possible to do so in the circumstances. Any search carried out without attempting to explain the reason to the occupier may mean the officers are not acting in the execution of their duty so that their entry may be lawfully resisted.

Q   What are your powers of entry, search and seizure following arrest for any other offence?

A   Other than at a police station, a constable may search any person who has been arrested if he has *reasonable grounds for believing* that he may present a danger to himself or others.

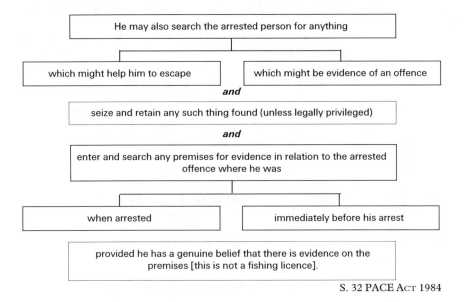

He may also search the arrested person for anything

which might help him to escape | which might be evidence of an offence

and

seize and retain any such thing found (unless legally privileged)

and

enter and search any premises for evidence in relation to the arrested offence where he was

when arrested | immediately before his arrest

provided he has a genuine belief that there is evidence on the premises [this is not a fishing licence].

S. 32 PACE ACT 1984

Q   What about premises containing two or more separate dwellings?

A

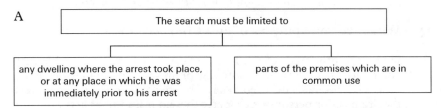

The search must be limited to

any dwelling where the arrest took place, or at any place in which he was immediately prior to his arrest | parts of the premises which are in common use

Q   Outline your powers of entry under S. 17 of PACE.

A   A constable may enter and search any premises for the purposes of:

[a]   executing a warrant for arrest or committal;
[b]   arresting for an arrestable offence;
[c]   arresting for offences under:

[i]   prohibition of uniforms (S. 1 Public Order Act 1936);
[ii]   offences of entering and remaining on property (Criminal Law Act 1977) [NB The constable must be in uniform];

[iii] fear or provocation of violence (S. 4 Public Order Act 1986);

[iiia] failing to stop when required to do so by a constable in uniform (S. 163 RTA 1988);

[iv] failing to comply with interim possession order (S. 76 CJ & PO Act 1994) [NB Must be in uniform].

[d] arresting any child or young person who is remanded to the care of the local authority (Children & Young Persons Act 1969);

[e] recapturing a person unlawfully at large;

[f] saving life and limb;

[g] preventing serious damage to property.

Q Must the officer have reasonable grounds for believing the person is on the premises before he can enter?

A Yes, except in the cases [f] & [g], above, when reasonable cause to suspect would suffice.

Q Is there a power of entry for a breach of the peace?

A Yes, where officers have a genuine and reasonable belief that a breach of the peace is happening or about to happen in the immediate future (*McLeod v. Cmr of Police for Metropolis (1994)*) and if need be by force.

Q What are your powers of entry in relation to fires?

A Under the provisions of the Fire Services Act 1947 a constable may enter and if necessary break into any premises or place in which a fire has, or is reasonably believed to have, broken out, or in order to protect the premises or persons or property therein from fire or acts done for fire-fighting reasons.

Q What is the offence of making a false fire alarm?

A It is an offence to knowingly give or cause to be given to a fire brigade or member of a fire brigade a false alarm of fire.

S. 31 FIRE SERVICES ACT 1947

Q What are your powers of seizure under S. 19 of PACE?

A

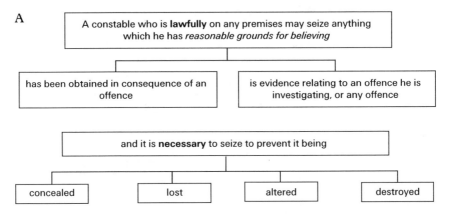

NB. Where the 'premises' searched are a vehicle, it can be seized.

Q Which material cannot be seized?

A [a] Legally privileged material;
[b] excluded material; and
[c] special procedure material.

Q What is 'excluded material'?

A [a] Personal records acquired or created in the course of any trade, business, profession or other occupation or in any paid or unpaid office and which are *held in confidence* [eg. medical records, records made by counsellors, priests or religious advisers];
[b] human tissue or tissue fluid which has been taken for the purpose of diagnosis or medical treatment and which are *held in confidence*;
[c] journalistic material *held in confidence*.

Q How can access to excluded material be obtained?

A By applying to a judge for a production order under the Schedule 1 PACE procedure and PACE Code B.

POLICE POWERS AND HUMAN RIGHTS

Q   **Outline the key features of the European Convention on Human Rights (ECHR).**

A   The ECHR protects certain rights which are considered by many to be fundamental civil liberties (i.e. human rights) within a democratic society. There are five key features:

[a]   the balancing of individual rights against the needs of democratic society;

[b]   the three tests of legitimate limitations on Convention rights;

[c]   the ECHR as a 'living instrument' [i.e. it must be interpreted by courts in the light of present-day conditions];

[d]   the 'margin of appreciation' [i.e. the recognition that because of social, political, economic and cultural differences throughout Europe some latitude in national interpretation of the ECHR must be given; and

[e]   derogations and reservations [Art. 15 allows States to derogate (i.e. restrict or disapply) aspects of the ECHR in time of war or public emergency].

Q   **Under the Human Rights Act 1998 and ECHR, what is meant by the three tests of legitimate limitations on a Convention right?**

A   Any limitation must be:

[a]   Prescribed by law;

[b]   intended to achieve a legitimate objective, and

[c]   proportionate to the end that is to be achieved.

Q   **Summarise test 1 – 'prescribed by law'**

A   An individual has the right to ask 'where did you get the power to act as you did?' and the public body concerned must be able to give an answer e.g. "from the Regulation of Investigatory Powers Act 2000". So that where an illegal telephone tap is made on a person at work, his employer may have breached his human rights (as occurred in *Halford v. UK (1997)*, which pre-dated the Act authorising such activities).

Q   **Summarise test 2 – 'intended to achieve a legitimate objective'**

A   Any limitation must be directed at achieving a legitimate goal, as set out in the ECHR itself e.g. the prevention of crime. The public body concerned must always be acting lawfully however.

Q   Summarise test 3 – 'proportionate to the end that is to be achieved'

A   The state cannot use a sledgehammer to crack a nut. The test is 'were the measures taken necessary in a democratic society?' Where police officers enter and search premises using more force than was necessary they might argue that they intended to:

[a]   achieve a legitimate objective by preventing crime; and
[b]   the objective was prescribed by law, ie PACE; but
[c]   the means employed by the officers would have to be in proportion to the crime that was to be prevented for the behaviour to be a legitimate limitation on the right to respect for private life.

Q   Under the Human Rights Act 1998, when is a Public Authority acting unlawfully?

A   It is unlawful for a public authority to act in a way that is incompatible with a Convention right.

S. 6 HRA 1998

Q   Under the Human Rights Act 1998, what is meant by a Public Authority ?

A   A public authority includes:

[a]   a court or tribunal, including the House of Lords in its judicial capacity;
[b]   police, fire and ambulance service; and
[c]   any person or body whose functions are of a public nature (but not including Parliament or persons exercising functions in connection with Parliamentary proceedings).

Q   Under the Human Rights Act 1998, who can bring proceedings?

A   Any 'victim' ie. person or organisation who believes that a public authority has acted unlawfully (i.e. breached their Convention rights). To be a victim the person/organisation must show that they are either directly affected or at risk of being directly affected by the behaviour complained of.

S.. 7 HRA 1998

Q **Under the Human Rights Act 1998, what are the time limits for commencing proceedings?**

A **One year** from the time of the act complained of, or a longer period if the court considers it equitable having regard to all the circumstances (subject to any stricter national time limits).

S. 7 HRA 1998

Q **Under the Human Rights Act 1998, what are the Convention Rights?**

A 1. *The right to life.* A life may be taken only by:

[a]   execution by order of a court;
[b]   when it results from the use of force which is *no more than absolutely necessary*:
    [i]   in defence of any person from unlawful violence;
    [ii]   in order to effect a lawful arrest or prevent escape from lawful detention; or
    [iii]   in action lawfully taken to quell a riot or insurrection.

[ART. 2]

2. *Freedom from torture.* No one shall be subjected to torture or to inhuman or degrading treatment or punishment. Oppressive interrogation techniques such as sleep deprivation, exposure to continuous loud noise and forcing suspects to adopt uncomfortable postures has been held to be degrading and inhuman.

[ART. 3]

3. *Freedom from slavery and forced labour.* This does not include:

[a]   work done in the ordinary course of detention;
[b]   military service;
[c]   service exacted during an emergency; or
[d]   work done as a civic obligation.

[ART. 4]

4. *The right to liberty and security.* This does not include:

[a]   lawful arrest; and
[b]   lawful detention.

[ART. 5]

5.   *The right to a fair trial.* Everyone is entitled to:

[a]   a fair and public hearing;
[b]   held within a reasonable time;
[c]   by an independent and impartial legal tribunal

[ART. 6]

6.   *No punishment without crime.* This effectively prohibits governments passing retrospective legislation making an offence of what was previously no offence, thus making crimes of otherwise lawful behaviour.

[ART. 7]

7.   *Right to a private life.* People are entitled to 'respect' for their

[a]   private life,
[b]   family life,
[c]   home, and
[d]   correspondence.

However, these may be interfered with if the three tests can successfully be applied:

[i]   there is a legal authority allowing the interference;
[ii]   there is a legitimate objective behind the actions; and
[iii]   there is a 'pressing social need' for the interference.

[ART. 8]

8.   *Freedom of thought.* This gives people the right to freedom of:

[a]   thought,
[b]   conscience, and
[c]   religion.

[ART. 9]

9.   *Freedom of expression.* This gives people the right to the freedom:

[a]   of expression,
[b]   to have opinions, and
[c]   to receive and impart information and ideas.

[ART. 10]

10. *Freedom of Assembly and Association.*

[ART. 11]

11. *The right to marry.*

[ART.12]

12. *The right to an effective remedy.* This Article is not incorporated into the HRA 1998 but UK courts will be obliged to take case-law considering this right into account when interpreting the ECHR.

[ART. 13]

13. *Prohibition of discrimination in Convention rights.* This provides a guarantee that access to the ECHR is enjoyed equally by everyone, regardless of:

[a]   sex;
[b]   race, colour;
[c]   language;
[d]   religion;
[e]   political or other opinion;
[f]   national or social origin;
[g]   association with a national minority;
[h]   property, birth or other status.

[ART. 14]

14. *Derogation in time of emergency.* This means that a State can derogate from some of its obligations (i.e. those rights which are Qualified not Absolute) under the convention during:

[a]   times of **war,** or
[b]   other public emergency **threatening the life of the nation.**

[ART. 15]

15. *Restrictions on political activities of aliens.* This permits limitations to be imposed upon certain non-European citizens.

[ART. 16]

Q   Summarise Articles 1, 2 & 3 of Protocol 1

A   **Article 1.** *Protection of property.* Every person is entitled to the peaceful enjoyment of his possessions. To prove a breach of this Article it must be shown that the State has:

[a]   interfered with the applicant's peaceful enjoyment of his possessions; or
[b]   deprived him of his possessions; or
[c]   subjected those possessions to some sort of control.

However, the State is entitled to enforce such laws as it deems necessary to control the use of property 'in the general interest' or to secure payment of taxes, contributions or penalties.

Article 2. *The right to education.* No person shall be denied the right to education.
This provision requires the State to have regard to:

[a]   religious, and
[b]   philosophical convictions of the parents.

Note. The UK has lodged a reservation (restriction) to this provision.

Article 3. *The right to free elections.* This Convention right applies not only to the holding of elections, but also to rights of participation eg. voting and standing for election.

Q   Summarise Protocol 6

A   *The Death Penalty.* The death penalty is abolished (although a State may apply it in time of war). NB. the UK has adopted Protocol 13 which abolishes the death penalty without *any* exception.

PUBLIC ORDER AND TERRORISM

Q   Define a Breach of the Peace

A   A breach is occasioned when an act is done or threatened which:

[a]   harms a person; or
[b]   harms his property [in his presence]; or
[c]   is likely to cause harm; or
[d]   puts him in fear of harm.

R v. HOWELL (1982)

There is no power to bail because a breach of the peace is not a criminal offence, and a person arrested for it is not technically in police detention. He may be held until any likelihood of a recurrence of the breach has gone [based on an officer's honest and reasonable belief that detention is necessary to prevent a breach] or be brought before a court ASAP to be bound over.

Q   What is the power of arrest for a Breach of the Peace?

A

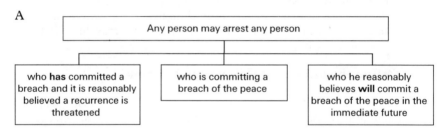

Any person may arrest any person

| who **has** committed a breach and it is reasonably believed a recurrence is threatened | who is committing a breach of the peace | who he reasonably believes **will** commit a breach of the peace in the immediate future |

Q   Where can the above power be exercised?

A   Anywhere, public or private (and if in private there is no requirement to show that the disturbance affected members of the public outside the property: *McQuade v. CC of Humberside Police (2001)*. An officer may enter premises to prevent a breach and remain in order to do so.

Q   When can it be exercised?

A   In *Bibby v. CC of Essex (2000)* the Court of Appeal held that the power to arrest for breach of the peace must only be exercised in the following circumstances:

[a]   where there is clearly a real and present threat to the peace;
[b]   the threat is coming from the person to be arrested;
[c]   his/her conduct must clearly be interfering with the rights of another; and
[d]   that conduct must be unreasonable.

Q   Who can be arrested for Drunk and Disorderly Behaviour?

A   Any person who is drunk *and* disorderly in a public place. Any person may arrest.

S. 91(1) CRIMINAL JUSTICE ACT 1967

Drunk. Means where the defendant has taken intoxicating *liquor* to an extent that affects his steady self-control: *Neale v. R.M.J.E. (a minor) (1984)*. *NB* Not drugs or any other intoxicant, but where there are several causes, one of which is alcohol, a court may find that this offence is made out.

Q   Define the offence of Being found Drunk

A   Any person found drunk in any highway or other public place, whether a building or not, or on any licensed premises, commits an offence.

S. 12 LICENSING ACT 1872

Arrest. Under S. 1 Licensing Act 1902 a person found drunk in a highway or public place is liable to arrest by any person where there is an honest and reasonable belief that s/he is incapable of taking care of himself/herself.

Q Define riot

A

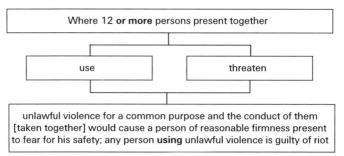

Where 12 **or more** persons present together

| use | threaten |

unlawful violence for a common purpose and the conduct of them [taken together] would cause a person of reasonable firmness present to fear for his safety; any person **using** unlawful violence is guilty of riot

S. 1 PUBLIC ORDER ACT 1986

Arrest. Arrestable offence.

Q Whose consent is required for the prosecution of riot?

A The DPP's.

Q Where can riot take place?

A Anywhere, public or private.

Q What does 'violence' include?

A Violence towards persons or property. It is not restricted to conduct causing or intended to cause injury or damage but includes any other violent conduct, e.g. throwing a missile of a kind capable of causing injury at a person: S. 8 Public Order Act 1986.

Q Can drunkenness be a defence?

A Only if the drunkenness (whether by drink, drugs or other means) was not self-induced e.g. 'spiked' drinks (Mickey Finns) or a result of medication. (Other general defences such as self-defence may also apply.)

PUBLIC ORDER AND TERRORISM

Q   Define violent disorder

A

Where **three or more persons** present together

use	threaten

unlawful violence and the conduct of them (taken together) would cause a reasonable person present to fear for his personal safety then each person using **or threatening** unlawful violence is guilty of violent disorder

S. 2 Public Order Act 1986

Arrest. Arrestable offence.

Q   Define affray

A

A person is guilty of affray if he

uses	threatens

unlawful violence towards another [present at the scene: *I and Others v. DPP (2002)*] and his conduct is such that it would cause a person of reasonable firmness present to fear for his personal safety

S. 3 Public Order Act 1986

Arrest. Statutory power: reasonably suspects is committing an offence.

Q   Can words alone constitute a threat?

A   No. But words accompanied by action e.g. shaking fist or threatening with a dog, would be sufficient.

Q   Compare riot, violent disorder and affray

Attribute	Riot	Violent disorder	Affray
Minimum number	12	3	1
Present together	Yes	Yes	N/A
Common purpose	Yes	Not required	N/A
Unlawful violence	Person or property	Person or property	Personal only
Reasonable person who fears for his safety	Need not be present	Need not be present	Need not be present but the threat of unlawful violence must be towards a person present
Who is guilty?	Actually use violence	Use or threaten violence	Use or threaten violence
Intoxication defence?	Only if medication or Mickey Finns	Only if medication or Mickey Finns	Only if medication or Mickey Finns
Private or public	Yes	Yes	Yes
Arrest	Arrestable offence	Arrestable offence	Statutory power: reasonably suspects is committing: S. 3(6) POA 1986

Q   Define S. 4 fear or provocation of violence

A

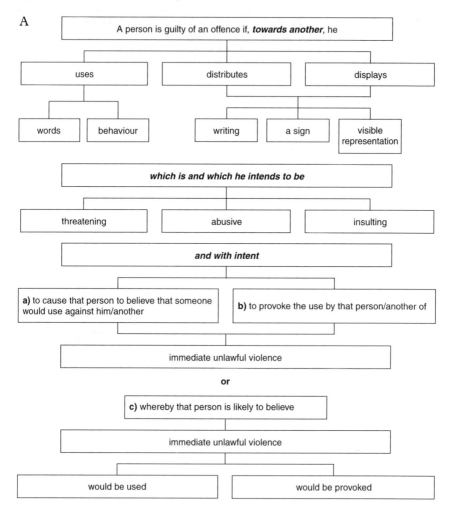

A person is guilty of an offence if, ***towards another***, he

| uses | distributes | displays |

| words | behaviour | writing | a sign | visible representation |

which is and which he intends to be

| threatening | abusive | insulting |

and with intent

a) to cause that person to believe that someone would use against him/another

b) to provoke the use by that person/another of

immediate unlawful violence

or

c) whereby that person is likely to believe

immediate unlawful violence

| would be used | would be provoked |

S. 4 PUBLIC ORDER ACT 1986

No offence where the things are done **inside a dwelling** and the other person is inside that *or another* dwelling.

Q   Define a 'dwelling'

A   Any structure or part thereof **occupied as a person's home** or as living accommodation (whether the occupation is separate or shared with others), but not any parts not so occupied (e.g. communal landings, stairwells, lobbies, garages etc.).
Structure includes tent, caravan, vehicle, vessel or other temporary or moveable structure, e.g. a treehouse occupied by an eco-protestor.

Q   What is the power of arrest for the Section 4 offence?

A   A constable may arrest anyone he reasonably suspects is committing the offence.

Q   Define the S. 4A intentional harassment, alarm or distress offence

A   It is an offence, **with intent** to cause a person harassment, alarm or distress, to:

[a]   use threatening, abusive or insulting words or behaviour, or disorderly behaviour, or

[b]   display any writing, sign or other visible representation which is threatening, abusive or insulting, *thereby causing* a person harassment, alarm or distress.

S. 4A PUBLIC ORDER ACT 1986

Arrest. Reasonably suspects is committing.

Defence. To prove that he was inside a dwelling and had no reason to believe that the activities would be heard or seen by a person outside that or any other dwelling, or his conduct was reasonable.

No offence. If the activity is by a person inside a dwelling and the other person is inside that or another dwelling.

Q   Define the S. 5 harassment, alarm or distress offence

A   It is an offence to:

[a]   use threatening, abusive or insulting words or behaviour, or disorderly conduct;

[b]   display any writing, sign or other visible representation which is threatening, abusive or insulting **within the hearing or sight** of a person likely to be caused harassment, alarm or distress.

Mens rea. The offender must **intend** his actions or **be aware** of their likely consequences (but it is not necessary for them to actually cause any harassment, alarm or distress [compare the S. 4A offence]).

No offence if the activity is by a person **inside a dwelling** and the other person is inside that or another dwelling.

Defence:
[a] he had no reason to believe that anyone likely to be caused harassment, alarm or distress could **hear or see** his activities;
[b] he was **inside a dwelling** and he had no reason to believe he would be heard or seen by anyone outside that or any other dwelling; or
[c] his conduct was reasonable.

Power of arrest. Where the defendant engages in offensive conduct which a constable **warns him to stop** and he engages in further offensive conduct immediately or shortly afterwards. The arresting officer need not be the warning officer.

Q **What effect has the Crime and Disorder Act 1998 made on racially aggravated offences ?**

A The Act does not create new offences but instead sets out the circumstances when an offence is racially aggravated. Post 11 September 2001, the Anti-terrorism, Crime and Security Act 2001 has extended the definition to include religiously aggravated offence.

Q **How does the Powers of Criminal Courts (Sentencing) Act 2000 relate to the above ?**

A The Act can increase the penalties for offences where they are shown to be racially or religiously aggravated.

Q **Which offences can be deemed to be racially or religiously aggravated?**

A [a] Wounding and GBH: Crime & Disorder Act 1998 S. 29(1)(a);
[b] ABH: Crime & Disorder Act 1998 S. 29(1)(b);
[c] common assault: Crime & Disorder Act 1998 S. 29(1)(c);
[d] simple criminal damage: Crime & Disorder Act 1998 S. 30(1);
[e] causing fear or provocation: S. 4 Public Order Act 1986;
[f] intentional harassment, alarm or distress: S. 4A Public Order Act 1986;

[g] causing harassment, alarm or distress: S. 5 Public Order Act 1986;

[h] harassment and putting in fear of violence (Protection from Harassment Act 1997 offences): Crime & Disorder Act 1998 SS. 32(1)(a) & (b).

Q Define racially or religiously aggravated

A [a] A **demonstration of hostility** by the defendant based on the victim's membership or presumed membership of a racial or religious group:

[i] immediately before the offence;
[ii] at the time of the offence; or
[iii] immediately after committing the offence; or

[b] **motivation by hostility** of the defendant based on the victim's membership of a racial or religious group.

Q What is a S. 42 direction?

A A power under the Criminal Justice & Police Act 2001 to deal with harassment of people in their homes. The *senior officer at the scene* may give directions to people in the vicinity to do anything the officer specifies as being necessary to prevent harassment, alarm or distress of the resident, such as leaving the vicinity (either immediately or after a specified time). The direction may be given orally and the officer giving it need not be in uniform. It is an offence to knowingly contravene a S. 42 direction, and a constable may arrest any person he reasonably suspects *to be committing* it but that constable **must be in uniform**.

Q When does the power to give a S. 42 direction arise?

A Where a person is outside or in the vicinity of any premises used by any individual (not a company) as his/her dwelling, and a constable reasonably believes
[i] the person is there to persuade the resident to
[a] not do something they are entitled to do, or
[b] do something they are not obliged to do, and
[ii] that that person's presence amounts to or may result in harassment of the resident or is likely to cause them alarm or distress.

Q   Define the racial hatred offence under S. 18 Public Order Act 1986

A   A person who uses threatening, abusive or insulting words or behaviour, or displays any written material which is threatening, abusive or insulting commits an offence if:

[a]   **he intends** thereby to stir up racial hatred, or
[b]   **it is likely** to stir up racial hatred.

Arrest. Arrestable offence.

No offence where the activity is **inside a dwelling** and is not heard or seen except by persons in that *or another* dwelling.

Defence. For the accused to prove he was inside a dwelling and had no reason to believe the behaviour would be heard or seen by a person outside that or any other dwelling.

Prosecution. The consent of the Attorney-General (or Solicitor-General) is required.

Q   Define the S. 19 racial hatred - publishing, distributing written material offence

A   A person who publishes or distributes written material which is threatening, abusive or insulting commits an offence if:

[a]   **he intends** to stir up racial hatred, or
[b]   **it is likely** to stir up racial hatred.

S. 19 PUBLIC ORDER ACT 1986

Defence. For a person who is not shown to have intended to stir up racial hatred to prove **he was not aware of the contents** of the material and did not suspect, or have a reason to suspect, it was threatening, abusive or insulting.

Arrest. Arrestable offence.

Prosecution. The consent of the Attorney-General (or Solicitor-General) is required.

Q What are the requirements of the written notice to be given for public processions?

A

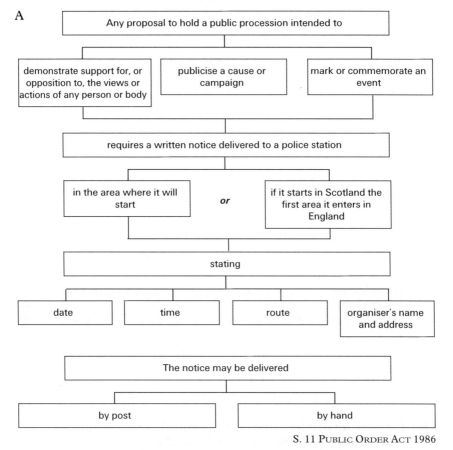

Any proposal to hold a public procession intended to

demonstrate support for, or opposition to, the views or actions of any person or body

publicise a cause or campaign

mark or commemorate an event

requires a written notice delivered to a police station

in the area where it will start

or

if it starts in Scotland the first area it enters in England

stating

date

time

route

organiser's name and address

The notice may be delivered

by post

by hand

S. 11 Public Order Act 1986

By post. Not less than **six clear days** by **recorded delivery.** [S. 7 of the Interpretation Act 1978 under which a document sent by post is deemed to have been served when posted and to have been delivered in the ordinary course of post does not apply]; or

By hand. Not less than **six clear days,** or as soon as is practicable.

Offence. Is committed by any organiser who fails to comply with the above.

Defence. To prove that he did not know and neither suspected nor had reason to suspect of the failure to satisfy the requirements. In the case of providing the wrong date, time or route, it is a defence to prove the difference arose from circumstances beyond his control or with the agreement of a police officer.

Q   What condition under S. 12 Public Order Act 1986 can a senior police officer make?

A

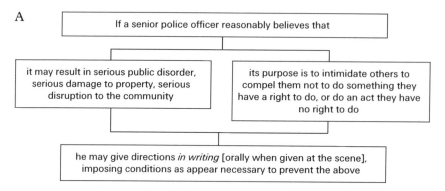

If a senior police officer reasonably believes that

it may result in serious public disorder, serious damage to property, serious disruption to the community

its purpose is to intimidate others to compel them not to do something they have a right to do, or do an act they have no right to do

he may give directions *in writing* [orally when given at the scene], imposing conditions as appear necessary to prevent the above

A senior police officer means the chief officer of police, unless the procession or meeting is in the process of being held, e.g. people forming up etc, in which case the **senior police officer present at the scene.**

Power of arrest. A constable **in uniform** may arrest anyone he reasonably suspects *is committing* an offence, i.e. organising or taking part in a procession whilst knowingly failing to comply with a condition, or inciting another to do so.

Q   Define the offence under S. 13 Public Order Act 1986 of taking part in a prohibited procession

A   Any person who:

[a]   organises a prohibited procession; or
[b]   who takes part in; or
[c]   incites another to take part in a prohibited procession knowing it is prohibited

commits an offence.

Power of arrest. A constable **in uniform** may arrest anyone he reasonably suspects *is committing* the offence.

Q   **Define the offence under S. 14 Public Order Act 1986 of organising a public assembly**

A   Any person who:

[a]   organises a public assembly and knowingly fails to comply with a condition; or

[b]   takes part in an assembly and knowingly fails to comply with a condition; or

[c]   incites another to take part in a public assembly which he knows does not comply with a condition

commits an offence.

Defence. To prove that the failure to comply arose from circumstances beyond his control.

Power of arrest. A constable **in uniform** may arrest anyone he reasonably suspects is committing the offence.

Q   **What is a public assembly?**

A   An assembly of 2 or more people in a public place that is wholly or partly open to the air (S. 16 Public Order Act 1986).

Q Outline the Power under S. 14B Public Order Act 1986 to prohibit a trespassory assembly

A

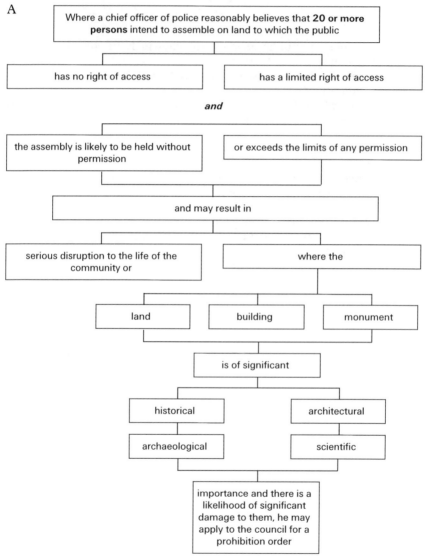

Where a chief officer of police reasonably believes that **20 or more persons** intend to assemble on land to which the public

| has no right of access | has a limited right of access |

and

| the assembly is likely to be held without permission | or exceeds the limits of any permission |

and may result in

| serious disruption to the life of the community or | where the |

| land | building | monument |

is of significant

| historical | architectural |
| archaeological | scientific |

importance and there is a likelihood of significant damage to them, he may apply to the council for a prohibition order

The order. May be granted by the council *with the consent of the Secretary of State.* It shall not exceed **four days** nor apply to more than a five mile radius from a specified centre.

Offence. Any person who organises or takes part in an assembly they *know* is prohibited, or incites another to, commits an offence.

Power of arrest. A constable in uniform may arrest anyone he reasonably suspects to be committing the offence.

Police powers. If a constable *in uniform* reasonably believes that a person is on his way to an assembly which is prohibited, he may:

[a]   stop that person; and

[b]   direct him not to proceed in the direction of the assembly.

The power must be exercised only in the area of the prohibitory order. Note that it applies to persons not vehicles. Use Road Traffic Act 1988 powers to stop vehicles.

Offence. Failure to comply is an offence.

Power of arrest. A constable **in uniform** may arrest anyone he reasonably suspects to be committing an offence (i.e. failing to comply with a direction). The arresting officer need not be the officer who gave the direction.

Q   Outline police powers under S. 1 Public Meeting Act 1908

A   Where a person at a lawful public meeting acts in a disorderly manner for the purpose of preventing the business of the meeting, he is guilty of an offence. If a constable reasonably suspects any person of committing this offence, he may *if requested by the chairman of the meeting,* require him to **declare his name and address immediately.** Failure to do so is a summary offence.

Arrest. Consider S. 25 PACE General arrest conditions.

Public meeting. Not defined in the Act and therefore there is no specific number of persons required to be present. Public Election meetings are excluded from this offence (but are covered by a similar specific offence under the Representation of the People Act 1983).

Q Outline the power to order Dispersal of Groups

A   Where a superintendent or above has reasonable grounds to believe

[a]   that any members of the public have been

[i]   intimidated
[ii]   harassed
[iii] alarmed or
[iv]   distressed

as a result of the presence or behaviour of groups of 2 or more persons in public places in any locality in his police area, and

[b]   that anti-social behaviour is a significant and persistent problem in that locality

s/he may, with the consent of the local authority(s) for that area, give an authorisation in writing conferring powers on constables **in uniform** who reasonably believe that ground (a) above has been or is likely to be satisfied, to direct

[i]   dispersal of the group
[ii]   any of those persons who do not reside in the locality to leave it, and
[iii] any such persons not to return within 24 hours of the direction to leave.

S. 30 ANTI-SOCIAL BEHAVIOUR ACT 2003

Offence. It is an offence knowingly to contravene any such direction (statutory power of arrest, in uniform: *reasonably suspects has committed.*)

Q How must the authorisation be notified to the Group?

A   The authorisation must be published, either in a local newspaper or by posting a notice in some conspicuous place(s) in the locality (or both). The direction to disperse may then be given (orally or otherwise) to any person individually or to 2 or more people together, and it may subsequently be withdrawn or varied by the person who gave it.

Q   Outline the power to remove under 16s

A   If, between the hours of 9 pm – 6 am, a constable **in uniform** finds in any public place a person under 16 who is not under the effective control of a parent or a responsible person aged 18 or over, s/he may remove the person to their place of residence (unless s/he has reasonable grounds for believing that the person would, if removed to that place, be likely to suffer significant harm. [In which case s/he should exercise police protection powers under S. 46 Children Act 1989]). In the event that an officer exercises this power, the local authority must be notified.

S. 30(6) ANTI-SOCIAL BEHAVIOUR ACT 2003

Q   What are 'designated' and 'regulated' football matches?

A

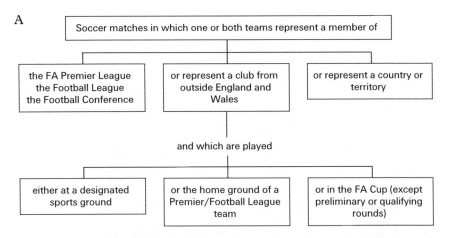

Q   Outline the three offences of misbehaviour at designated football matches

A   [a]   **Throwing.** It is an offence to throw anything at or towards:

[i]   the playing area or any area adjacent to it where spectators are not admitted;

[ii]   any area in which spectators or other persons may be present [without lawful authority or reasonable excuse - onus of proof [on a balance of probabilities] lies on him].

[b] **Chanting.** It is an offence to engage or take part in chanting of an **indecent or racist** nature.

  [i] 'Chant' means the *repeated* uttering of words or sounds whether alone or in concert with others; and

  [ii] 'racist' means threatening, abusive or insulting to a person by reason of colour, race, nationality or ethnic origins.

[c] **Entering playing area.** It is an offence to go on to the playing area or place adjacent to it where spectators are not normally allowed [without lawful authority or reasonable excuse - onus of proof lies on him].

SS. 2, 3, 4 FOOTBALL (OFFENCES) ACT 1991

Power of arrest. All three are arrestable offences.

Q Define the offence of Ticket Touts

A It is an offence for **an unauthorised person** to sell [offer/expose] a ticket for a designated football match in a public place [or any place if in the course of a business].

S. 116 CRIMINAL JUSTICE AND PUBLIC ORDER ACT 1994

Who is unauthorised? Anyone who does not have written authorisation from the home club or organisers.

Power of arrest. Arrestable offence [S. 24 PACE].

Search. The power to search extends to vehicles believed to be used by touts.

Ticket. Means anything which purports to be a ticket.

Q What is the purpose of the Football (Disorder) Act 2000?

A The regulation of Football Banning Orders.

Q   **In what two ways can be a Banning Order be obtained?**

A   [i]   Upon conviction for a 'relevant' offence under S. 14A Football Spectators Act 1989. Courts are under a duty to make an Order when satisfied that there are reasonable grounds to believe that an Order would help prevent violence or disorder at or in connection with a regulated football match. An order is in addition to any sentence imposed by the court for the relevant offence, and may be made even if the offence is dealt with by an absolute or conditional discharge.

  [ii]   Following complaint by a chief officer of police for the area in which a person resides under S. 14 B Football Spectators Act 1989, if the court is satisfied that the person has, at any time, caused or contributed to any violence or disorder in the UK or elsewhere.

Q   **What power has the court in relation to banning orders?**

A   The court can impose any appropriate conditions and [save in exceptional circumstances] **must** require the **surrender of the person's passport** in connection with matches **outside the UK.**

Q   **When must a person who is the subject of a banning order first report to a police station?**

A   Within five days of the day on which the order was made (or five days of release if in custody).

Q   **Is there a power of arrest for breaching a Banning Order?**

A   Arrestable offence.

Q   **What is the duration of a Banning Order?**

A   [a]   A minimum of 6 years and a maximum of 10 years, where the order is imposed in addition to an immediate custodial sentence;

  [b]   a minimum of 3 years and a maximum of 5 years when imposed in addition to a non-custodial sentence;

  [c]   a minimum of 2 years and a maximum of 3 years when imposed following a police complaint.

Q   **What powers of detention exist in relation to Banning Orders?**

A   During any 'control period' in relation to any match or tournament outside England and Wales a constable in uniform who has reasonable cause to *suspect* that a person has caused/contributed at any time to any violence or disorder in the UK or elsewhere, and reasonable cause to *believe* that making a Banning Order would help prevent violence or disorder at or in connection with a regulated football match, may detain a **British citizen** for a maximum of **4 hours (6 hours** if authorised by an **inspector** or above) in order to decide whether to issue him with a S. 21B notice.

Q   **What is a S. 21B notice?**

A   A constable in uniform who is authorised by an inspector or above may give a person a written notice requiring him
[a]   to appear before a magistrates' court at a specified time (within 24 hours of the notice or detention, whichever is earlier);
[b]   not to leave England and Wales before that time, and
[c]   to surrender his passport.

Q   **What is the 'control period' during which these powers may be exercised?**

A   In relation to any match/tournament outside England and Wales, the period commencing 5 days before the match/tournament begins and ending when the match/tournament ends.

Q   **Is there any power of arrest?**

A   Yes, a constable may arrest the person to whom he is giving the notice if he has reasonable grounds to believe that it is necessary in order to secure compliance with the notice. It is also an arrestable offence to fail to comply with the notice once it is given.

Q   **To which vehicles does S. 1 of the Sporting Events (Control of Alcohol etc.) Act 1985 apply?**

A   **Public Service Vehicles (PSVs) and trains** being used for the *principal purpose* of carrying passengers to or from a designated sporting event.

Q Who commits alcohol-related offences in relation to such vehicles?

A [a] The operator of a PSV, or his servant/agent, who knowingly causes or permits alcohol to be carried on it;

[b] the hirer of any PSV or train, or his servant/agent, who knowingly causes or permits alcohol to be carried on it;

[c] any person who has intoxicating liquor in his possession while on the vehicle;

[d] any person who is drunk on the vehicle.

Police powers. A constable may stop and search a PSV (or search a railway carrriage, *not* stop the train) if he has reasonable grounds to suspect an offence under this section is being or has been committed on the vehicle.

Q Outline the alcohol-related offences at sports grounds

A

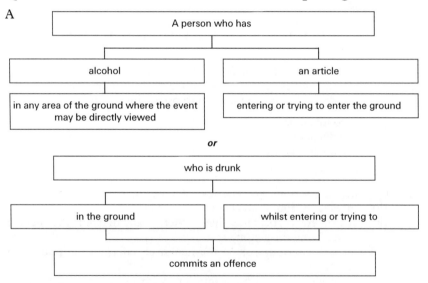

S. 2 SPORTING EVENTS (CONTROL OF ALCOHOL ETC.) ACT 1985

Q Define an 'article'

A It must be capable of **causing injury** to a person struck by it, being:

[a] a bottle, can or portable container, or part of such [whether crushed or broken] which

[i] is for holding any drink, and
[ii] is normally discarded or returned when empty.

But not. Medical containers.

Q During what times may these offences be committed?

A During the period beginning 2 hours before the start of the event or (if earlier) the advertised time, and ending 1 hour after the event. Where the event is postponed to a later date the time limits still apply on the originally advertised date [because spectators may have attended the ground].

Q Terrorism. Under S. 1 of the Terrorism Act 2000, what is terrorism?

A Terrorism is defined as the use or threat of *action* which is designed to influence the government or intimidate the public or a section of the public and which is made for the purpose of advancing:

[a] a political; or
[b] religious; or
[c] ideological cause.

'Action' means it:

[i] involves serious violence against a person; or
[ii] involves serious damage to property; or
[iii] endangers a person's life, other than that of the person committing the action; or
[iv] creates a serious risk to the health or safety of the public [or section]; or
[v] is designed seriously to interfere with or seriously disrupt an electronic system.

Note. This is a very broad definition which may apply to offences such as blackmail, contamination of goods and threats to kill.

Firearms. Where action involves the use of firearms or explosives for the purpose of advancing a political, religious or ideological cause, there is no additional requirement for it to be designed to influence or intimidate.

Q   Outline the main offences involving Proscribed Organisations

A   [a]   Belonging or professing to belong to a proscribed organisation (S. 11(1));

[b]   inviting support for a proscribed organisation (S. 12(1));

[c]   arranging or managing [or assisting] a meeting of three or more people (in public or private) which the defendant knows is:

[i]   to support a proscribed organisation;

[ii]   to further the activities of a proscribed organisation; or

[iii]   to be addressed by a person who belongs [or professes] to a proscribed organisation [or addressing such a meeting] (S. 12(2)(3)).

Arrest. Arrestable offences.

Q   What additional police powers are given to constables by the 2000 Act?

A   [a]   The power to arrest without warrant (anywhere in the UK) any person whom he/she reasonably suspects to be a terrorist;

[b]   the power to stop and search (anywhere in the UK) any person whom he/she reasonably suspects to be a terrorist to discover whether they have in their possession anything which may constitute evidence that they are a terrorist; and

[c]   the power to seize and retain anything which he/she discovers in the course of the search which he/she reasonably suspects may constitute evidence that the person is a terrorist.

SS. 41, 43 TERRORISM ACT 2000

Terrorist. Means a person who has committed a terrorism offence or is or has been concerned in the commission, preparation or instigation of acts of terrorism.

Q **Outline the offence of Causing Explosion likely to Endanger Life/Property**

A A person in the UK or a UK citizen in the Republic of Ireland who unlawfully and maliciously causes by any explosive substance an explosion which is likely to endanger life or cause serious injury to property is guilty of an offence.

Arrest. Serious arrestable offence.

Explosive. Includes fireworks, petrol bombs, shotguns, electronic timers etc.

Prosecution. The consent of the Attorney-General (or Solicitor-General) is required.

S. 2 EXPLOSIVE SUBSTANCES ACT 1883

Q **Outline the offence of Attempting to Cause an Explosion**

A A person in the UK or elsewhere (if a UK or colonial citizen) who unlawfully and maliciously:

[a] does any act with intent to cause or conspires to cause an explosion likely to endanger life or cause serious damage to property in the UK or Republic of Ireland; or
[b] makes, has in his possession or under his control, any explosive with intent to endanger life or cause serious damage to property in the UK or Republic of Ireland or to enable another to do so, commits an offence.

Arrest. Arrestable offence.

Prosecution. The consent of the Attorney-General (or Solicitor-General) is required.

S. 3 EXPLOSIVE SUBSTANCES ACT 1883

Q   **Outline the offence of Possessing Explosives under Suspicious Circumstances**

A   Any person who makes or knowingly has in his possession or under his control any explosive under circumstances as to give rise to a reasonable suspicion that it is **not for a lawful object** [onus of proof lies on him] commits an offence.

Arrest. Arrestable offence.

Prosecution. The consent of the Attorney-General (or Solicitor-General) is required.

S. 4 EXPLOSIVE SUBSTANCES ACT 1883

Q   **Outline the gunpowder offences under the Offences Against the Person Act 1861**

A   [a]   Causing bodily injury by use of gunpowder or other explosive substance: S. 28;
[b]   causing gunpowder or other explosive, corrosive, dangerous or noxious thing intentionally to do bodily harm: S. 29;
[c]   placing gunpowder or explosives near buildings or ships with intent to do bodily harm: S. 30

Arrest. All are arrestable offences.

HARASSMENT AND ANTI-SOCIAL BEHAVIOUR

Q Define the offence of Harassment

A

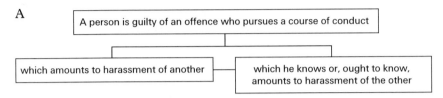

Course of conduct. On at least two occasions.

Harassment. Includes alarming the person or causing them distress.

Another. Does not include companies or corporations. However individual employees etc are covered.

The test. Is objective. Did the defendant know, or *ought he have known*, that his conduct amounted to harassment? He ought to have known if a reasonable person in possession of the same information would think it amounted to harassment.

Defence. If done for the purposes of preventing or detecting crime, under a rule of law or if the conduct was reasonable.

Arrest. Arrestable offence.

SS. 1 & 2 PROTECTION FROM HARASSMENT ACT 1997

Q Outline the offence of Putting People in Fear of Violence

A   A person whose course of conduct causes another to fear, on at least **two occasions**, that violence will be used against him is guilty of an offence if he knows or ought to know that his course of conduct will cause the other so to fear *on each occasion.*

The test. Is objective. The defendant must know or ought to have known that his conduct would cause the other person to fear violence.

Defence. If done for the purposes of preventing or detecting crime, under a rule of law, or was reasonable for the **protection of himself/ another** or **protection of property.**

Arrest. Arrestable offence.

S. 4 PROTECTION FROM HARASSMENT ACT 1997

The Secretary of State may issue a certificate that the conduct was carried out by a specified person on a specified occasion relating to:

[a]   national security;
[b]   the economic well-being of the UK; or
[c]   the prevention and detection of serious crime

on behalf of the Crown. Such a certificate negates any offence under the 1997 Act.

S. 12 PROTECTION FROM HARASSMENT ACT 1997

Q   Who may apply for a Harassment Injunction?

A   Anyone who fears an actual or potential breach of S. 1 (i.e. a course of conduct amounting to harassment) may apply to a civil court for an injunction prohibiting such conduct. Following any breach of such an injunction the claimant may apply for the issue of a warrant for the arrest of the defendant.

S. 3(1) PROTECTION FROM HARASSMENT ACT 1997

Q   Outline the Breach of Injunction offence under S. 3(6).

A   Where a court has granted an injunction to restrain any harassment by the defendant, if, without reasonable excuse, he does any act which is prohibited by the injunction, he is guilty of an offence.

Arrest. Arrestable offence.

Q   What is a Restraining Order?

A   An order made by a court dealing with a person convicted of a harassment offence and which is made for the purpose of protecting the victim, or any other specified person, from further harassment. It has a similar effect to a civil injunction, but can be made by a criminal court. Breach of a restraining order, without reasonable excuse, is an arrestable offence.

S. 5 PROTECTION FROM HARASSMENT ACT 1997

Q   Who can apply for an Anti-Social Behaviour Order [ASBO]?

A   The 'relevant authority', which is either:
[a]   the local authority, or
[b]   the chief officer of police of any police area forming part of the local authority, or
[c]   the chief constable of the British Transport Police, or
[d]   any registered social landlord providing housing in the area.
They **must consult** each other before making the application.

Q   When can an ASBO be applied for?

A   When it appears to the relevant authority that a relevant person acted in a manner that caused, or was likely to cause, harassment, alarm or distress to one or more people who are not of the same household as the relevant person, **and** such an order is necessary to protect people in the local goverment area in which the consequence of that person's behaviour was suffered from further anti-social acts by that person.

Q   At least how old must the 'relevant person' be?

A   10 years.

Q   Can an ASBO be applied for by someone in the same household?

A   No, only relevant authorities can apply, and only in relation to acts against people of a different household. The ASBO cannot be used to solve domestic disputes.

Q   At which court should the application for an ASBO be made?

A   Usually by way of complaint to a magistrates' court in the local government or police area concerned (which need not necessarily be where the anti-social behaviour occurred). ASBOs may also be sought in county courts when the relevant authorities are a party to the proceedings therein.

Q   What standard of proof is required?

A   ASBOs are civil complaints, so the civil standard applies [ie. on the balance of probabilities].

Q   How long does an ASBO last?

A   A minimum period of two years. It may be discharged before then with the consent of **both parties.**

Q   What can the ASBO prohibit?

A   Anything considered necessary to prevent further misconduct. E.g. communicating with a particular person, or creating noise (either generally or in a particular place or between particular times).

Q   Is there a power of arrest for breaching an ASBO?

A   Yes, breach of an ASBO without reasonable excuse is an arrestable offence under S. 1(10) Crime and Disorder Act 1998.

Q   Who can appeal in the case of a magistrates' court ASBO?

A   Only the defendant to the Crown Court. The applicant cannot appeal against a refusal to make an order (though it may ask the court to 'state a case' for the consideration of the Divisional Court).

COMMUNICATIONS

Q Outline the offence of Bomb Threats (Placing or Sending Articles)

A

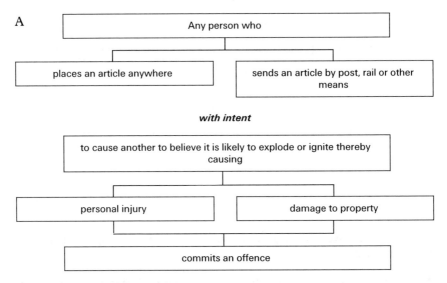

Any person who

| places an article anywhere | sends an article by post, rail or other means |

with intent

to cause another to believe it is likely to explode or ignite thereby causing

| personal injury | damage to property |

commits an offence

Arrest. Arrestable offence

S. 51(1) CRIMINAL LAW ACT 1977

Q Define the offence of Communicating Hoax Bomb Threats

A   A person who communicates information which he knows or believes to be false intending to induce in any person a belief that a bomb or anything liable to explode is in any place, commits an offence.

Arrest. Arrestable offence.

S. 51(2) CRIMINAL LAW ACT 1977

Q   Outline the offence of Placing or Sending Substances under the Anti-terrorism, Crime and Security Act 2001

A

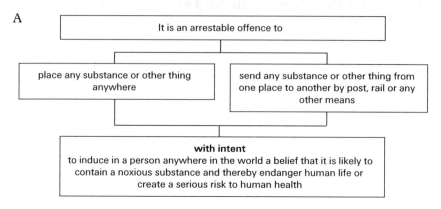

It is an arrestable offence to

| place any substance or other thing anywhere | send any substance or other thing from one place to another by post, rail or any other means |

with intent
to induce in a person anywhere in the world a belief that it is likely to contain a noxious substance and thereby endanger human life or create a serious risk to human health

S. 114(1) ANTI-TERRORISM, CRIME AND SECURITY ACT 2001

Q   Outline the offence of Hoax Threats involving Noxious Substances

A   A person is guilty of an offence if he communicates any information which he knows or believes to be false with the intention of inducing in a person anywhere a belief that a noxious substance or other noxious thing is likely to be present (whether at the time of the communication or later) in any place and thereby endanger human life or create a serious risk to human health.

S. 114(2) ANTI-TERRORISM, CRIME AND SECURITY ACT 2001

Future threats. Note that this offence covers both present and future threats, whereas the equivalent offence concerning bomb hoaxes covers only present threats (e.g. 'there is a bomb in the City' not 'there will be a bomb next week').

Q   Outline the offence of Interfering with Mail under the Postal Services Act 2000

A   Any person who, without reasonable excuse, intentionally delays or opens a postal packet in the course of its transmission by post, or intentionally opens a mailbag, commits an offence.

Further, a person commits an offence if, intending to act to a person's detriment and without reasonable excuse, he opens a postal packet which he knows or reasonably suspects has been incorrectly delivered to him.

No offence. Where the actions were carried out under a lawful warrant or statutory provision.

S. 84 POSTAL SERVICES ACT 2000

Q   Outline the offence of Sending Prohibited Articles by Post under S. 85 Postal Services Act 2000

A   It is an offence to send by post a postal packet which encloses any creature, article or thing of any kind which is *likely to injure* other postal packets in the post or any postal operator (unless the contents are permitted by the postal operator concerned).

It is also an offence to send by post a postal packet which encloses:

[a]   any *indecent or obscene* print, painting, photograph, lithograph, engraving, cinematograph film or other record of a picture or pictures, book, card or written communication, or

[b]   any other indecent or obscene article

or to send any postal packet which has on the cover any words, marks or designs which are of an indecent or obscene character.

Q   Outline the offence under S. 1 of the Malicious Communications Act 1988

A   Any person who sends to another a letter, electronic communication or any other article which he intends should cause distress or anxiety to the recipient or another conveying:

[a]   a message which is indecent or grossly offensive;
[b]   a threat; or
[c]   information which he knows or believes is false
[d]   any article or e-communication which is, in whole or part, of an indecent or grossly offensive nature

commits an offence.

Defence. It is a defence to prove that the threat was used to reinforce a demand which he had reasonable grounds for making and the threat was the proper means of reinforcing demand.

Sends. Includes transmitting and would cover putting dog faeces through a neighbour's letterbox.

Q   Define the offence of Making a Threat to Kill

A   A person who without lawful excuse makes to another a threat to kill that person or a third person intending that the other would fear it would be carried out, commits an offence.

Note. It does not matter that the recipient of the threat does not actually fear that it would be carried out. It is the intention of the threatener which is important.

Arrest. Arrestable offence.

S. 16 OFFENCES AGAINST THE PERSON ACT 1861

Q   Outline the offence of Improper Use of Public Telecommunication Systems

A   A person who:

[a]   sends by means of a **public** telecommunication system, a message or matter that is grossly offensive or indecent, obscene or menacing; or

[b]   for the purpose of causing annoyance, inconvenience or needless anxiety to another, sends (or causes to be sent) a message or matter that he knows to be false, or persistently makes use of a public telecoms system for that purpose

commits an offence.

S. 43 TELECOMMUNICATIONS ACT 1984

Note. This offence applies to 'nuisance' calls on public systems such as the public telephone system or Internet. It does not apply to internal calls in the workplace.

Persistent misuse. Requires proof of sufficient occasions to amount either to a pattern of behaviour, or recklessness as to whether someone suffers anxiety etc.

Q   Outline the offence of Sending Unsolicited Publications

A   It is a summary offence to send unsolicited material or advertising material which describes or illustrates human sexual techniques.

Prosecution. The consent of the DPP is required for prosecution.

S. 4 UNSOLICITED GOODS AND SERVICES ACT 1971

FIREARMS

Q   Define a firearm

A

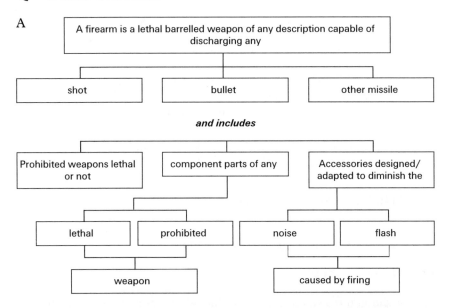

A firearm is a lethal barrelled weapon of any description capable of discharging any

| shot | bullet | other missile |

and includes

| Prohibited weapons lethal or not | component parts of any | Accessories designed/ adapted to diminish the |

| lethal | prohibited | noise | flash |

| weapon | caused by firing |

S. 57 FIREARMS ACT 1968

Component parts such as triggers, barrel etc are included. Telescopic sights are not. Note that where accessories such as silencers and flash eliminators are concerned, they will only be considered firearms in themselves if they can be shown to be capable of use with a weapon in the defendant's possession, and were held for that purpose:

R v. Buckfield (1998)

Q   When is a firearm not a firearm?

A   It may cease to be a firearm if it is de-activated by proving:

[a]   it bears a mark [approved by the Secretary of State] denoting the fact that it has been de-activated by an approved company; and

[b]   the company has certified in writing that the work has been carried out in an approved manner for rendering it incapable.

S. 8 FIREARMS (AMENDMENT) ACT 1988

Q Summarise the list of prohibited weapons under the Firearms Acts

A [a] Automatic weapons;
   [b] most self-loading or pump-action weapons;
   [c] any firearm which is less than **60 cm** long or whose barrel is less than **30 cm** long e.g. most handguns;
   [d] most smooth-bore revolvers;
   [e] any weapon designed or adapted for the discharge of noxious liquid, gas or thing;
   [f] military weapons and ammunition, including grenades and mortars.

   Empty washing up bottles filled with noxious liquid [acid] do not amount to 'being adapted': *R v. Formosa (1991)*

   FIREARMS ACTS 1968 & 1997

Q What are 'Section 1 firearms'?

A All firearms except shotguns (not sawn-off shotguns) and conventional (ie. not 'specially dangerous') air weapons.

Q Define a shotgun

A A shotgun is a smooth-bore gun [not air weapon or revolver] which:

   [a] has a barrel not less than **24 inches;**
   [b] whose bore does not exceed **2 inches;** and
   [c] whose magazine [if any] does not hold more than **2 cartridges.**

   S. 1(3)(A) FIREARMS ACT 1968

Q When is an air weapon 'specially dangerous'?

A [a] When the kinetic energy exceeds 6 ft lb [air pistol];
   [b] when the kinetic energy exceeds 12 ft lb [air weapon]; or
   [c] when it is disguised as another object.

   Note. [b] does not apply to underwater guns.

Q What ammunition is exempt from Section 1 Firearms?

A [a] Cartridges containing five or more shots, none bigger than **0.36 inch** diameter;
   [b] ammunition for an airgun, air rifle or air pistol; and
   [c] blank cartridges not more than **1 inch** diameter.

Q   Outline the offence of Possessing a S. 1 Firearm/Ammo without a Certificate

A

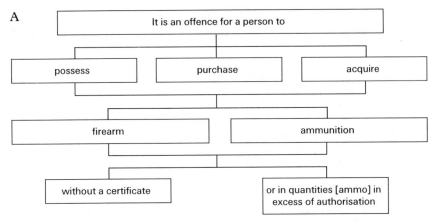

S. 1 FIREARMS ACT 1968

Q   Summarise who is generally exempt from holding a firearms certificate

A   [a]   Police permit holders;
     [b]   clubs, athletics and sporting purposes;
     [c]   borrowed rifle on private premises;
     [d]   holders of visitors permits;
     [e]   antiques as ornaments or curiosities;
     [f]   authorised firearm dealers;
     [g]   auctioneers, carriers or warehouse staff;
     [h]   licensed slaughterers;
     [i]   theatrical performers;
     [j]   ship or aircraft equipment;
     [k]   crown servants;
     [l]   proof houses; and
     [m]   museum licences.

Q   What are the two main shotgun offences?

A   [a]   It is an offence to possess, purchase or acquire a shotgun without a certificate; or
     [b]   to fail to comply with a condition of a shotgun certificate.

SS. 2(1) & (2) FIREARMS ACT 1968

Arrest. [a] Arrestable offence; [b] no specific power of arrest.

Q Define the offence of Possessing or Distributing Prohibited Weapons or Ammunition

A It is an offence, without the authority of the Secretary of State, to possess, purchase, acquire, manufacture, sell or transfer a prohibited weapon or ammunition.

S. 5 FIREARMS ACT 1968

Arrest. Arrestable offence.

Q Outline the eight offences of Firearms – Criminal Use

A 1. **Possession with intent to endanger life.** It is an offence for a person to have in his possession a firearm or ammunition with intent to endanger life or cause serious injury to property or to enable another to do so. *Serious Arrestable.*

S. 16

2. **Possession with intent to cause fear of violence.** It is an offence for a person to have in his possession a firearm [or imitation] with intent to cause, or enable another to cause, any person to believe that **unlawful violence** will be used against him or another. *Arrestable.*

S. 16A

3. **Using a firearm to resist arrest.** It is an offence for a person to make [or attempt to make] use of a firearm [or imitation] to prevent the lawful arrest of himself or another. *Serious Arrestable.*

Note. 'Firearm' here does not include component parts and silencers/flash eliminators.

S. 17(1)

4. **Possession of a firearm while committing/being arrested for a Schedule 1 offence.** If a person, at the time of committing or being arrested for an offence in Schedule 1 to the Act, has in his possession a firearm [or imitation] he commits an offence unless he can show he has it for a **lawful object.** *Arrestable.*

S. 17(2)

Schedule 1 offences are:

[a] criminal damage;
[b] theft, robbery, blackmail, burglary, taking conveyance;
[c] assaults and wounding;
[d] rape;
[e] child abduction;
[f] aiding and abetting any of the above.

5. **Having a firearm with intent to commit indictable offence or resist arrest.** It is an offence to have a firearm [or imitation] with intent to commit an indictable offence, or resist or prevent arrest of another while in possession of a firearm. *Serious Arrestable.*

S. 18(1)

6. **Having a loaded firearm in a public place.** A person commits an offence if, without lawful authority or reasonable excuse [onus of proof lies on him], he has in a public place, a loaded shotgun, a loaded air weapon, or any other **firearm** [loaded or not] **together with ammunition** for it. *Arrestable unless air weapon.*

S. 19

7. **Trespassing with firearm in building.** A person commits an offence if, while he has a firearm or imitation firearm with him, he enters or is in any building or part of a building as a trespasser and without reasonable excuse (the proof of which lies on him). *Arrestable unless imitation firearm or air weapon.*

S. 20(1)

8. **Trespassing with firearm on land.** A person commits an offence if, while he has a firearm or imitation firearm with him, he enters or is on any land as a trespasser and without reasonable excuse (the proof of which lies on him). *No specific power of arrest.*

S. 20(2)

Q What firearms restrictions are placed on convicted persons?

A Any person who has been sentenced to custody for life or to any form of detention for 3 years or more is prohibited from having any firearms or ammunition in his possession **at any time.** Any person sentenced to any form of detention for between 3 months and 3 years is prohibited for 5 years (beginning on the day of release).

S. 21 FIREARMS ACT 1968

Q What are Police Stop and Search powers under S. 47 Firearms Act 1968?

A

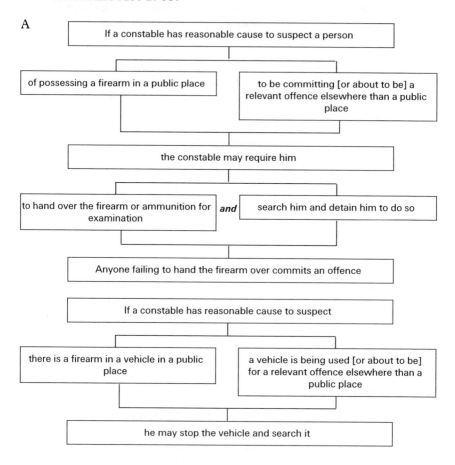

If a constable has reasonable cause to suspect a person

of possessing a firearm in a public place

to be committing [or about to be] a relevant offence elsewhere than a public place

the constable may require him

to hand over the firearm or ammunition for examination *and* search him and detain him to do so

Anyone failing to hand the firearm over commits an offence

If a constable has reasonable cause to suspect

there is a firearm in a vehicle in a public place

a vehicle is being used [or about to be] for a relevant offence elsewhere than a public place

he may stop the vehicle and search it

Q   What are police powers to demand certificates under S. 48 Firearms Act 1968?

A

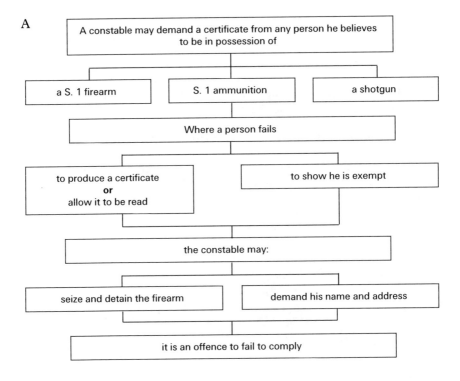

A constable may demand a certificate from any person he believes to be in possession of

| a S. 1 firearm | S. 1 ammunition | a shotgun |

Where a person fails

| to produce a certificate **or** allow it to be read | to show he is exempt |

the constable may:

| seize and detain the firearm | demand his name and address |

it is an offence to fail to comply

Q   It is an offence to shorten the barrel of a shotgun to a length less than?

A   24 inches.

S. 4(1) FIREARMS ACT 1968

Arrest. Arrestable offence.

Measurement. The length of the barrel is measured from its muzzle to the point at which the charge is exploded.

Q   Define the offence of Converting an Imitation Firearm

A   It is an offence for a person [other than a registered firearms dealer] to convert an imitation firearm into a firearm.

S. 4(3) FIREARMS ACT 1968

Arrest. Arrestable offence.

OFFENSIVE WEAPONS

Q Outline the offence of Having an Offensive Weapon in a Public Place

A

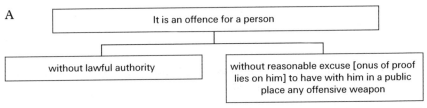

S. 1 PREVENTION OF CRIME ACT 1953

Arrest. Arrestable offence.

Lawful authority. Police officers, members of the military. **Not security guards** although they may have reasonable excuse on a particular occasion.

Reasonable excuse. Possession of tools of your trade, fancy dress incorporating, say, a policeman's truncheon. It is **not reasonable** to carry an offensive weapon 'just in case'. It may be reasonable if you have good grounds for fearing an unlawful attack, e.g. whilst guarding money in transit.

Has with him. Means actual physical possession or at least readily accessible.

Q Define an Offensive Weapon

A

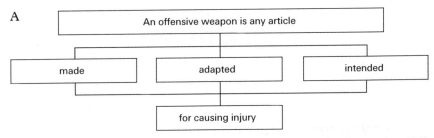

S. 1(4) PREVENTION OF CRIME ACT 1953

Made. Articles made for causing injury, e.g. knuckle dusters, swordsticks, bayonets, flick-knives etc are offensive per se [without further proof] and there is no need for the prosecution to show further proof of intent, possession is enough.

Adapted. Where an article is adapted for causing injury, e.g. broken bottle, chair leg containing nails, etc, the prosecution must show that injury was intended.

Intended. An article may be inoffensive in itself, e.g. an umbrella, but if it is intended for use as an offensive weapon it becomes an offensive weapon.

S. 1 PREVENTION OF CRIME ACT 1953

Q **Outline the offence of Having Blades or Sharply Pointed Articles in a public place**

A

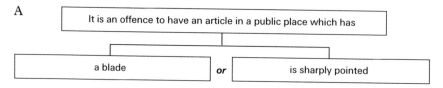

It is an offence to have an article in a public place which has

a blade *or* is sharply pointed

S. 139(1) CRIMINAL JUSTICE ACT 1988

Blade. Folding pocket knives with a blade which does not exceed 3 inches are exempt. If the folding pocket knife locks in the open position, it is not exempt.

Defence.

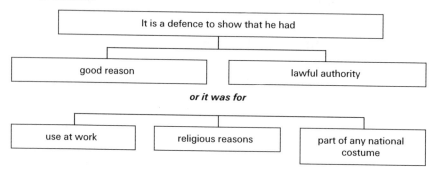

It is a defence to show that he had

good reason lawful authority

or it was for

use at work religious reasons part of any national costume

Religious reasons. E.g. a member of the Sikh religion may carry a small knife (kirpan).

National costume. E.g. someone in Highland dress with a skean dhu, [knife in sock].

Arrest. Arrestable offence.

Q   Define the offence of Having Bladed or Sharply Pointed Articles on School Premises

A

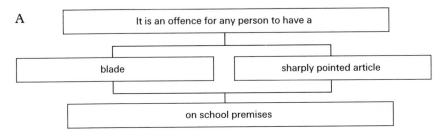

It is an offence for any person to have a

blade | sharply pointed article

on school premises

S. 139A(1) Criminal Justice Act 1988

School premises. Means land used for primary or secondary education. Not further or higher education.

Defence. It is a defence to show that he had good reason or lawful authority or that he had it for use at work, for religious reasons or as part of any national costume.

Arrest. Arrestable offence.

Q   What is the power of entry for the above offence?

A

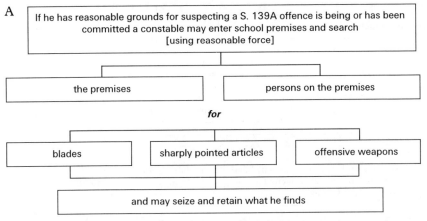

If he has reasonable grounds for suspecting a S. 139A offence is being or has been committed a constable may enter school premises and search [using reasonable force]

the premises | persons on the premises

for

blades | sharply pointed articles | offensive weapons

and may seize and retain what he finds

S. 139B Criminal Justice Act 1988

Arrest. Arrestable offence.

School premises. Means land used for school purposes, but not land occupied solely as a dwelling by a person employed by the school.

Q **Define the offence of Trespassing with an Offensive Weapon**

A Any person who is on any premises as a trespasser, after having entered as such, and who has with him any offensive weapon without lawful authority or reasonable excuse, commits an offence.

S. 8(1) CRIMINAL LAW ACT 1977

Arrest. A constable in uniform may arrest someone committing or reasonably suspected to be committing the offence.

Trespasser. The offence is restricted to a person who **entered** as a trespasser, not someone who entered lawfully but who later becomes a trespasser.

Premises. Any building; any part of a building under separate occupation; any land adjacent to and used/intended for use in connection with a building; any site comprising any building together with ancillary land; any fixed structure; any movable structure, vehicle or vessel designed or adapted for residential use.

Q **Define the offence of Manufacture, Sale/Hire of Weapons**

A

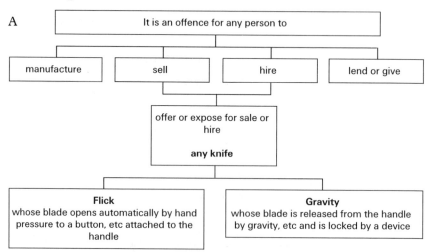

Note 1. This Act (Restriction of Offensive Weapons Act 1959) does not create an offence of possession. The Act was designed to stop trading in such knives only.

Note 2. S. 141 of the Criminal Justice Act 1988 makes similar provisions for a whole range of martial arts weapons.

Q What is the offence of Selling Knives and Articles to under 16s?

A

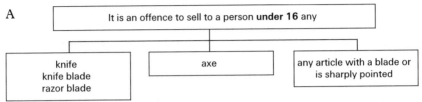

It is an offence to sell to a person **under 16** any

knife	axe	any article with a blade or
knife blade		is sharply pointed
razor blade		

S. 141A CRIMINAL JUSTICE ACT 1988

Defence. To prove that he took all reasonable precautions and exercised due diligence to avoid committing the offence.

Note. The offence does not apply to folding pocket knives with a cutting edge not exceeding 3 inches nor to razor blades in cartridges where no more than 2 mm of blade is exposed (e.g. 'Bic' type razors): Criminal Justice Act 1988 (Offensive Weapons) (Exemptions) Order 1996.

Q Outline the offence of Unlawful Marketing of Knives under S. 1 Knives Act 1997

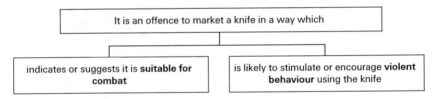

It is an offence to market a knife in a way which

indicates or suggests it is **suitable for combat**

is likely to stimulate or encourage **violent behaviour** using the knife

Marketing. Includes selling, hiring [offering or exposing] and possession for marketing.

Q Outline the offence of Publishing Marketing Material under S. 2 Knives Act 1997

A

It is an offence to publish marketing material which

indicates or suggests a knife is **suitable for combat**

is likely to stimulate or encourage **violent behaviour** using the knife

Q   What are the defences to Marketing and Publishing?

A   [a]   The knife was marketed for use by the armed forces of any country or as an antique or curio; and

[b]   it was reasonable to market it that way; and

[c]   there were no reasonable grounds for believing it would be used unlawfully.

It is also a defence to prove that he did not know or suspect that the way in which the knife was marketed [published] indicated that it was **suitable for combat** or would stimulate or encourage **violent behaviour** using the knife as a weapon, or that he took reasonable precautions and exercised due diligence to avoid committing the offence.

SS. 3,4 KNIVES ACT 1997

Q   Outline the three offences involving Crossbows and persons under 17 years of age

A   1.

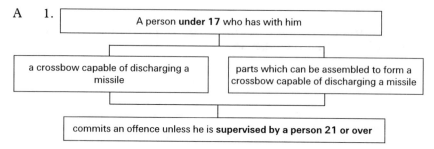

2.   It is an offence for a person to sell or hire a crossbow or a part of a crossbow to a person **under 17,** unless he believes and has reasonable grounds for believing he is 17 or over.

3.   A person **under 17** who buys or hires a crossbow or part of a crossbow commits an offence.

Q   When is a crossbow not a crossbow?

A   When the draw weight is **less than 1.4 kg.**

SS. 1-3 CROSSBOWS ACT 1987

Q   What are the Powers of Search and Seizure of Crossbows?

A

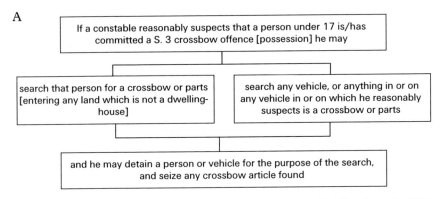

If a constable reasonably suspects that a person under 17 is/has committed a S. 3 crossbow offence [possession] he may

search that person for a crossbow or parts [entering any land which is not a dwelling-house]

search any vehicle, or anything in or on any vehicle in or on which he reasonably suspects is a crossbow or parts

and he may detain a person or vehicle for the purpose of the search, and seize any crossbow article found

S. 4 Crossbows Act 1987

NUISANCE

Q Outline the offences of Dangerous Activities on Highways

A [a] Any person who [without lawful authority or excuse] **deposits** anything on a highway whereby a user is **injured or endangered** commits an offence;

[b] any person who [without lawful authority or excuse] **lights a fire, discharges a firearm or firework, within 50 feet** of the centre of the highway whereby a user is **injured, interrupted or endangered** commits an offence;

[c] any person who plays **games** on a highway to the **annoyance** of a user commits an offence;

[d] any person who [without lawful authority or excuse] allows **offensive matter** to flow onto a highway from adjoining premises commits an offence;

[e] any person who **lights a fire on land [not a highway],** or directs or permits it whereby a user is **injured, interrupted or endangered** by the fire or smoke, commits an offence; and

[f] any person who places any **rope, wire or anything** across a highway whereby it is likely to cause **danger** to a user commits an offence, unless he proves he has given adequate warning of the danger.

Fire defence. At the time the fire was lit he was satisfied that it was unlikely that users would be injured, interrupted or endangered by the fire or smoke and either :

[i] both before and after the fire was lit he did what he reasonably could to prevent users being injured etc, or

[ii] he had a reasonable excuse for not doing so.

SS. 161-162 Highways Act 1980

Q Give some examples of the common law offence of causing a Public Nuisance

A [a] Allowing a rave to take place in a field: *R v. Shorrock (1994)*;

[b] making hundreds of nuisance telephone calls to at least 13 women: *R v. Johnson (1996)*;

[c] contaminating 30 houses with noise and quarry dust: *AG v. PYA Quarries Ltd. (1957)*;

[d] selling meat unfit for human consumption: *R v. Stephens (1866)*.

Q   Define the offence of Exceeding Noise Level after Service of Notice

A   Where a warning notice has been served in respect of noise from a dwelling, any person responsible for noise which is emitted from the dwelling during the **period specified** and exceeding the prescribed limit **measured from the complainant's dwelling,** commits an offence.

S. 4(1) Noise Act 1996

Defence. To show that there was a reasonable excuse for the noise.

Q   Define the offence of Leaving Litter

A

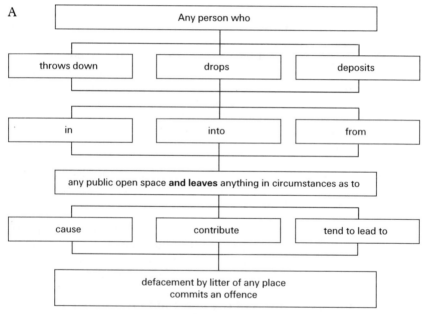

S. 87(1) Environmental Protection Act 1990

Public open space. Means where the public are entitled to access **without payment** and any **covered space** open to the public **open to the air on at least one side.**

Note. This offence can also be committed on relevant land belonging to: Local authority, the Crown, Statutory undertakers [railway, tramway, docks etc] and designated educational institutions.

Defence. When authorised by law or with the consent of the land owner.

Litter. Includes animal droppings.

Q   Define the offence of Throwing Fireworks into a Highway or Street

A   If any person throws, casts or fires any fireworks in or into any highway, street, thoroughfare, or public place, he shall be guilty of an offence.
S. 80 EXPLOSIVES ACT 1875

Q   Outline the Possession of Fireworks offences

A   It is an offence for any person under 18 to possess (unless exempted) an adult firework in a public place. It is also an offence for any person (of any age) to possess (unless exempted) a category 4 firework.
REGS 3 & 4 FIREWORKS REGULATIONS 2003

Fireworks. The definitions and categories of fireworks are set out in the British Standards Specification BS 7114. Adult fireworks are generally those which have some explosive material except, for example, caps, cracker snaps, party poppers, sparklers etc. Category 4 fireworks are certain large powerful fireworks. General exemptions are provided for those who have such fireworks in the course of their work or business, or are properly authorised to conduct displays.

Q   Outline the offence of Begging

A   It is a summary offence under the Vagrancy Act 1824 to beg or gather alms in a street or public place. Caselaw indicates that the Act is intended to deal with conduct that forces passers-by to deal with the defendant's activities rather than simply ignoring it (e.g. 'aggressive' begging), and it is necessary to prove more than a single act of approaching a person and asking for money.

OFFENCES RELATED TO LAND

Q   **What is an Interim Possession Order?**

A   An order made by a court during proceedings for the recovery of premises occupied by trespassers. Wilful obstruction of anyone executing such an order is a summary offence.

CRIMINAL JUSTICE AND PUBLIC ORDER ACT 1994

Q   Outline the Interim Possession Order Trespass Offence

Q   When an interim possession order has been made and served then a person commits an offence if he:

[a]   is present on the premises as a trespasser during the currency of the order unless:

[i]   he leaves **within 24 hours** of its service and does not return; or

[ii]   the order is void by reason of not being fixed to the premises;

[b]   having been in occupation when the order was served he re-enters as a trespasser after the order expired but **within one year** of it being served.

S. 76 CRIMINAL JUSTICE AND PUBLIC ORDER ACT 1994

Arrest. A constable *in uniform* may arrest anyone who is, or he reasonably suspects to be, guilty of an offence.

Q   Define the offence of Making False Statement to Obtain Interim Possession Order

A

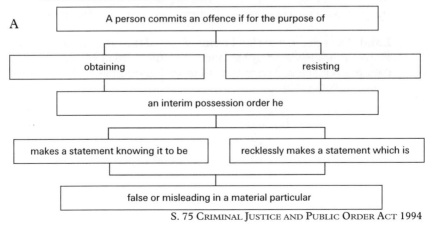

S. 75 CRIMINAL JUSTICE AND PUBLIC ORDER ACT 1994

Q   Outline the offence of Aggravated Trespass

A

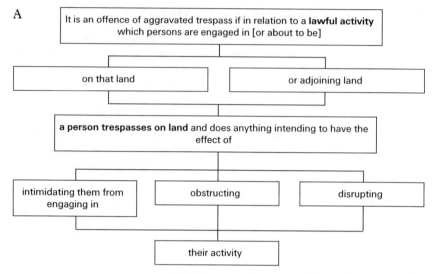

It is an offence of aggravated trespass if in relation to a **lawful activity** which persons are engaged in [or about to be]

on that land

or adjoining land

a person trespasses on land and does anything intending to have the effect of

intimidating them from engaging in

obstructing

disrupting

their activity

S. 68 CRIMINAL JUSTICE AND PUBLIC ORDER ACT 1994

Arrest. A constable *in uniform* who reasonably suspects a person is committing an offence.

Purpose. This offence was primarily intended to cover the activities of e.g. hunt saboteurs disrupting a hunt (which, at the time of writing, remains a lawful activity). Notice that it only applies to persons who are trespassing on land, and therefore does not encompass protesters who stand on highways or other land where they have permission to be.

Land. Does not include land forming part of the highway unless it is a footpath, bridleway or byway open to traffic or road used as a public path or cycle track. Trespassing in or on buildings as well as on open land is now covered.

Q **Outline police powers in relation to Aggravated Trespass**

A The senior police officer present **at the scene** (who need not be in uniform) may direct a person to leave land if he reasonably believes:

[a] he is or is intending to commit the offence of aggravated trespass on land; or

[b] **two or more persons are trespassing** on land in the open air with the common purpose of intimidating, obstructing or disrupting a lawful activity.

S. 69 CRIMINAL JUSTICE AND PUBLIC ORDER ACT 1994

Offence. Knowing a direction has been given, fails to leave the land as soon as possible, or having left, re-enters as a trespasser **within three months** of the direction being given.

Defence. To prove he was not a trespasser or that he had reasonable cause for failing to leave, or re-enter.

Arrest. A constable *in uniform.*

Q **Outline the police powers where two or more people are Trespassing for Residence**

A The senior police officer present **at the scene (who need not be in uniform) may direct persons to leave land if he reasonably believes:**

[a] **two or more persons are trespassing** on land; and

[b] that their common purpose is to **reside there**; and

[c] they have been **asked to leave** [or reasonable steps have been taken by occupier]; and

that any of those persons have:

[a] caused damage to land or property; or

[b] have used threatening, abusive or insulting words or behaviour towards the occupier, his family, employee, or agent; or

[c] they have **six or more vehicles** on the land.

he may direct them to leave the land together with their vehicles and property. The direction may be communicated by any officer at the scene (who need not be in uniform). It is an offence to knowingly

[a]   fail to leave as soon as reasonably practicable; or

[b]   having left, to re-enter as a trespasser within 3 months.

S. 61 CRIMINAL JUSTICE AND PUBLIC ORDER ACT 1994

Trespasser? Where persons were not trespassers at the outset but have subsequently become trespassers the police officer must believe that they have caused damage, used threatening words or behaviour or have six or more vehicles **since becoming trespassers.**

Arrest. A constable *in uniform.* Vehicles may be seized and removed.

Land. Does not include buildings, except farm buildings or scheduled monuments. Nor does it include a footpath, bridleway or byway open to traffic or road used as a public path or cycle track.

Damage to land. Includes any pollution, e.g. oil from vehicles.

Vehicles. Includes parts, such as a chassis or body appearing to have formed part of a vehicle. Also includes caravans.

Defence. To prove [a] that he was not trespassing; or [b] that he had a reasonable excuse for failing to leave as soon as reasonably practicable, or for re-entering as a trespasser.

Q   Outline the S. 62A trespassing offence and police powers

A   This is a power designed to enable officers to order persons (e.g. 'travellers' or gypsies) to leave land on which they are trespassing with vehicles and to remove any caravan(s), when there is a suitable and legal alternative site available for them to use.

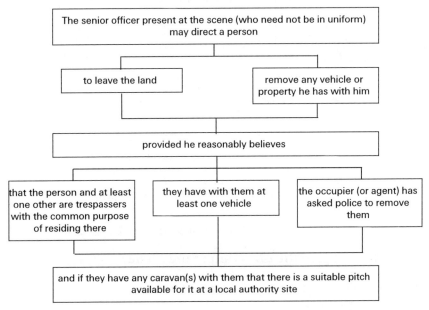

S. 62A CRIMINAL JUSTICE AND PUBLIC ORDER ACT 1994

Offence. It is an offence for anyone who knows of such a direction which applies to him, to fail without reasonable excuse to leave the land as soon as reasonably practicable, or re-enter *any land in the local authority area as a trespasser* and with intention to reside **within 3 months**. A constable **in uniform** may arrest and/or seize/remove a vehicle.

S. 63 CRIMINAL JUSTICE AND PUBLIC ORDER ACT 1994

Q   Outline police powers in relation to Raves

A

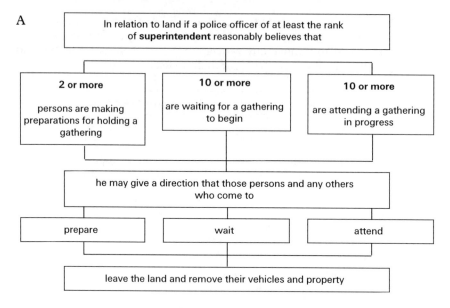

In relation to land if a police officer of at least the rank of **superintendent** reasonably believes that

2 or more

persons are making preparations for holding a gathering

10 or more

are waiting for a gathering to begin

10 or more

are attending a gathering in progress

he may give a direction that those persons and any others who come to

prepare

wait

attend

leave the land and remove their vehicles and property

S. 63 Criminal Justice and Public Order Act 1994

Q   Who can give the direction at the scene?

A   Any constable. He need not be in uniform.

Q   What is meant by a gathering?

A   [a]   On land;
[b]   100 persons or more trespassing or not, or
[c]   20 or more trespassers;
[d]   at which amplified music is played during the night; and by reason of its loudness, duration and time it is played
[e]   is likely to cause serious distress to the inhabitants of the locality.

The gathering continues during intermissions, and **music** includes sounds of a succession of repetitive beats.

Arrest. If a person knows a direction has been given which applies to him and:

    [i]   fails to leave the land as soon as possible, or
    [ii] having left, re-enters **within seven days,** or
    [iii] makes preparations for or attends a gathering within 24 hours of the direction he may be arrested by a constable in uniform.

Defence. For the accused to show he had a reasonable excuse for not leaving the land, or for re-entering.

Exempt. The occupier, his family, employees etc or anyone whose home is on the land.

Q   Outline the powers of the Local Authority in relation to Residing in Vehicles on land

A   If it appears to a Local Authority that persons are residing **in a vehicle** on any land:

    [a] forming part of a highway;
    [b] other unoccupied land; or
    [c] occupied land without the consent of the occupier,

the authority may give a direction to leave and remove their vehicles and property.
                       S. 77 Criminal Justice and Public Order Act 1994

Arrest. If a person knowing that a direction has been given which applies to him:

    [i]   fails to leave the land as soon as possible; or
    [ii] having left, re-enters the land **within three months,**
he may be arrested by a constable **in uniform.**

Defence. To prove that his failure to leave/re-entry was due to illness, mechanical breakdown, or other immediate emergency.

Removal order. The local authority can apply to a magistrates' court for a removal order if people ignore the direction. The local authority can enforce the order.

Notice. 24 hours' notice must be given to the owner of the land and the residents of their intention to enforce the order.

Q Define the offence of Depriving Residential Occupier of Premises - [unlawful eviction]

A A person shall be guilty of an offence who:

unlawfully deprives the residential occupier of any premises of his occupation of them or any part [or attempts] unless he proves that he believed, and had reasonable cause to believe, that the residential occupier had ceased to reside there.

S. 1(2) PROTECTION FROM EVICTION ACT 1977

Q Define the offence of Harassment of Residential Occupiers under the Protection from Eviction Act 1977

A A person commits an offence if, with intent to cause the residential occupier of any premises to:

[a] give up the occupation of the premises [or part]; or
[b] refrain from exercising any right or from pursuing a remedy in respect of the premises,

he does acts likely to interfere with the peace or comfort of the residential occupier or his household, or persistently withdraws or withholds services reasonably required for his occupation, **and in the case of a landlord or his agent,** he knows that his conduct is likely to cause the residential occupier to give up occupation or refrain from exercising any right to pursue any remedy.

S. 1(3) PROTECTION FROM EVICTION ACT 1977

Note. This offence is aimed at acts done by landlords (and others) with the objective of causing occupiers to leave the premises, e.g. cutting off electricity, gas supplies etc.

Residential occupier. Means a person occupying the premises as a resident [under a contract or rule of law] giving him the right to remain in occupation, or restricting the right of any person to recover the premises.

Defence. To prove that he had reasonable grounds for doing the act.

Q **Define the offence of Using or Threatening Violence to Enter Premises**

A It is an offence, without lawful authority, to use or threaten violence to secure entry to premises where **there is someone present** at the time who opposes the entry which the violence is intended to secure, and the person using the violence knows this is the case.

Defence. This section does not apply to a **displaced residential occupier** or a protected intended residential occupier.

Arrest. A constable *in uniform*.

S. 6 CRIMINAL LAW ACT 1977

Q **Who is a Displaced Residential Occupier?**

A Any person who was occupying any premises as a resident immediately before being excluded from occupation by anyone who entered as a trespasser, **but not** a displaced trespasser.

Q **Outline the offence of Failing to Leave Premises**

A Any trespasser is guilty of an offence if he fails to leave the premises on being required by [or on behalf of]:

[a] a displaced residential occupier; or
[b] a protected intended occupier.

S. 7 CRIMINAL LAW ACT 1977

Defence. To prove that he believed that the person requiring him to leave was not one of the two above.

Non-residential premises. This section does not apply to premises used **mainly** for non-residential premises, [e.g. factories, offices etc].

Power of arrest. A constable *in uniform* may arrest without warrant anyone whom he reasonably suspects to be guilty of an offence under this section.

Q   Outline the offence of Causing or Permitting Nuisance on Educational Premises

A   Any person who without lawful authority is present on relevant premises and who causes or permits nuisance or disturbance to the annoyance of persons who lawfully use those premises (whether or not any such persons are present at the time) commits an offence.

Which premises? Either premises that provide further or higher education and which are maintained by a local education authority (S. 40(1) Local Government (Misc. Prov.) Act 1982) or premises that provide primary or secondary education and which are LEA or grant maintained (S. 547(1) Education Act 1996). 'Premises' includes playing fields and other outdoor areas.

Police powers. If a constable (or other person authorised by a LEA) has reasonable cause to suspect that a person is committing or has committed an offence under these provisions he may remove him from the premises.

LICENSED PREMISES

Q Define Intoxicating Liquor

A   It means any spirits, wine, beer, cider and any fermented, distilled or spirituous liquor.

Excluding
[a]   liquor less than 0.5% proof; [at the time of sale]
[b]   flavouring essences;
[c]   liquor intended as medicine;
[d]   perfumes.

S. 201 Licensing Act 1964

At the time of sale. Where a shandy is poured in a pub and the beer is say 3.5% but is reduced in strength to less than 0.5% when the lemonade is added, it is intoxicating liquor because it was over 0.5% at the time of sale: *Hall v. Hyder (1966)*

Q Define Licensed Premises and Bar

A   **Licensed premises** means premises for which a justices' licence [or occasional licence] is in force.

Bar is any place exclusively or mainly used for both the **sale *and* consumption** of intoxicating liquor.

SS. 200 & 201(1) 1964 Act

Q What is an Occasional Permission?

A   A temporary licence granted by licensing justices for the sale of liquor by an organisation not operating for gain e.g. Parent Teachers Association, church committees etc.

Licensing (Occasional Permission) Act 1983

Q What is an Occasional Licence?

A   A temporary licence for the sale of liquor by **a licensee** other than at his premises, e.g. village hall, trade fair etc. Granted by a magistrates court (not necessarily licensing JPs) and must **not exceed three weeks.**

If the applicant applies in person he must:

[a]   give at least **24 hours' notice** to the police;
[b]   provide name and address;

[c]   provide details of the place and location;
[d]   state the period and the hours the licence is to run.

A licence may be granted without a hearing. In order to apply, the applicant must submit to the Justices' clerk **two copies** in writing **at least one month** before the event. One copy is sent to the police.

S. 180 LICENSING ACT 1964

Note. There is no offence of sale outside permitted hours during an occasional licence nor is there an offence of children under 14 being on the premises. However evidence of children aged under 14 years being on the premises and 'sale after hours' could be used to object to further applications by the licensee.

Q   What are Permitted Hours in Licensed Premises?

A

On-licences	
Weekdays	11 am - 11 pm
Sundays Good Friday	12 noon - 10.30 pm
Christmas Day	12 noon - 3 pm 7 pm - 10.30 pm
Off-licences	
Weekdays Good Friday	8 am - 11 pm
Sundays	10 am - 10.30 pm
Christmas Day	12 noon - 3 pm 7 pm - 10.30 pm

Magistrates may modify the hours to begin earlier than 11 am but not earlier than 10 am.

S. 60(1) LICENSING ACT 1964 (AS AMENDED)

Q   What is meant by Vicarious Liability of Licensees?

A   Where a licensee is himself in charge, he shall not be responsible for acts done by his employees without his knowledge [if the offence requires knowledge on his part.]

However, where the licensee **delegates all responsibility** to his employee [e.g. away on holiday] he is liable for acts done by his employee without his knowledge.

Q Outline the main exceptions to drinking after 11 pm

A

First 20 minutes	After permitted hours end
30 minutes	If drinking was ancillary to a meal
At any time	By residents
At any time	By friends of the resident (including the licensee) entertained at resident's expense
After hours	Employees at the expense of the licensee or the person in charge of the business

Sham friendships. Ordinary (paying) customers cannot be transformed into 'friends' in order to evade the permitted hours provisions. A person who was a customer before 'time' remains a customer after 'time'.

Q What are the offences relating to failing to abide by the terms of an Off-Licence?

A

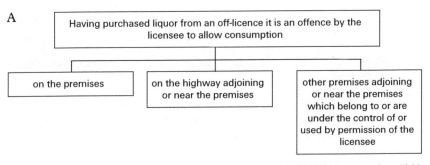

Having purchased liquor from an off-licence it is an offence by the licensee to allow consumption

on the premises

on the highway adjoining or near the premises

other premises adjoining or near the premises which belong to or are under the control of or used by permission of the licensee

S. 164(1) LICENSING ACT 1964

LICENSED PREMISES

Q What is the offence of allowing under 14s in a bar?

A A licensee shall not allow persons aged under 14 years to be in a bar during permitted hours.

S. 168(3) LICENSING ACT 1964

Defence. The person was **apparently** aged 14 years or he exercised due diligence to prevent it. It is also a defence to prove that the person under 14 was in the company of someone aged 18 or over and a children's certificate is in force.

Q Which children aged under 14 years may be in a bar?

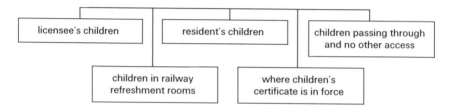

Q What is a Children's Certificate?

A A licensee may apply under S. 168A(1) of the Licensing Act 1964 to the licensing justices for a certificate in relation to any part of his premises which includes a bar. The justices may grant a certificate if it appears appropriate and they are satisfied that:

[a] the area is a suitable environment for under 14 year olds; and
[b] that meals and soft drinks will be available.

When granted the licensee must keep posted in a conspicuous place a certificate:

[i] stating a children's certificate is in force; and
[ii] explaining the effect of the certificate and any conditions attached to it

then, children aged under 14 years **accompanied by a person aged 18 years or over** may be in the area or bar and the person aged under 14 years may be in the bar for up to 30 minutes after the certificate expires if he or the adult is eating a meal bought before the certificate ceased to operate.

Offence. To fail to comply with the conditions of a children's certificate and where it is alleged that a person was under 14 and it appears to the court that he was aged under 14 years, he shall be deemed to be aged under 14 years unless the contrary is proven.

Defence. To prove that he took all reasonable precautions and exercised due diligence.

Q **What are the offences of Providing Liquor to Under 18s?**

A The licensee/servant shall not **sell** liquor to a person aged under 18 years or knowingly **allow the sale** to a person aged under 18 years.

SS. 169A(1), 169B(1) LICENSING ACT 1964

Defence. For the offence of selling it is a defence to prove that he exercised due diligence to avoid the offence or that nobody could reasonably have suspected from his appearance that he was under 18 and that he believed he was aged 18 years or over. The licensee may claim the defence of due diligence for acts of his servants.

No offence. If the person under 18 is at least 16 and the drink involved is:

[a] beer, porter or cider;
[b] for consumption with a meal;
[c] in a part of the licensed premises that is not a 'bar'; and which
[d] is set apart for the service of meals

then this offence does not apply: S. 169D.

Buying aged under 18 years. It is an offence for a person aged under 18 years to buy [or attempt to] or consume liquor in a bar. No person shall buy [or attempt to] for a person aged under 18 years in a bar.

S. 169C LICENSING ACT 1964

Q **Outline the offences of Delivery/Sending liquor for/to under 18s**

A [a] The licensee/servant shall not knowingly deliver, or allow any person to deliver, to a person aged under 18 years liquor for consumption off the premises, unless the delivery is made at the residence or workplace of the purchaser.
   [b] A person shall not knowingly send a person aged under 18 years to licensed premises or other premises for liquor for consumption off the premises.

SS. 169F, 169G LICENSING ACT 1964

No offence. Where the under 18 is a member of the licensee's family or employee and is acting as a messenger to deliver the liquor.

Q   **Can an under 18 year old work behind a bar?**

A   Yes, but only if he is a member of an Approved Training Scheme, and he complies with the conditions of the scheme.

S. 170A LICENSING ACT 1964

Q   **Outline the provisions of the Confiscation of Alcohol (Young Persons) Act 1997**

A

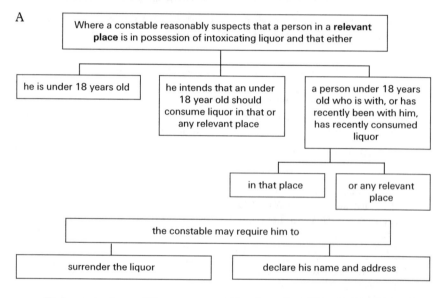

Relevant place. Means any public place [not licensed premises] or any place [other than a public place] to which he has **unlawfully gained access.**

Offence. Failure to comply with the constable's requirements without reasonable excuse is an offence.

Warning. Where a constable requires liquor/name and address, he must inform the person of his suspicions and warn that to fail to supply is an offence.

Arrest. A constable may arrest any person failing the requirement.

Disposal of alcohol. The Constable may dispose of anything surrendered in a manner he considers appropriate.

Q   Outline the drunkenness offences

Offence	Who is liable	Conditions	Arrest
Drunkenness	Licensee Bar staff	permitting drunkenness, or any violent, quarrelsome or riotous behaviour on licensed premises	S. 25 PACE Act 1984
Selling to a drunk	Licensee/staff		No
Procuring liquor for a drunk	any person	in licensed premises	No
Aiding a drunk	any person	to obtain or consume on licensed premises	No
Found drunk	Drunk	on a highway or public place or licensed premises	Yes if he is incapable of taking care of himself

S. 172 Licensing Act 1964

Q   What is the power to exclude drunks?

A   A Licensee or his employee/agent may **refuse to admit, or expel** any person who is drunk, violent, quarrelsome or disorderly, and a Licensee (not his employee/agent) may refuse to admit or expel any person whose presence in the premises would subject him to a penalty.

S. 174 Licensing Act 1964

Offence. To fail to leave the premises, without reasonable excuse.

A constable is there to **help** *the licensee* to expel, not to remove the drunk himself. He may use reasonable necessary force.

Q **What is the power to deal with Alcohol Consumption in a Designated Public Place?**

A

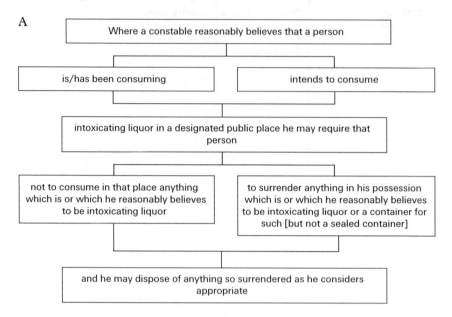

Where a constable reasonably believes that a person

is/has been consuming

intends to consume

intoxicating liquor in a designated public place he may require that person

not to consume in that place anything which is or which he reasonably believes to be intoxicating liquor

to surrender anything in his possession which is or which he reasonably believes to be intoxicating liquor or a container for such [but not a sealed container]

and he may dispose of anything so surrendered as he considers appropriate

Designated public place. Identified by local authorities as places where consumption of intoxicating liquor has been associated with disorder or public nuisance or annoyance. **Not** licensed premises, clubs or places covered by occasional permissions/licences.

Offence. It is an arrestable offence to fail, without reasonable excuse, to comply with a requirement not to consume/to surrender. The constable **must** first inform the person concerned that failure to comply is an offence.

Q   What is the power of a constable to enter licensed premises?

A

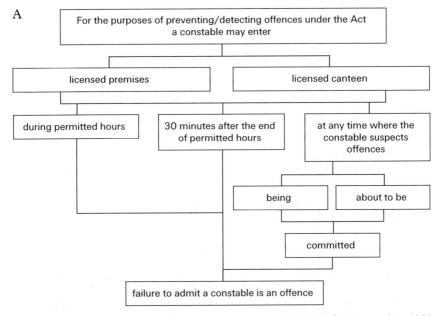

For the purposes of preventing/detecting offences under the Act a constable may enter

| licensed premises | licensed canteen |

| during permitted hours | 30 minutes after the end of permitted hours | at any time where the constable suspects offences |

| being | about to be |

committed

failure to admit a constable is an offence

S. 186(1) LICENSING ACT 1964

Q   What if a Special Hours Certificate is in force?

A   The power to enter is during the hours beginning at **11 pm** to **30 minutes after** the end of the hours **permitted in the certificate.**

Q   What is an Exclusion Order?

A   Under the Licensed Premises (Exclusion of Certain Persons) Act 1980, a court may order persons to be excluded from licensed premises for offences involving violence. The order may exclude persons for any period between **three months** and **two years.** The licensee may however give express consent for the person to enter.

Offence. To enter the premises in breach of the order.

Power to expel. The licensee/servant may expel such a person and a constable shall, at the request of the licensee/agent **help to expel.**

Q   What is the power to make a Closure Order in respect of Licensed Premises?

A   An officer of at least the rank of **Inspector** may make an order requiring specified licensed premises to close for **up to 24 hours** if he reasonably believes that

[a]   there is disorder on, or in the vicinity of and related to the premises; or

[b]   there is likely to be disorder on, or in the vicinity of and related to the premises, and in either case he reasonably believes an order is necessary

[i]   in the interests of public safety; or

[ii]   to prevent excessive noise disturbance.

S. 179A LICENSING ACT 1964

Q   What are police powers of Entry and to Expel from Licensed Betting Offices?

A   A constable may enter any licensed betting office to ascertain whether it is being run in accordance with the rules and a constable may, on the request of the licensee/servant, **help to expel** from a licensed betting office any person who is liable to be expelled, e.g. persons aged under 18 years, persons who are drunk, violent, quarrelsome or disorderly, or whose presence would subject the licensee to a penalty.

S. 10 BETTING, GAMING AND LOTTERIES ACT 1963

Q   Outline police powers of Entry and Inspection of Gaming Machines

A

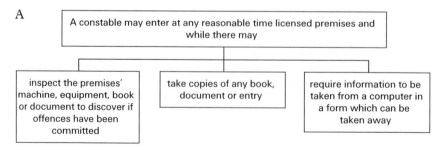

A constable may enter at any reasonable time licensed premises and while there may

| inspect the premises' machine, equipment, book or document to discover if offences have been committed | take copies of any book, document or entry | require information to be taken from a computer in a form which can be taken away |

S. 43 GAMING ACT 1968

Offence. It is an offence if the licensee/servant:

[a]   fails to admit a constable without reasonable excuse;

[b]   fails to permit him to inspect the premises/equipment, without reasonable excuse;

[c]   fails to produce any book or document which the constable wishes to inspect or copy, without reasonable excuse; or

[d]   fails to obtain a computer printout if required, without reasonable excuse.

CIVIL DISPUTES

Q Under the Family Law Act 1996 what is a Non-Molestation order?

A
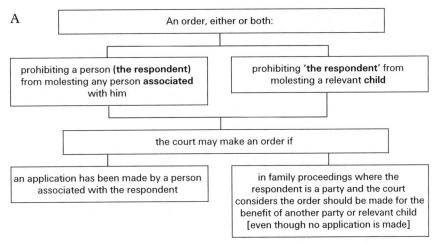

An order, either or both:

prohibiting a person (**the respondent**) from molesting any person **associated** with him

prohibiting '**the respondent**' from molesting a relevant **child**

the court may make an order if

an application has been made by a person associated with the respondent

in family proceedings where the respondent is a party and the court considers the order should be made for the benefit of another party or relevant child [even though no application is made]

S. 42 FAMILY LAW ACT 1996

Associated. Means:

[a] they are or have been married to each other;
[b] they are cohabitees, or former cohabitees;
[c] they live or have lived in the same household [but not as employee, tenant, lodger or boarder];
[d] they are relatives;
[e] they have agreed to marry [whether or not the agreement is terminated];
[f] they are parties to the same family proceedings.

In relation to a child they are both:

[i]   its parents; or
[ii] have or had parental responsibility.

S. 62 FAMILY LAW ACT 1996

Arrest. Where a court makes an order and it appears that the respondent has used or threatened **violence** against the applicant or relevant child it **shall attach a power of arrest** to one or more provisions of the order **unless** satisfied the applicant or child will be adequately protected. A constable may arrest where he has reasonable cause to suspect a breach of such an order.

S. 47 FAMILY LAW ACT 1996

Ex parte. The ability to attach a power of arrest ex parte [in the absence of the other person attendance at the hearing] exists only if:

[a]   the respondent has used or threatened violence against the applicant or child; or

[b]   there is a risk of significant harm to the applicant or relevant child if a power of arrest is not attached immediately.

After arrest. Where the respondent is arrested he shall be brought before the court which made the order **within 24 hours;** and if the matter is not dealt with he may be remanded.

S. 47(7) FAMILY LAW ACT 1996

24 hours. Does not take account of Christmas Day, Good Friday or Sundays. If it is not possible to bring the respondent to a courtroom within the 24 hours, the judge or magistrate may sit in any suitable and convenient place to hear the case.

TRADE DISPUTES

Q What is meant by Peaceful Picketing?

A

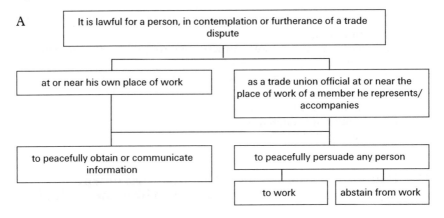

It is lawful for a person, in contemplation or furtherance of a trade dispute

at or near his own place of work

as a trade union official at or near the place of work of a member he represents/accompanies

to peacefully obtain or communicate information

to peacefully persuade any person

to work

abstain from work

S. 220 Trade Union and Labour Relations (Consolidation) Act 1992

Q What if he works elsewhere?

A If he works:

[a] other than at any one place; or
[b] it is impracticable to picket there,

then his place of work shall be deemed to be any premises of his employer from which he works or from which his work is administered.

What if he no longer works? If his last employment was terminated in connection with the trade dispute, or gave rise to the dispute, his place of work shall be deemed to be **his last place of work.**

What if the workplace has moved? A person's place of work does not include new premises of an employer who has moved since dismissing him: *News Group Newspapers Ltd. v. SOGAT '82 (1987)*

Q What is meant by a Trade Dispute?

A   A dispute between employers and workers relating mainly to:

[a]   terms and conditions of employment, including physical conditions;

[b]   engagement [or not] suspension/termination of employment/ duties of one or more workers;

[c]   allocation of work or duties;

[d]   discipline;

[e]   membership of a trade union;

[f]   facilities for union officials; and

[g]   machinery for negotiation or consultation.

S. 244(1) 1992 ACT

Q Can a dispute between workers in a government department and the Minister come within the section?

A   Yes, even though he/she is not the workers' 'employer'.

Q   **Outline the offence of Intimidation by Violence or otherwise in relation to Labour Relations**

A

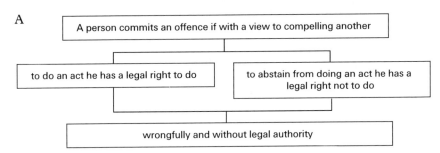

He:
[a]   uses violence or intimidates him, his wife or children or damages his property;
[b]   persistently follows him;
[c]   hides his tools or property or deprives him of their use;
[d]   watches or besets his house or work business or where he is [or the approaches];
[e]   **three or more** follow him in a disorderly manner in any street or road.

S. 241 TRADE UNION AND LABOUR RELATIONS (CONSOLIDATION) ACT 1992

Arrest. A constable may arrest anyone he reasonably suspects to be committing an offence under this section.

Seamen. This offence does not apply to seamen.

Intent. 'With a view to compelling' means with intent to compel the other person.

OFFENCES INVOLVING INFORMATION

Q **What is the offence of Unauthorised Access to Computers (Hacking)?**

A A person is guilty of an offence if:

[a] he **causes a computer to perform any function** intending to secure unauthorised access to any program or data; and
[b] he knows that the access is **unauthorised.**

S. 1 COMPUTER MISUSE ACT 1990

The intent. Need not be directed at:

[i] any particular program or data;
[ii] a program or data of a particular kind; or
[iii] a program or data held in any particular computer.

Secure access. Means by causing the computer to perform a function, he:

[a] alters or erases the program or data;
[b] copies or moves to a different storage;
[c] uses it; or
[d] has it printed from the computer which holds it.

Time limit. Any prosection for a S. 1 offence must be brought within six months from the date on which evidence sufficient to warrant prosecution comes to the knowledge of the prosecutor: S. 11(2).

Q **Outline the offence of Unauthorised Access with Intent to commit an arrestable offence**

A

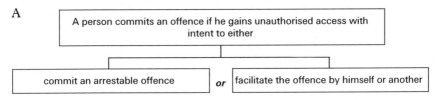

S. 2 COMPUTER MISUSE ACT 1990

Arrest. Arrestable offence.

Q Outline the offence of unauthorised Modification of Computer Material

A A person commits an offence if:

[a] he does any act which causes unauthorised modification of the contents of any computer; with intent to cause a modification to the contents of any computer and thereby to impair its operation, prevent or hinder access to any program or data, or impair the operation or reliability of a program; and

[b] he knows that any such modification is unauthorised.

S. 3 COMPUTER MISUSE ACT 1990

Arrest. Arrestable offence.

Virus implantation. Is an offence under this section.

Q Under the Data Protection Act 1998 what is the meaning of Data?

A 'Data' means information recorded in a form in which it can be processed by equipment operating automatically in response to instruction given for that purpose or which is recorded as part of a relevant filing system.

Relevant filing system. Means any set of information relating to **individuals** to the extent that, although not processed by equipment operating automatically, the set is structured in a way that information relating to a **particular individual** is readily accessible.

S. 1 1998 ACT

Q   Outline the offence of Obtaining, Disclosure and Sale of Personal Data

A   A person must not knowingly or recklessly, without the consent of the data controller

[a]   obtain or disclose personal data; or
[b]   procure the disclosure for another, unless:

[i]   it was for preventing or detecting crime; or
[ii]   authorised by an enactment, rule of law, or order of a court; or
[iii]   he believed he had a right in law to obtain, disclose etc; or
[iv]   he believed he would have had the consent of the data controller; or
[v]   it was justified as being in the public interest.

[c]   it is an offence **to offer for sale personal data** unlawfully obtained.

Prosecution. Offences under the 1998 Act may not be prosecuted by anyone other than the Data Protection Commissioner or with the consent of the DPP.

Q   What is a Covert Human Intelligence Source (CHIS) under the Regulation of Investigatory Powers Act 2000?

A   A CHIS is someone who establishes and develops a relationship with another person for the covert purpose of obtaining information or providing access to information or covertly disclosing information obtained as a result of the relationship. A 'covert' relationship is one which is calculated to ensure that one of the parties is unaware of its true purpose.

Part 2 - Crime

INTRODUCTION

Q What does S.8 Criminal Justice Act 1967 say about Intent?

A   A court or jury in deciding whether a person has committed an offence :

[a]   shall **not be bound to infer that he intended or foresaw** a result of his actions by reason only of it being *a natural and probable consequence;* but

[b]   shall decide whether **he did intend or foresee** that result by *reference to all the evidence,* drawing such inferences as appear proper.

Q Define subjective (*Cunningham*) recklessness

A   Where the defendant actually foresees that there is a risk of the consequence resulting from his act, and in all the circumstances it is unreasonable for him to take that risk, but he takes it anyway.

Q Give an example of transferred malice

A   'A' throws a rock at 'B' intending him injury, but misses and causes injury to 'C'. (So long as the defendant has the required state of mind for a particular offence it does not matter whether the actual target/ victim was unintended or unforeseen).

Q What is meant by actus reus and mens rea?

A   *Actus reus* is the physical act of the crime and *mens rea* is the guilty state of mind, e.g. intent.

Q Distinguish between a principal and an accessory

A   The principal is one who has met all the requirements of an offence whilst an accessory is a person who aids, abets, counsels or procures the commission of an offence. An aider and abetter is guilty as a principal.

Q When can an omission amount to an offence?

A When the 'offender' has a **duty of care** to act in favour of the 'victim' e.g. where a police officer voluntarily fails to intervene to prevent an assault.

Q Define incitement

A It is a common law offence unlawfully to incite (or encourage) another to commit an offence. The substantive offence need not be committed; incitement to commit is the offence. (If the substantive offence is committed the inciter will be an accessory.) If the substantive offence is indictable incitement is an arrestable offence.

Q Define Statutory Conspiracy

A It is an offence to be involved in any agreement between two or more persons to pursue a course of conduct, which, if carried out either:

[a] will involve committing an offence; or
[b] would do so, but in the event it is impossible to commit.

SS. 1, 2 CRIMINAL LAW ACT 1977

Arrest. Arrestable offence if the substantive offence is arrestable.

No conviction. A defendant cannot be convicted of conspiracy if the only other party to the agreement is his spouse, child under 10, or the intended victim. However a husband and wife can both be convicted if they conspire with a third party.

Prosecution. Conspiracy is triable only on indictment even if the substantive offence is summary, but in such a case, the consent of the DPP is required for prosecution.

Q Define conspiracy to defraud at Common Law

A Any agreement by two or more persons by dishonesty to deprive a person of what is his or to which he is entitled or to harm his proprietary rights: *Scott v. Met. Police Cmr (1975)*

Q   Define a criminal attempt

A   If, with intent to commit an offence, a person **does an act which is more than merely preparatory** to the commission of the offence he is guilty of attempt.

S. 1(1) Criminal Attempts Act 1981

Impossible offences. Where the above definition fits, a person may be charged with an attempt even though the offence is impossible. [e.g. searching an empty purse for money].

Q   Define the offence of Interfering with Motor Vehicles

A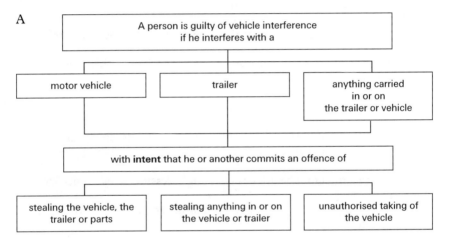

Which charge? Where it is shown that a person accused under this section intended that one of the offences should be committed, it is immaterial that it cannot be shown which one it actually was.

S. 9 Criminal Attempts Act 1981

Q   Who can authorise the use of a CHIS?

A   A superintendent (or above). In urgent cases (not involving juveniles or the obtaining of confidential material) an inspector may give authority.

INTRODUCTION

Q Can an inspector give oral authority in an urgent case?

A No. Inspectors' authorities must always be in writing. Only a superintendent (or above) can give oral authority, and then only in urgent cases.

Q For how long can a CHIS authority last?

A A superintendent's written authority will ordinarily last for 12 months. A superintendent's urgent oral authority lasts for 72 hours, as does an inspector's urgent written authority, unless renewed. Strict controls govern the use of juveniles (under 18s) as CHISs. A written authority in such a case will last for 1 month.

Q For what purposes may the use of a CHIS be authorised?

A When the superintendent/inspector believes it is both necessary and proportionate:

[a] for the prevention/detection of crime/disorder;

[b] in the interests of national security, public safety and/or the economic well-being of the UK;

[c] for protecting health or collecting/assessing taxes, duties etc. or

[d] for any other purpose specified by order made by the Secretary of State.

Q What is 'covert surveillance'?

A Surveillance which is carried out in a manner calculated to ensure that people subject to it are unaware that it is taking place. 'Surveillance' covers monitoring, observing, listening to and recording people and their conversations, activities and communications.

Q   What is 'directed surveillance'?

A   Surveillance which is

[a]   covert (but not 'intrusive')
[b]   for the purposes of a specific investigation or operation
[c]   likely to result in the obtaining of private information about a person (whether or not they have been previously identified for the purposes of the investigation)
[d]   not carried out in immediate response to events/circumstances where it would not be reasonably practicable to seek prior authorisation.

Q   What is 'intrusive surveillance'?

A   Surveillance which is

[a]   covert
[b]   carried out in relation to anything taking place on any residential premises (including hotel rooms) or in any private vehicle (i.e. for domestic not business use)
[c]   involves the presence of an individual on the premises or in the vehicle, or is carried out by means of a surveillance device.

Q   What is <u>not</u> intrusive surveillance?

A   A location tracking device attached to a vehicle: S. 26(4)(a) RIPA 2000.

Q   What is <u>neither</u> directed nor intrusive surveillance?

A   Covert TV detector equipment: S.26(6) RIPA 2000.

Q   Who can authorise directed surveillance?

A   A superintendent (or above). In an urgent case, an inspector. As with
CHIS authorities, the superintendent's authority should generally be
in writing but a superintendent may give oral authority in an urgent
case. Inspectors' urgent authorities must always be in writing. The
purposes for which authority can be given are broadly the same as for a
CHIS.

Q   How long will directed surveillance authorisations last?

A   A superintendent's written authority will ordinarily cease to have effect
after 3 months. A superintendent's urgent oral authority will last for 72
hours unless renewed, as will an inspector's urgent written authority.

Q   Who can authorise intrusive surveillance?

A   For the police (and military police) it is the 'senior authorising officer'
e.g. chief officers, the Commissioner/Asst. Commissioner of the Met &
City police, and the DGs of NCS/NCIS [Provost Marshall for the
military police]. Authorisation must only be made where it is believed
to be necessary and proportionate

[a]   in the interests of national security,
[b]   for preventing/detecting **serious** crime, or
[c]   for safeguarding the economic well-being of the UK.

Any such authority must be notified in writing to a surveillance
commissioner as soon as practicable. Except in urgent cases, the
authority will only take effect when approval from the surveillance
commissioner has been received in writing by the chief officer.

**Q   What is the offence of Unlawful Interception of Public
Communications?**

A   It is an offence to *intentionally* and *without lawful authority* intercept,
anywhere in the UK, any communication in the course of its
transmission by means of:

[a]   a public postal service; or
[b]   a public telecommunication system.

S. 1(1) REGULATION OF INVESTIGATORY POWERS ACT 2000

Prosecution. The consent of the DPP is required for any prosecution.

Lawful authority. Means:

[a]   conduct in accordance with any statutory power;
[b]   conduct authorised under the Act (i.e. where both sender and intended recipient consent; the interception is on behalf of the communications provider for its legitimate business purposes; or the interception is authorised under the Wireless Telegraphy Act 1949 S. 5);
[c]   conduct in accordance with an interception warrant issued by the Secretary of State.

Q   When may the Secretary of State issue an interception warrant?

A   Only if he/she believes it is necessary
   [a]   in the interests of national security;
   [b]   for the prevention/detection of serious crime;
   [c]   in order to safeguard the economic well-being of the UK, or
   [d]   for the purposes of international mutual assistance.

Q   For how long does an interception warrant last?

A   Generally 3 months. In urgent cases a warrant may be signed by a senior official expressly authorised by the Secretary of State, and such urgent warrants are valid for 5 working days.

DEFENCES

Q Outline the general defences to crime

A **Automatism.** Involuntary reflex action - e.g. a driver being attacked by a swarm of bees.

Intoxication. There is no general defence of intoxication but intoxication (voluntary or involuntary) may be relied upon to negate *mens rea* in offences of specific intent if the intoxication prevented the offender from forming the specific intent required (unless the offender deliberately became intoxicated simply to give him courage to commit the offence). For some offences involuntary intoxication (eg. through medication or 'spiked' drinks) is a specific defence eg. riot and violent disorder.

Insanity. The test for insanity was established by the **M'Naghten Rules** (1843):

*... to establish a defence on the ground of insanity, it must be clearly proved that, at the time of the committing of the act, the accused was labouring under such a **defect of reason, from disease of mind,** as not to know the nature and quality of the act he was doing, or if he did know it, that he did not know he was doing wrong.*

Mistake. Mistake may be claimed where the mistake would negate the required *mens rea* for a particular offence e.g. mistakenly picking up someone else's coat and walking off with it may negate the requirement of dishonesty for theft.

Duress by threats. Where a person is threatened with **death or serious physical injury** unless they commit an offence, they may raise this defence, but:

[a] the threat must have caused the defendant to commit the crime;
[b] he must have acted as would a reasonable person with his characteristics;
[c] the threat or injury must be more or less immediate;
[d] he must not have voluntarily exposed himself to an otherwise avoidable risk of duress; and
[e] it is no defence to murder or attempted murder.

Duress of circumstances. Where a person commits an offence to avoid serious consequences because he has no real alternative, e.g. a disqualified driver driving a dying man to hospital, the court will decide the reasonableness of the offender's behaviour.

Defence of self, another, or property. A person may use such force as is reasonable in the circumstances in the prevention of crime, or in effecting or assisting in the lawful arrest of offenders or suspected offenders or of persons unlawfully at large.

S. 3(1) Criminal Law Act 1967

A 'pre-emptive' strike may be justified in all the circumstances.

Infancy. A child under 10 is presumed incapable of committing crime [*doli incapax*].

HOMICIDE

Q Define murder

A A person is guilty of murder who

[a] being of sound mind and of the age of discretion
[b] unlawfully kills
[c] another human being
[d] under the Queen's Peace
[e] with malice aforethought.

COMMON LAW

Arrest. Serious arrestable offence.

Sentence. Murder carries the mandatory fixed penalty of life imprisonment.

Sound mind. Sane (i.e. not legally insane under the McNaghten Rules)

Age of discretion. A person at least 10 years old.

Unlawfully kills. Actively causes the death of another without justification (and may include omissions to act when a person has a duty to act but fails to, and the failure is a substantial cause of the death). Acting in self-defence, or in the prevention of crime etc. may amount to justification.

Another human being. Includes babies which have fully emerged from their mother's body and have an independent existence from their mother.

Under the Queen's Peace. Excludes deaths caused during the legitimate prosecution of warfare.

Malice aforethought. Intention to kill or cause GBH. (Note that for *attempted* murder only intention to kill will do.)

Q   What is the 'year and day rule'?

A   An ancient common law rule which stated that no prosecution for murder could be brought unless the victim died within a year and a day of the defendant's actions. It has now been abolished.

However, under the Law Reform (Year and a Day Rule) Act 1996 the Attorney-General's (or Solicitor-General's) consent is required to prosecute in the following cases:

[a]   where the victim dies more than 3 years after the injury;
[b]   where the defendant has already been convicted of an offence committed under the circumstances connected with the death (e.g. GBH).

Q   What is the position regarding murders committed overseas?

A   A British citizen who commits murder (or manslaughter) anywhere in the world may be tried for it in England and Wales: S.9 Offences Against the Person Act 1861.

Q   Define the special defences to murder of Diminished Responsibility, Provocation and Suicide Pact

A   **Diminished responsibility.** Where a person is suffering from an **abnormality of mind** so as to substantially **impair his mental responsibility** he shall not be convicted of murder, but manslaughter.
S. 2 HOMICIDE ACT 1957

Provocation. Where a jury can find evidence that he was provoked to lose self-control the question whether it was enough to make **a reasonable man do as he did** shall be left to the jury and they shall take into account things said and done.

The test. The jury must consider how a reasonable person **sharing the defendant's characteristics** would have reacted to the provocation. The defendant may be liable for manslaughter, not murder.
S. 3 HOMICIDE ACT 1957

Suicide pact. A common agreement between two or more persons, having for its object the death of them all, whether or not each is to take his own life, and each must have the **settled intention of dying** in pursuance of the pact.

S. 4 HOMICIDE ACT 1957

Where 'A' and 'B' form a suicide pact and 'A', in pursuance of the pact, kills 'B' but does not kill himself, 'A' will be guilty of manslaughter under S. 4 Homicide Act 1957. Where 'B' kills himself, 'A' will have committed an offence of aiding and abetting under S. 2 Suicide Act 1961 (see below).

Q   Define manslaughter

A   Manslaughter is the unlawful killing of another, either by an unlawful act which was likely to cause bodily harm, or by gross negligence.

COMMON LAW

Distinguished from murder. On the grounds that there is no malice aforethought.

Unlawful act. The defendant must have the required *mens rea* for the act, e.g. assault.

Gross negligence. Such cases arise where there is a duty of care which is breached, e.g. medical staff, train drivers, machine operators.

Arrest. Serious arrestable offence.

Q   Define the offence of Aiding Suicide

A   A person who aids, abets, counsels or procures the suicide [or attempted suicide] of another, commits an offence.

Alternative verdict. This offence is an alternative verdict on a charge of murder or manslaughter, and requires the DPP's consent for prosecution.

Arrest. Arrestable offence.

S. 2 SUICIDE ACT 1961

Q Define Solicitation of Murder

A Whosoever shall solicit, encourage, persuade or endeavour to persuade, or propose to any person, to murder another shall be guilty of an offence.

S. 4 Offences Against the Person Act 1861

'Contract killings'. It is irrelevant whether a 'contract' is actually concluded, it is sufficient to prove that someone has attempted to arrange such a contract. Therefore this offence will be made out when a person 'endeavours to persuade' an undercover police officer to carry out a 'hit'.

Arrest. Arrestable offence.

MISUSE OF DRUGS

Q **Give examples of Class A, B and C drugs**

A **Class A,** includes the most dangerous drugs: heroin, morphine, opiates, cocaine, LSD;

Class B, includes codeine and some amphetamines;

Class C, includes many commonly abused prescription drugs, e.g. diazepam, and now also includes cannabis and cannabis resin.

Q **According to the Misuse of Drugs Act 1971, what does Cannabis not include?**

A [a] Cannabis resin;
 •[b] the mature stalk of any cannabis plant [or fibre from it]; and
 [c] seed from the plant.

Q **What two conditions must be satisfied in order to prove possession of a controlled drug?**

A [a] That a person has or had a controlled drug under his possession (physical control); and
 [b] he knew that he had something in his possession which was in fact a controlled drug.

Q **Define the offence of possession**

A It is an offence to unlawfully possess a controlled drug.

S. 5(2) MISUSE OF DRUGS ACT 1971

Arrest. Arrestable offence.

Q **Outline the two specific statutory defences to Possession of a controlled drug**

A [a] **To prevent an offence being committed:**

 [i] knowing or suspecting it to be a controlled drug;
 [ii] he took possession **to prevent another person committing an offence**; and
 [iii] as soon as possible took steps to **destroy the drug**; or
 [iv] **to deliver to lawful custody.**

[b] **To deliver to lawful custody:**

[i] knowing or suspecting it to be a controlled drug;
[ii] he took possession **to deliver it to a person lawfully entitled** to receive the drug; and
[iii] as soon as he took possession he took all steps reasonable **to deliver it to such a person.**

S. 5 Misuse of Drugs Act 1971

Q Outline the General Defence under S. 28 of the Misuse of Drugs Act 1971

A In relation to unlawful production, unlawful supply, unlawful possession, possession with intent to supply, unlawful cultivation of cannabis and offences connected with opium, it will be a defence to prove:

[a] **Lack of knowledge of a fact:**

[i] he did not know or suspect, [nor had reason to suspect]
[ii] the existence of a fact alleged by the prosecution which it must prove.

Who is protected? E.g. an innocent messenger.

[b] **Lack of knowledge of Controlled Drug:**

Where it is necessary for the prosecution to prove it was *a particular controlled drug* and it has been proved that it *was* that drug, it will be a defence to prove:

[i] he thought the substance was **something other than a controlled drug,** and had no reason to believe it to be a controlled drug; or
[ii] he thought it was a controlled drug **which he could lawfully possess,**

but he shall not escape conviction by only proving:

[i] he did not suspect or believe [nor have reason to]
[ii] that the substance was **the particular drug** in question.

Who is protected? E.g. a person mistakenly believing a white substance [heroin] to be salt, or that it was a drug prescribed for him by his doctor (though in fact it was a different drug). **But not** simply that he thought it was one drug when in fact it was another.

Q Define the offence of Producing a Controlled Drug

A   It is an offence to:

[a]   unlawfully produce a controlled drug; or
[b]   to be concerned in the production of the drug.

S. 4(2) MISUSE OF DRUGS ACT 1971

Arrest. Serious arrestable offence.

Produce. Means by manufacture, cultivation or by any other method.

Q Define the offence of Supplying Controlled Drugs

A   It is an offence to:

[a]   supply or **offer to supply** a controlled drug to another;
[b]   to be concerned in the supply; or
[c]   to be concerned in the making of an offer to supply.

S. 4(3) MISUSE OF DRUGS ACT 1971

Arrest. Serious arrestable offence.

Supply. Includes distribute.

Offer to supply. The offence is complete once the **offer** is made.

Q Define the offence of Possession with Intent to Supply

A   It is an offence to possess [lawfully or not] a controlled drug with intent to supply.

S. 5(3) MISUSE OF DRUGS ACT 1971

Arrest. Serious arrestable offence.

Intent. A person in lawful possession, e.g. doctor, who intends to unlawfully supply is guilty of this offence.

Q Define the offence of Cannabis Cultivation

A It is an offence to unlawfully cultivate cannabis.

S. 6 Misuse of Drugs Act 1971

Arrest. Arrestable offence.

Cultivate. Includes watering, feeding. It is not necessary for the defendant to know that the plant is cannabis, the offence is complete simply upon proof of cultivation.

Q Define the offence of Supplying Articles for Administering or Preparing Drugs

A A person commits an offence who supplies or offers to supply:

[a] any article which may be used or adapted for use [on its own or in conjunction with other articles] in the unlawful **administration** by a person of a controlled drug to himself or another, in the knowledge that the article is to be used unlawfully; or

[b] any article which may be used to **prepare** a controlled drug for unlawful administration by himself or another, in the knowledge that the article is to be used unlawfully.

S. 9A Misuse of Drugs Act 1971

Unlawful. Any administration of a controlled drug will be unlawful **except** when the

[i] administration to self or another is not an offence of unlawful supply;

[ii] administration to himself is not an offence of unlawful possession.

Note. Hypodermic syringes and needles are not covered: S. 9A(2).

Q Outline the offence of Opium Misuse

A It is an offence for a person to:

[a] smoke or otherwise use prepared opium; or
[b] to frequent a place used for opium smoking; or
[c] to possess:

[i] any pipes or other utensils made or adapted for use in connection with the **smoking of opium:**

which have been used in that connection, either by him, or with his knowledge and permission, or which he intends to use or permit others to use in that connection;

[ii] any utensils which have been used by him or with his knowledge and permission for the preparation of **opium for smoking.**

S. 9 Misuse of Drugs Act 1971

Arrest. Arrestable offence.

Q Outline the offence of Drugs Misuse by Occupiers of Premises

A

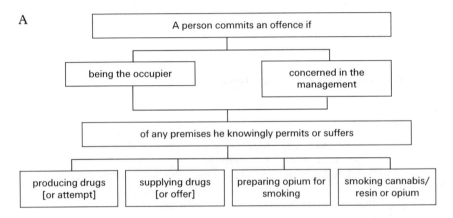

S. 8 Misuse of Drugs Act 1971

Arrest. Arrestable offence.

Management. Means someone involved in the planning, organising and actual use of the premises.

Permit/suffer. Turning a 'blind eye' to the activities will do.

Q   What is a 'closure notice'?

A   This is a power to close 'drug dens', 'crack houses' etc. Under S.1 of the Anti-Social Behaviour Act 2003, if a superintendent (or above) reasonably believes that premises have been used during the previous 3 months in connection with the unlawful use, production or supply of a Class A controlled drug, and that the use of the premises is associated with the occurrence of disorder or serious nuisance to members of the public, s/he may authorise the issue of a closure notice in respect of the premises if s/he is satisfied:

[a]   that the local authority has been consulted, and
[b]   reasonable steps have been taken to discover the identity of anyone residing on the premises, or with control of or responsibility for, or an interest in, the premises.

Q   What must the closure notice say?

A   The notice must state the following:

[i]   that an application will be made to close the premises,
[ii]   that access to the premises by any person (other than an habitual resident or owner) is prohibited,
[iii]   the date and time and place where the application will be heard,
[iv]   the effects of a closure order,
[v]   that failure to comply with the notice is an offence, and
[vi]   information about housing and legal advisers in the area who may be contacted for assistance.

Q   How is a closure notice served?

A   It must be served by a police officer, by fixing a copy to

[i]   at least one prominent place on the premises,
[ii]   each normal means of access to the premises,
[iii]   any outbuildings which appear to the constable to be used with or as part of the premises

and by giving a copy to

[i]   at least one person who appears to the constable to have control/responsibility for the premises,
[ii]   any person who lives on the premises.

Q   How is a closure order obtained?

A   Following the issue of a closure notice a police officer must apply to a magistrates' court for a closure order. The application must be heard not later than 48 hours after the notice has been served (although the application may then be adjourned for up to 14 days to allow persons with an interest in the premises to contest the application). A closure order may be made only if the magistrates are satisfied:

[a]   the premises have been used in connection with the unlawful use, production or supply of a Class A controlled drug,

[b]   use of the premises is associated with the occurrence of disorder or nuisance during the period of the notice, and

[c]   making an order is necessary to prevent a reoccurrence of such disorder or nuisance during the period of the notice.

Q   For how long does a closure order last?

A   The order closes the premises (or any specified parts of it) to all persons for such period as decided by the court, but no longer than 3 months. An extension for a further 3 months may be applied for at any time before the order expires, with a superindent's authority (following consultation with the local authority). No further extensions may be sought thereafter.

Q   What is the power to enter under a closure order?

A   A police officer (or other authorised person) may enter the premises, using reasonable force if necessary, and/or secure the premises against entry, again using reasonable force if necessary. In addition a police officer (or other authorised person) may enter at any time during the period of the order to carry out essential maintenance or repairs (but must produce evidence of ID and authority if challenged by the owner/occupier).

Q   Outline the breach of closure order offences

A   It is an offence, without reasonable excuse, to remain on or enter premises in contravention of a closure notice or closure order. It is also an offence to obstruct a constable or other authorised person exercising his powers of entry.

S. 4 ANTI-SOCIAL BEHAVIOUR ACT 2003

Arrest. A constable *in uniform* may arrest any person s/he reasonably suspects of committing or having committed these offences.

Q   Define the offence of Misuse of Drugs Outside the UK

A   A person commits an offence if **in the UK** he assists or induces the commission in any place **outside the UK** of an offence under the law in force in that other place.

S. 20 MISUSE OF DRUGS ACT 1971

Arrest. Arrestable offence.

Q   Outline Police Powers of Entry etc

A

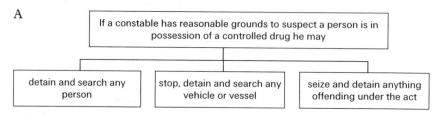

Vehicle/vessel. Includes hovercraft.

S. 23 MISUSE OF DRUGS ACT 1971

Q   What are the grounds for the issue of a Warrant?

A   A magistrate may issue a warrant if satisfied on information on oath that there are reasonable grounds to suspect :

[a]   that any **controlled drug** is unlawfully in the possession of a person on the premises;

[b]   or that **a document** relating to an unlawful transaction or dealing is in possession of a person on the premises.

Q   **What are the powers under the Warrant?**

A   [a]   At any time **within one month** from the date of the warrant;
    [b]   enter, search the premises and persons; and

        [i]   if there are grounds for suspecting that an offence has been committed in respect of **controlled drugs found**; or
        [ii]   there is reason to believe that **any document found** relates to an unlawful transaction,

    seize and detain the drugs or document.

S. 23 MISUSE OF DRUGS ACT 1971

Obstruction. It is an offence to intentionally obstruct a constable exercising these powers.

Unlawful transaction. The document is any document in relation to a transaction in the UK or, if carried out abroad, would be an offence under the foreign law.

Q   **What is the offence of Supply of Intoxicating Substances?**

A

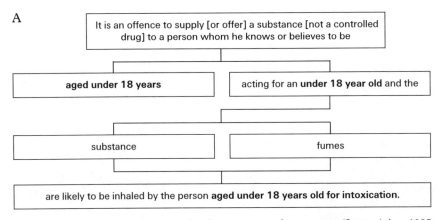

S. 1 INTOXICATING SUBSTANCES (SUPPLY) ACT 1985

Defence. It is a defence to show that at the time of the supply or offer the defendant was both under 18 himself and not acting in the course or furtherance of a business.

S. 1(2) INTOXICATING SUBSTANCES (SUPPLY) ACT 1985

Q   What is the offence of Supplying Butane Lighter Refills?

A   It is an offence to supply any cigarette lighter refill cannister containing butane to any person under 18 years old.

Q   What is a Travel Restriction Order?

A   The courts may impose travel restrictions on offenders convicted of drug trafficking which may prohibit the offender from leaving the UK at any time during a specified period commencing with the date of his release from custody. The minimum duration of such an order is 2 years. It is an arrestable offence to breach such an order.

OFFENCES AGAINST THE PERSON

Q Define Common Assault and Battery

A **Assault** is any act whereby the defendant, intentionally or recklessly, causes another **to apprehend** immediate and unlawful personal violence and **battery** is the actual **application of force.**

S. 39 CRIMINAL JUSTICE ACT 1988

Q Define Assault with Intent to Resist Arrest

A It is an offence to assault any other person with intent to resist or prevent the lawful apprehension of himself or another for any offence.

S. 38 OFFENCES AGAINST THE PERSON ACT 1861

Who is protected? Police, store detectives, bailiffs etc.

Note. The arrest must be lawful and the defendant must be aware of that for the offence to be proved.

Q Define the offence of Assault on Police

A A person commits an offence who assaults a constable in the execution of his duty or a **person assisting a constable** in the execution of his duty.

S. 89(1) POLICE ACT 1996

Q Define the offence of Obstructing Police

A Any person who resists or wilfully obstructs a Constable in the execution of his duty or a **person assisting a Constable** in the execution of his duty, commits an offence.

S. 89(2) POLICE ACT 1996

Obstruction. 'Resistance' suggests physical opposition. Obstruction is wider, and may be interpreted as 'making it more difficult for a constable to carry out his duties'.

Arrest. Only if the obstruction involves a breach of the peace.

Q Define the offence of Assaulting/Obstructing Accredited Persons

A It is an offence to assault, resist or wilfully obstruct a designated or accredited person in the execution of his duty, or a person assisting such a person in the execution of his duty.

S. 46 POLICE REFORM ACT 2002

Designated/accredited persons. Eg. PCSOs, Investigating Officers, Detention Officers, Escort Officers, persons accredited under Community Safety Accreditation Schemes.

Q Define ABH

A A person commits an offence if he assaults another person so as to cause actual bodily harm.

ABH. Means any hurt or injury calculated to interfere with the health or comfort of the victim, it can include shock and mental 'injury'.

Arrest. Arrestable offence.

S. 47 OFFENCES AGAINST THE PERSON ACT 1871

Q   **Define Unlawful Wounding Contrary to S. 20 Offences Against the Person Act 1861**

A

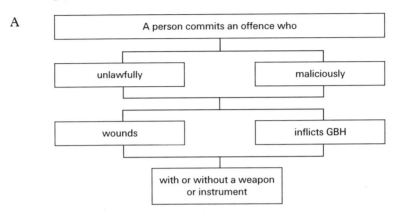

Arrest. Arrestable offence.

Wound. Is the breaking of the whole skin [internally or externally].

GBH. Means really serious harm including psychiatric harm.

Maliciously. Means that the defendant must realise that there is a risk of harm.

Inflicts. The harm may be inflicted indirectly and without physical contact e.g. psychiatric injury following harassment, or infecting someone with a disease.

Q   Outline Wounding with Intent contrary to S. 18 Offences Against the Person Act 1861

A

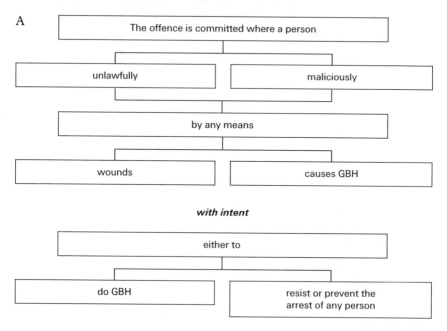

The offence is committed where a person

unlawfully   maliciously

by any means

wounds   causes GBH

with intent

either to

do GBH   resist or prevent the arrest of any person

Arrest. Arrestable offence.

By any means. No actual contact is required, e.g. woman jumping from a train to escape a rapist.

Intent. There must be an intention to cause really serious harm or to resist or prevent arrest.

Q Define Torture

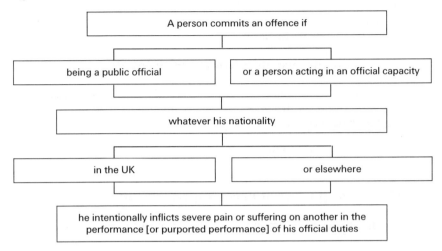

Defence. To prove he had lawful authority, justification or excuse. (But note that in the light of the absolute prohibition against torture under Art. 3 ECHR, any such defence will be incompatible with the ECHR.)

Arrest. Serious arrestable offence.

Prosecution. Consent of Attorney-General (or Solicitor-General) is needed to prosecute.

Non-public officials. Commit this offence if done at the instigation of or with the consent or acquiescence of a public official and the public official was performing [purporting] his duties when he instigated or consented to the offence.

Pain and suffering. It is immaterial whether the pain or suffering is physical/mental or caused by an act or omission.

S. 134 CRIMINAL JUSTICE ACT 1988

Q Define the offence of Poisoning

A   It is an offence to unlawfully and maliciously administer [or cause to be] any poison, destructive or noxious thing so as to **endanger life** or cause **GBH.**

S. 23 OFFENCES AGAINST THE PERSON ACT 1861

Arrest. Arrestable offence.

Cause to be administered. Covers indirect poisoning and inducing someone to poison themselves.

Q Define the offence of Poisoning with Intent

A It is an offence to unlawfully and maliciously administer [or cause to be] any poison, destructive or noxious thing **with intent to injure, aggrieve or annoy.**

Arrest. Arrestable offence.

S. 24 Offences Against the Person Act 1861

Q Define the offence of False Imprisonment

A It is an offence at common law to falsely imprison any person.

Arrest. Arrestable offence.

Imprison. Keeping someone in a place unlawfully is imprisonment.

Mens rea. Intentional or subjectively reckless restraint of a person's freedom of movement is required.

Q Define the offence of Kidnapping at common law

A It is an offence of kidnapping to take or carry away another without their consent and without lawful excuse.

Arrest. Serious arrestable offence.

Taking or carrying away. This physical movement must be either by force or fraud. Force need not be physical force, mentally overpowering someone by the exercise of a position of dominance or influence may be enough.

Prosecution. Consent of the DPP is required when the victim is under 16 or where the prosecution is against a parent/guardian (Child Abduction Act 1984 S. 5)

Q   Outline the offence of Hostage Taking

A

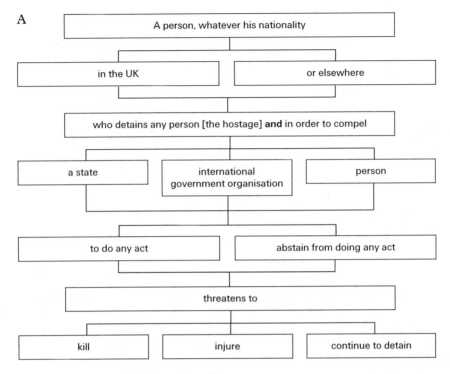

Arrest. Serious arrestable offence.

Prosecution. Consent of the Attorney-General (or Solicitor-General) is required to prosecute.

S. 1 TAKING OF HOSTAGES ACT 1982

Q Compare False Imprisonment, Kidnapping and Hostage Taking

OFFENCE	ACTUS REUS	MENS REA	ARREST	CONSENT TO PROSECUTE
FALSE IMPRISONMENT	Detention without lawful excuse	Intention or subjective recklessness	Arrestable	None required
KIDNAPPING	Taking or carrying away without consent or lawful excuse	Intention or subjective recklessness	Serious Arrestable	DPP if victim under 16 or parent/ guardian offender
HOSTAGE TAKING	Detention plus threats to kill, injure or continued detention	Intention	Serious Arrestable	AG or SG

SEXUAL OFFENCES

Q   **What is the definition of 'sexual' under the Sexual Offences Act 2003?**

A   Penetration, touching or any other activity will be sexual *if a reasonable person would consider that*

[a]   whatever its circumstances or any person's purpose in relation to it, it is **sexual by its very nature**, or

[b]   because of its nature it may be **sexual** and **because of its circumstances or the purpose** of any person in relation to it, it is sexual.

S. 78 SEXUAL OFFENCES ACT 2003

In other words, category (a) covers those activities which a reasonable person would always consider sexual (e.g. intercourse, masturbation) whilst category (b) covers activities that may or may not be considered sexual by a reasonable person, it will depend on the particular circumstances or intention of the perpetrator (e.g. a doctor inserting a finger into a vagina may be sexual, or it may be non-sexual if it is done simply to carry out a medical inspection). If a reasonable person would not consider the activity to be sexual then it will not be a sexual activity, regardless of any particular sexual gratification an individual may derive from it (e.g. a shoe fetishist deriving pleasure from placing shoes on people's feet in the shoe shop in which he works).

Q   **What is the definition of 'touching' under the Sexual Offences Act 2003?**

A   Touching includes touching:

[a]   with any part of the body
[b]   with anything else
[c]   through anything

and in particular, touching amounting to penetration.

S. 79(8) SEXUAL OFFENCES ACT 2003

SEXUAL OFFENCES

Q Outline the offence of Rape

A

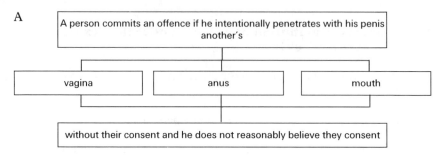

A person commits an offence if he intentionally penetrates with his penis another's

| vagina | anus | mouth |

without their consent and he does not reasonably believe they consent

S. 1 Sexual Offences Act 2003

Arrest. Serious arrestable offence.

Reasonable belief in consent. Is to be determined having regard to all the circumstances. Consent is a question of fact.

Victim under 13. If the victim is a child under 13 it is sufficient to prove penetration and the child's age. The issue of consent does not arise: S.5 Sexual Offences Act 2003.

Q Outline the presumptions about consent

A   [a]   The 'evidential presumption': the victim can be taken not to have consented where it is proved that the defendant did the act and:

       [i]   immediately before, or at the time of the act, *any person* was using violence against the victim or causing the victim to fear that immediate violence would be used against him/her;

       [ii]   immediately before, or at the time of the act, *any person* was causing the victim to fear that violence was being used, or that immediate violence would be used, against *any person;*

       [iii]   the victim was, and the defendant was not, unlawfully detained at the time of the act;

       [iv]   the victim was asleep or unconscious at the time of the act;

       [v]   because of the victim's physical disability they would not have been able at the time of the act to communicate consent to the defendant, or

[vi] *any person* had administered to or caused to be taken by the victim, witout the victim's consent, a substance capable of causing or enabling the victim to be stupefied or overpowered at the time of the act.

However in any such case the defence is entitled to bring evidence to rebut the presumption.

S. 75 SEXUAL OFFENCES ACT 2003

[b] The 'conclusive presumption': if its proved that the defendant did the act and that s/he:
[i] intentionally deceived the victim as to the nature or purpose of the act, or
[ii] intentionally induced the victim to consent by impersonating a person *known personally* by the victim,

then there will be a conclusive presumption both that the victim did not consent and that the defendant did not believe that s/he consented.

S. 76 SEXUAL OFFENCES ACT 2003

Q Define the offence of Assault by Penetration

A   A person (A) commits an offence if
[a] he *intentionally penetrates* the vagina or anus of another person (B) with *a part of his body or anything else*,
[b] the penetration is sexual,
[c] B *does not consent* to the penetration, and
[d] A *does not reasonably believe* that B consents.

S. 2 SEXUAL OFFENCES ACT 2003

Arrest. Serious arrestable offence.

Victim under 13. Where the victim is a child under 13 it is only necessary to prove intentional sexual penetration and the child's age. The issue of consent does not arise: S. 6 Sexual Offences Act 2003.

Q Define the offence of Sexual Touching

A   A person (A) commits an offence if

[a]   he *intentionally* touches another person (B),
[b]   the touching is sexual,
[c]   B *does not consent* to the touching, and
[d]   A *does not reasonably believe* that B consents.

S. 3 SEXUAL OFFENCES ACT 2003

Arrest. Arrestable offence.

Victim under 13. Where the victim is a child under 13 it is only necessary to prove intentional sexual touching and the child's age. The issue of consent does not arise: S. 7 Sexual Offences Act 2003.

Q Define the offence of Causing a person to Engage in Sexual Activity without consent

A   A person (A) commits an offence if

[a]   he *intentionally* causes another person (B) to engage in an activity,
[b]   the activity is sexual,
[c]   B *does not consent* to engaging in the activity, and
[d]   A *does not reasonably believe* that B consents.

S. 4 SEXUAL OFFENCES ACT 2003

Arrest. Serious arrestable offence if indictable only (i.e. where it involves penetration of the victim's anus or vagina or mouth with the defendant's penis, of any other person's anus or vagina with a part of the victim's body or by the victim, or of any person's mouth by the victim's penis), otherwise arrestable.

Victim under 13. Under S. 8 it is an offence to cause *or incite* a child under 13 to engage in sexual activity. The issue of consent is irrelevant in such cases.

Q Define the offence of Sexual Activity with a Child under 16

A A person *aged 18 or over* (A) commits an offence if

[a] he intentionally touches another person (B),
[b] the touching is sexual, and
[c] either

[i] B is under 16 and A does not reasonably believe B is 16 or over, or
[ii] B is under 13.

S. 9 SEXUAL OFFENCES ACT 2003

Arrest. Arrestable offence.

Age of offender. Must be 18 or over for this offence. If offender is under 18 s/he commits an offence under S. 13, which is punishable (on indictment) by up to 5 years' imprisonment (rather than 14 years' under S. 9).

Q Define the offence of Engaging in Sexual Activity in the Presence of a Child under 16

A A person *aged 18 or over* (A) commits an offence if

[a] he intentionally engages in an activity,
[b] the activity is sexual,
[c] for the purpose of obtaining sexual gratification, he engages in it

[i] when another person (B) is present or is in a place from which A can be observed, and
[ii] knowing or believing that B is aware, or intending that B should be aware, that he is engaging in it, and

[d] either

[i] B is under 16 and A does not reasonably believe that B is 16 or over, or
[ii] B is under 13.

S. 11 SEXUAL OFFENCES ACT 2003

Arrest. Arrestable offence.

Purpose. This offence would cover, for example, a person masturbating in front of a child, or masturbating in the presence of a child to whom he is describing what he is doing, perhaps because the child is covering his face. It would also cover the situation where A performs a sexual act in a place where he knows he can be seen by a child, for example via a webcam.

Q Define the offence of Causing a Child under 16 to Watch a Sexual Act

A A person *aged 18 or over* (A) commits an offence if

[a] for the purpose of obtaining sexual gratification, he intentionally causes another person (B) to watch a third person engaging in an activity, or to look at an image of any person engaging in an activity,

[b] the activity is sexual, and

[c] either

[i] B is under 16 and A does not reasonably believe that B is 16 or over, or

[ii] B is under 13.

S. 12 Sexual Offences Act 2003

Arrest. Arrestable offence.

Purpose. While the previous offence under S. 11 is concerned with engaging in sexual activity which the person knows, believes or intends to be observed by a child, the S. 12 offence is concerned with intentionally causing a child to watch a *third person* engaging in such activity, or to look at an image of a person engaging in such activity. For example, a person who forces a child to watch a pornographic film or a couple have sex.

Q Define the offence of Arranging or Facilitating Child sex offences

A A person (A) commits an offence if

[a] he intentionally arranges or facilitates something that he intends to do, intends another person to do, or believes that another person will do, *in any part of the world,* and

[b] doing it will involve the commission of an offence under SS. 9 – 11 (i.e. sexual activity with a child, causing or inciting a child to engage in sexual activity or engaging in sexual activity in the presence of a child).

S. 14 SEXUAL OFFENCES ACT 2003

Arrest. Arrestable offence.

Purpose. The first 2 limbs of the offence will cover, for example, where A approaches an agency to procure a child for the purpose of sexual activity either with himself or with a friend. The offence is complete whether or not the sex takes place. An example of the 3rd limb of the offence is where A intentionally drives another person (X) to meet a child with whom he knows X is going to have sexual activity. A may not intend X to have child sexual activity, but he believes that X will do so if he meets that child.

Q Define the offence of Meeting a Child following Sexual Grooming

A A person *aged 18 or over* (A) commits an offence if

[a] having met or communicated with another person (B) on at least *2 earlier occasions* he

[i] intentionally meets B, or
[ii] travels with the intention of meeting B *in any part of the world,*

[b] at the time, he intends to do anything to or in respect of B, during or after the meeting and in any part of the world, which if done will involve the commission by A of a relevant offence,

[c] B is under 16, and

[d] A does not reasonably believe that B is 16 or over.

S. 15 SEXUAL OFFENCES ACT 2003

Arrest. Arrestable offence.

Communicated. By any method, including electronic methods e.g. text, MSN, internet chatrooms etc.

Relevant offence. Any offence under Part 1 of the Act (i.e. any of the principal sexual offences).

Q Outline the Abuse of Position of Trust offences

A   It is an offence for a person *aged 18 or over* (A) to

[a]   intentionally sexually touch another person (B); or

[b]   intentionally cause or incite B to engage in a sexual activity; or

[c]   for the purpose of sexual gratification, intentionally engage in any sexual activity when B is present, or in a place from which A can be observed, knowing or believing that B is aware or intending that B should be aware that he is engaging in it; or

[d]   for the purpose of sexual gratification, intentionally cause B to watch a third person engaging in a sexual activity, or look at an image of any person engaging in sexual activity

if he is in a position of trust in relation to B.

SS. 16-19 SEXUAL OFFENCES ACT 2003

Arrest. Arrestable offence.

Q What is a 'position of trust'?

A   A looks after (i.e. cares for, trains, supervises, is in sole charge of) persons under 18 who are accommodated and cared for in any of the following settings:

[i]   detained in an institution under a court order;

[ii]   local authority accommodation or accommodation provided by a voluntary organisation;

[iii]   hospital;

[iv]   independent clinic;

[v]   care home, residential care home or private hospital;

[vi]   community home, voluntary home or children's home;

[vii] home provided under S. 82(5) Children Act 1989;
[viii] residential family centre;
[ix]   educational establishment.

Q   Define the offence of Sexual Activity with Child Family Member

A   A person (A) commits an offence if

[a]   he intentionally touches another person (B),
[b]   the touching is sexual,
[c]   the relationship of A to B is any of the following:

   [i]   parent
   [ii]   grandparent
   [iii] brother or sister
   [iv]   half-brother or half-sister
   [v]   aunt or uncle
   [vi]   is or has been foster parent
   [vii] where A and B live or lived in the same household, or A is or has been regularly involved in caring for, training, supervising or being in sole charge of B and

      [aa] one of them is or has been the other's step-parent, or
      [bb] they are cousins, or
      [cc] one of them is or has been the other's step-brother or step-sister, or
      [dd] they have the same parent or foster parent

[d]   A knows or could reasonably be expected to know that his relation to B is one of the above, and
[e]   either

   [i]   B is under 18 and A does not reasonably believe that B is 18 or over, or
   [ii]   B is under 13.

SS. 25-26 SEXUAL OFFENCES ACT 2003

Arrest. Arrestable offence.

Q Outline the Making Indecent Photographs offence

A It is an offence for a person

[a] *to take,* or permit to be taken, or make, any indecent photograph or pseudo-photograph of a child; or

[b] *to distribute* or show such indecent photographs or pseudo-photographs; or

[c] *to have in his possession* such indecent photographs or pseudo-photographs, with a view to their being distributed or shown; or

[d] *to publish* or cause to be published any advertisement likely to be understood as conveying that the advertiser distributes or shows such indecent photographs or pseudo-photographs, or intends to do so.

S. 1 PROTECTION OF CHILDREN ACT 1978

Arrest. Serious arrestable offence.

Defence. It is a defence to prove that he had a legitimate reason for distributing or showing the photos *or* that he had not himself seen the photos and did not know, nor had any cause to suspect, that they were indecent *or* they were lawfully married or partners in an enduring family relationship. (There is a further special exception for persons making such photos for crime investigation/prosecution purposes).

Pseudo-photographs. Includes computer images.

Prosecution. The consent of the DDP is required for any prosecution.

Q Outline the Possessing Indecent Photographs offence

A It is an offence for a person to have any indecent photograph or pseudo-photograph of a child in his possession.

S. 160 CRIMINAL JUSTICE ACT 1988

Arrest. Arrestable offence.

Defence. It is a defence to prove that he had a legitimate reason or having the photograph or pseudo-photograph in his possession *or* that he had not himself seen the photograph or pseudo-photograph and did not know, nor have any cause to suspect, it to be indecent *or* that the photograph or pseudo-photograph was sent to him without any prior request made by him or on his behalf and he did not keep it for an unreasonable time *or* he was married to the child or lived with him as partners in an enduring family relationship.

Q Define the offence of Paying for Sexual Services of a Child

A   A person (A) commits an offence if

[a]   he intentionally obtains for himself the sexual services of another person (B),

[b]   before obtaining those services, he has made or promised payment for those services to B or a third person, or knows that another person has made or promised such a payment, and

[c]   either

[i]   B is under 18, and A does not reasonably believe that B is 18 or over, or

[ii]   B is under 13.

S. 47 SEXUAL OFFENCES ACT 2003

Arrest. Arrestable offence.

Payment. Includes any financial advantage.

Q Outline the offences of Causing, Inciting, Controlling Child etc. Prostitution or Pornography

A   It is an offence for a person (A) to

[a]   intentionally cause or incite another person (B) to become a prostitute, or to be involved in pornography *in any part of the world*;

[b] intentionally control any of the activities of B relating to B's prostitution or involvement in pornography *in any part of the world*;

[c] intentionally arrange or facilitate the prostitution or involvement in pornography *in any part of the world* of B.

SS. 48-50 SEXUAL OFFENCES ACT 2003

Arrest. Arrestable offence.

Prostitute. Means a person who, on at least 1 occasion, and whether or not compelled to do so, offers or provides sexual services to another person in return for payment or a promise of payment to themselves or a third person.

Q What is meant by a 'disqualification order'?

A An order under the Criminal Justice and Court Services Act 2000 which is aimed at disqualifying people who present a threat to children from working in certain jobs and positions. A court must impose a disqualification order on a person convicted of certain offences against children (such as those involving sexual activity, violence or drugs) unless, having regard to all the evidence, the court is satisfied that it is unlikely that the defendant will commit any further offences against *any* child. It is an arrestable offence for a disqualified person to apply for, offer to do, accept or do any work in a job which involves working with children.

Q Define the offence of Sexual Activity with a Person with a Mental Disorder

A A person (A) commits an offence if

[a] he intentionally touches another person (B),
[b] the touching is sexual,
[c] B is unable to refuse because of or for a reason related to a mental disorder, and
[d] A knows or could reasonably be expected to know that B has a mental disorder and that because of it or for a reason related to it B is likely to be unable to refuse.

S. 30 SEXUAL OFFENCES ACT 2003

Arrest. Serious arrestable offence where it involves penetration. Otherwise arrestable.

Mental disorder. "Mental illness, arrested or incomplete development of mind, psychopathic disorder and any other disorder or disability of mind": S. 1(2) Mental Health Act 1983.

Q Define the offence of Sexual Activity in the Presence of a Person with a Mental Disorder

A   A person (A) commits an offence if

[a]   he intentionally engages in an activity,
[b]   the activity is sexual,
[c]   for the purpose of obtaining sexual gratification, he engages in it

[i]   when another person (B) is present, or is in a place from which A can be observed, and
[ii]   knowing or believing that B is aware, or intending that B should be aware, that he is engaging in it,

[d]   B is unable to refuse because of or for a reason related to a mental disorder, and
[e]   A knows or could reasonably be expected to know that B has a mental disorder and that because of it or for a reason related to it B is likely to be unable to refuse.

S. 32 SEXUAL OFFENCES ACT 2003

Arrest. Arrestable offence.

Q Define the offence of Causing a Person with a Mental Disorder to Watch a Sexual Act

A   A person (A) commits an offence if

[a]   for the purpose of obtaining sexual gratification, he *intentionally* causes another person (B) to watch a third person engaging in an activity, or to look at an image of any person engaging in an activity,
[b]   the activity is sexual, and
[c]   B is unable to refuse because of or for a reason related to a mental disorder, and
[d]   A knows or could reasonably be expected to know that B has a mental disorder and that because of it or for a reason related to it B is likely to be unable to refuse.

S. 33 SEXUAL OFFENCES ACT 2003

Arrest. Arrestable offence.

Inducements. Causing a person with a mental disorder to watch a sexual act by offering inducements, threats or deception is an arrestable offence under S. 37, and is in the same terms as above, except that it is not necessary to show that B was unable to refuse.

Q Define the offence of Outraging Public Decency

A It is an offence at common law to commit an act of a lewd, obscene or disgusting nature and outrage public decency.

COMMON LAW

Arrest. Arrestable offence.

Deliberate act. The offence requires the deliberate commission of a lewd, obscene or disgusting act. Whether something is lewd etc. is a question of fact. If the act done is not lewd then the defendant's intention or motive in doing the act will not make it so. For example, if the defendant leaves messages in a public toilet asking young boys to contact him and those messages are not lewd etc. themselves, then the offence is not committed, no matter that by leaving the notes the defendant intended to induce boys to commit grossly indecent acts with him.

Q Define the offence of Exposure

A A person commits an offence if

[a] s/he intentionally exposes his/her genitals, and
[b] s/he intends that someone will see them and be caused alarm or distress.

S. 66 SEXUAL OFFENCES ACT 2003

Arrest. Arrestable offence.

Offence complete. It is not necessary for A's genitals to have been seen by anyone or for anyone to have been alarmed or distressed. The offence is complete upon proof of exposure with the necessary intent.

Q Outline the offence of Voyeurism

A A person commits an offence if

[a] for the purpose of obtaining sexual gratification, he observes another person doing a private act, and he knows that that person does not consent to being observed for his sexual gratification; or

[b] he operates equipment with the intention of enabling another person to observe, for the purpose of obtaining sexual gratification, a third person (B) doing a private act, and he knows that B does not consent to his operating equipment with that intention; or

[c] he records another person (B) doing a private act, he does so with the intention that he or a third person will, for the purpose of obtaining sexual gratification, look at an image of B doing the act, and he knows B does not consent to his recording the act with that intention; or

[d] he installs equipment or constructs or adapts a structure or part of a structure, with the intention of enabling himself or another person to commit an offence under (a) above.

S. 67 SEXUAL OFFENCES ACT 2003

Arrest. Arrestable offence.

Private act. A person is doing a private act if they are in a place which would reasonably be expected to provide privacy and their genitals, buttocks or breasts are exposed or covered only with underwear; or they are using a lavatory; or they are doing a sexual act of a kind not ordinarily done in public.

Examples. (a) Looking through a window or peephole at someone having sex, where A knows the person observed does not consent to being looked at; (b) a landlord (A) operating a webcam to allow people on the internet for their sexual gratification to view live images of his tenant (B) getting undressed, if A knew that B did not consent to this; (c) A secretly films B masturbating in B's bedroom to show to others for their sexual gratification. Proof that the intention was the sexual gratification of others could be obtained by the fact that the images were uploaded to a website, or sent to a pornographic magazine; (d) A drilled a spyhole or installed a 2-way mirror in a house with the intention of spying on someone for sexual gratification or allowing others to do so. A would be covered by the offence even if the spyhole or mirror was discovered before it was used.

Q Define the offence of Sexual Activity in a Public Lavatory

A   A person commits an offence if

[a]   he is in a lavatory to which the public or a section of the public has or is permitted to have access, whether on payment or otherwise,
[b]   he intentionally engages in an activity, and
[c]   the activity is sexual.

S. 71 SEXUAL OFFENCES ACT 2003

Arrest. Arrestable offence.

Sexual activity. The usual definition of sexual activity is replaced for this offence with a narrower test: "an activity is sexual if a reasonable person would, in all the circumstances but regardless of any person's purpose, consider it to be sexual": S. 71(2).

Q Define the offence of committing a criminal offence with intent to commit a sexual offence

A   It is an offence for a person to commit any offence with the intention of committing a relevant sexual offence.

S. 62 SEXUAL OFFENCES ACT 2003

Arrest. Arrestable offence.

Relevant offence. Offences under Part 1 of the Sexual Offences Act 2003 (i.e. the principal sexual offences).

Purpose. This offence is intended to cover the situation where A commits a criminal offence but does so with the intention of committing a subsequent sexual offence, regardless of whether the substantive sexual offence is actually committed. e.g. A kidnaps B so that he can rape him but is caught by the police before committing the rape. Obviously if A does commit the substantive sexual offence he can be charged with that in addition.

Q **Define trespassing with intent to commit a sexual offence**

A A person commits an offence if

[a] he is a trespasser on any premises,
[b] he intends to commit a relevant sexual offence *on the premises*, and
[c] he knows that, or is reckless as to whether he is, a trespasser.

S. 63 SEXUAL OFFENCES ACT 2003

Arrest. Arrestable offence.

Trespasser. On premises without the owner or occupier's consent, whether express or implied.

Premises. Any structure or part of a structure, including tents, vehicles, vessels, or other temporary or movable structures.

Q **Define the offence of Administering a Substance with intent**

A A person commits an offence if he intentionally administers a substance to, or causes a substance to be taken by, another person (B)

[a] knowing B does not consent, and
[b] with the intention of stupefying or overpowering B, so as to enable *any person* to engage in a sexual activity that involves B.

S. 61 SEXUAL OFFENCES ACT 2003

Arrest. Arrestable offence.

Intent. There is no need for B to actually be stupefied or overpowered or for any sexual activity to take place. The offence is complete at the point of administration with the necessary intent.

Q **Which persons are subject to Notification Requirements regulating sex offenders?**

A 'Relevant offenders' under Part 2 of the Sexual Offences Act 2003. These are persons who are

[a] convicted of a Schedule 3 sexual offence (i.e. the main sexual offences); or

[b] found not guilty of such an offence by reason of insanity; or

[c] found to be under a disability and to have done the act charged against them in respect of such an offence; or

[d] cautioned in respect of such an offence.

Q **What are the notification periods?**

A [i] For persons sentenced to imprisonment for life, or 30 months or more: **indefinite**

[ii] For persons admitted to a hospital subject to a restriction order: **indefinite**

[iii] For persons sentenced to between 6 months and 30 months imprisonment: **10 years**

[iv] For persons sentenced to less than 6 months imprisonment: **7 years**

[v] For persons admitted to hospital without a restriction order: **7 years**

[vi] For persons cautioned: **2 years**

[vii] For persons given a conditional discharge: **the period of the discharge**

[viii] For any other persons: **5 years**

In the case of persons under 18, the 10, 7, 5 or 2 year periods are halved.

Q   Outline the notification procedure

A   A relevant offender must, *within 3 days* of the date of conviction, finding or caution ('the relevant date') notify the police of (a) their date of birth (b) their national insurance number (c) their name(s) on the relevant date and on the date of notification (d) their home address on the relevant date and on the date of notification (e) the address of any other premises in the UK at which, at the time of notification, they regularly reside or stay. Thereafter, *within 3 days* of any change of home address or any use of a name which has not been previously notified to the police, or any stay for a 'qualifying period' at any address which has not been previously notified (i.e. any stay of 7 days or more *or* 2 or more periods in any 12 months which together amount to 7 days), or any release from custody, detention or hospital detention, the relevant offender must notify the police the new details. The relevant offender must then re-notify the police of their details *within 1 year* of either the initial notification or notification of change of details (unless they already did so when they notified of the change) i.e. a relevant offender who does not change their details has to re-notify within a year *and every year thereafter*. Failure to notify without a reasonable excuse is an arrestable offence under S. 91 Sexual Offences Act 2003.

Q   What is a 'sexual offences prevention order'?

A   A SOPO is a civil order which is designed to prevent offending and provide protection for the public. A court may make a SOPO in certain circumstances (e.g. when dealing with a schedule 3 offence) where it is satisfied that it is necessary to do so for the purpose of protecting the public (or any particular person) from serious sexual harm from the defendant. The order will last for at least 5 years and can be indefinite, provided that that is specified in the order, and will prohibit the defendant from doing anything specified in the order. Breach of a SOPO, without reasonable excuse, is an arrestable offence.

Q   What is a 'risk of sexual harm order'?

A   A civil preventative order which may be applied for *by a chief officer* from a magistrates' court in respect of a person aged 18 or over who resides in his police area or who the chief officer believes is in, or is intending to come to, his police area. The order may only be sought if it appears to the chief officer that the defendant has *on at least 2 occasions* done any of the following acts:

[i]   engaged in sexual activity involving a child or in the presence of a child,

[ii]   caused or incited a child to watch a person engaging in sexual activity or to look at a moving or still sexual image,

[iii]   given a child anything relating to sexual activity or containing references to such activity,

[iv]   communicated with a child, where any part of the communication is sexual

The court can then make a RSHO if satisfied that the defendant did commit such an act on at least 2 occasions and that the order is necessary to protect children generally (or a specific child) from harm from the defendant. The order will last for a fixed period not less than 2 years, or until further order, and prevents the defendant from doing anything specified in the order. Breach of a RSHO, without reasonable excuse, is an arrestable offence.

Q   What is a 'prostitute'?

A   A man or woman who, on at least 1 occasion and whether or not compelled to do so, offers or provides sexual services to another person in return for payment or a promise of payment to themselves or another: S. 51(2) Sexual Offences Act 2003.

Q   Define the offence of causing, inciting, controlling prostitution for gain

A   A person commits an offence if

[a]   he intentionally causes or incites another to become a prostitute *in any part of the world* and he does so for or in the expectation of gain for himself or a third person, or

[b]   he intentionally controls any of the activities of another person relating to that person's prostitution *in any part of the world*, and he does so for or in the expectation of gain for himself or a third person.

SS. 52 & 53 SEXUAL OFFENCES ACT 2003

Arrest. Arrestable offence.

Q   Define the offence of Keeping a Brothel

A   It is an offence for a person to keep, or to manage, or act or assist in the management of, a brothel to which people resort for practices involving prostitution (whether or not also for other practices).

S. 33A Sexual Offences Act 1956

Arrest. Arrestable offence.

Q   Outline the common law offence of Keeping a Disorderly House

A   It is an offence to keep a disorderly house.

Arrest. Arrestable offence.

Disorderly. Means unregulated by the restraints of morality, and run in a way that violates law and good order. It is necessary to show a degree of persistence in the behaviour, rather that just a one-off incident, and it is also necessary to prove that the house is open to customers and that the defendant knows it is being so used.

Q   Define the offence of Soliciting by a common prostitute

A   It is an offence for a common prostitute, *whether male or female*, to loiter or solicit in a street or public place for the purpose of prostitution.

S. 1 Street Offences Act 1959

Arrest. Preserved power: a constable may arrest without warrant anyone he finds in a street or public place and reasonably suspects to be committing the offence.

Common prostitute. To establish that a person is a 'common' prostitute it is usual to maintain a register of cautions given for soliciting, then where at least 2 cautions have been given in the previous 12 months, the evidence of the register will help to establish the prostitute's 'common' (i.e. repeat offender) status.

Q Define the offence of 'kerb-crawling'

A A person *whether male or female* commits an offence if he solicits another person(s) for prostitution

[a] from a motor vehicle while it is in a street or public place; or

[b] in a street or public place while in the immediate vicinity of a motor vehicle that he has just got out of or off,

persistently or in such manner or in such circumstances as to be likely to cause annoyance to the person(s) solicited, or nuisance to persons in the neighbourhood.

S. 1 SEXUAL OFFENCES ACT 1985

Arrest. Arrestable offence.

Further, a person *whether male or female* commits an offence if in a street or public place he persistently solicits a person(s) for prostitution.

S. 2 SEXUAL OFFENCES ACT 1985

Arrest. No specific power.

Persistently. More than once.

Q Define the offence of Placing Adverts relating to Prostitution

A It is an offence to place an advert relating to prostitution on, or in the immediate vicinity of, a public telephone, with the intention that it should come to the attention of any other person.

S. 46 CRIMINAL JUSTICE AND POLICE ACT 2001

Arrest. Arrestable offence.

Q **Outline the Trafficking offences**

A   A person commits an offence if he intentionally arranges or facilitates the arrival in (or travel within, or departure from) the UK of another person (B) and either

[a]   he intends to do anything to or in respect of B, after B's arrival but in any part of the world, which, if done will involve the commission of a relevant sexual offence, or

[b]   he believes that another person is likely to do something to or in respect of B, after B's arrival but in any part of the world, which if done will involve the commission of a relevant sexual offence.

SS. 57-59 SEXUAL OFFENCES ACT 2003

Arrest. Arrestable offence.

Relevant sexual offence. Any of the main sexual offences (Part 1 Sexual Offences Act 2003).

OFFENCES AGAINST CHILDREN AND VULNERABLE PERSONS

Q Outline the offence of Child Abduction [Person Connected with the Child]

A It is an offence for a person **connected with a child aged under 16 years of age** to take or send the child **outside the UK** without the appropriate consent.

S. 1 CHILD ABDUCTION ACT 1984

Connected with:

[a] parent;
[b] [where not married at the birth] father;
[c] guardian;
[d] person with a residence order; or
[e] with custody.

Appropriate consent means the consent of *each* of the following:

[a] mother;
[b] father [if he has parental responsibility];
[c] guardian;
[d] person with a residence order;
[e] person with custody; or
[f] with permission of a court under the Children Act 1989; or
[g] where a person has custody, permission of the court which awarded custody.

Arrest. Arrestable offence.

Prosecution. Consent of the DPP is required for a prosecution.

Defence.

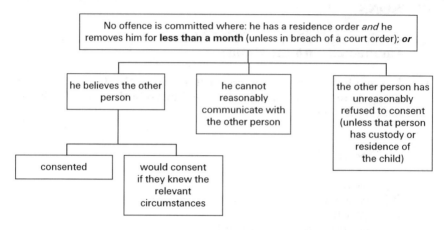

Q Outline the offence of Child Abduction [Person NOT connected with the child]

A It is an offence for a person **not connected with the child,** without lawful authority to take or detain a child **aged under 16 years of age so** as to remove him or keep him from the lawful control of a person entitled to lawful control.

S. 2 CHILD ABDUCTION ACT 1984

Arrest. Arrestable offence.

Who commits the offence? Anyone who **is not:**

[a] mother;
[b] father [if married at the time of birth];
[c] guardian, person with custody or residence order.

Defence. It shall be a defence to prove:

[a] At the time he believed the child **had attained 16 years of age;**
[b] [where the father and mother were not married at the time of his birth]:

  [i] he is the father; or
  [ii] he believed on reasonable grounds that he was the father.

Q Give an example of when both S. 1 & 2 offences can be committed together

A 'A' and his wife are separated, and the wife has custody. 'A' hires 'B' to collect the child from school and deliver the child to the airport where 'A' takes the child to Belgium. Therefore 'A' commits the S. 1 [connected to] offence and 'B' commits the S. 2 [not connected to] offence.

Q Define the offence of Child Cruelty

A An offence is committed where any person who has attained **16 years of age** and who has responsibility for a **child aged under 16 years of age**, wilfully:

[a] assaults;
[b] ill-treats;
[c] neglects;
[d] abandons;
[e] exposes;
[f] or causes or procures any of the above

in a manner likely to cause **unnecessary suffering or injury to the health of the child.**

Arrest. Arrestable offence.

Q Define the offence of Harmful Publications

A A person who prints, publishes, sells or hires out works likely to fall into the hands of a child or young person, portraying:

[a] the commission of crimes; or
[b] acts of violence or cruelty; or
[c] incidents of a repulsive or horrible nature,
in such a way that the work would **tend to corrupt a child or young person,** commits an offence.

Prosecution. The consent of the Attorney-General (or Solicitor-General) is required for a prosecution.

S. 2 CHILDREN AND YOUNG PERSONS (HARMFUL PUBLICATIONS) ACT 1955

Q   When is a child deemed to be under Police Protection?

A

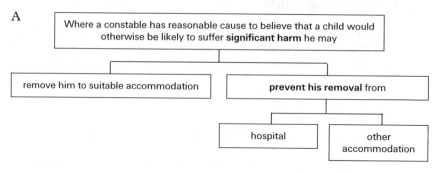

S. 46 CHILDREN ACT 1989

Q   What subsequent action must the constable take?

A   [a]   Inform local authority [where child found] of action taken/proposed/reasons;

[b]   inform local authority [where child usually lives] of his whereabouts;

[c]   inform the child of steps taken/proposed/reasons;

[d]   discover how the child feels about this;

[e]   tell parents or person with whom he was living of action taken/proposed/reasons;

[f]   if child removed from a place, arrange a refuge or local authority accommodation; and

[g]   inform the **designated officer.**

Q   What is the role of the Designated Officer?

A   [a]   To enquire into the case, then **release the child unless** he considers that there is still reason to believe that the child would still suffer **significant harm** if released;

[b]   do what is reasonable for the child's welfare;

[c]   allow such contact with the child as he believes is reasonable and in the child's interest [which may be no contact].

Contact (if considered reasonable and in the child's best interests) may be by:

[i]   the child's parents;
[ii] a person having parental responsibility;
[iii] the person the child was living with before police protection;
[iv] persons who have a right to contact; or
[v]   someone acting on behalf of any of these.

Q   How old is a 'child' for the purposes of the Children Act 1989?

A   Under 18 years of age.

Q   What is the maximum duration of police protection?

A   72 hours.

Q   Outline the offence of Contravention of Protection or Care Order

A

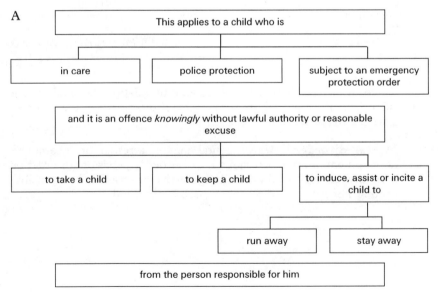

Arrest. S. 25 PACE General arrest conditions.

S. 49 CHILDREN ACT 1989

Q   Outline police powers to remove Mentally Disordered People from Public Places

A

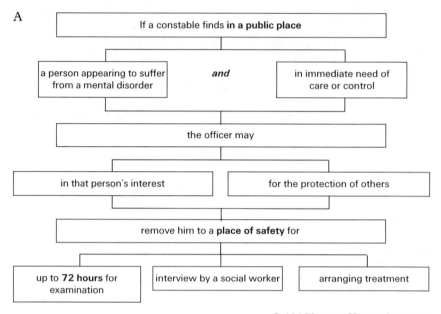

If a constable finds **in a public place**

a person appearing to suffer from a mental disorder   ***and***   in immediate need of care or control

the officer may

in that person's interest   for the protection of others

remove him to a **place of safety** for

up to **72 hours** for examination   interview by a social worker   arranging treatment

S. 136 MENTAL HEATH ACT 1953

Place of safety. Is social services accommodation, hospital, police station, mental nursing home or anywhere suitable where the occupier is willing to receive him.

Mental disorder. Means mental illness, arrested or incomplete development of mind, psychopathic disorder (a persistent disorder or disability resulting in abnormally aggressive or seriously irresponsible conduct) or any other disorder or disability of mind.

Q   What are the conditions of a Warrant to Search for Patients?

A   Where there is reasonable cause to suspect that a person believed to be suffering from a mental disorder has been, or is being, ill-treated or neglected or is unable to care for himself and is living alone, a warrant may be issued by a magistrate to a constable who may enter the premises and take him to a place of safety and **the officer *must be accompanied* by a social worker and doctor.**

S. 135 MENTAL HEALTH ACT 1983

Q   How long do police powers last for the retaking of an Escaped Patient?

A   A person taken to a place of safety by a constable, or under a warrant, who subsequently escapes cannot be retaken after **72 hours.**

When does the time begin?

At the place of safety	Escapes before arrival
time of arrival	time of escape

S. 138 MENTAL HEALTH ACT 1983

THEFT AND RELATED OFFENCES

Q Define Theft

A A person is guilty of theft if he dishonestly appropriates property belonging to another with the intention of permanently depriving the other of it.

S. 1 THEFT ACT 1968

Arrest. Arrestable offence.

Q What is not Dishonesty?

A

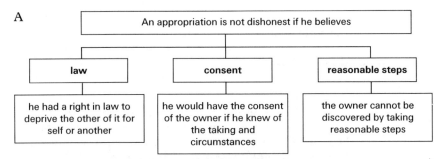

Willingness to pay. Behaviour may however be regarded as dishonest notwithstanding a willingness to pay for the goods. [A stranger removing a pint of milk from your doorstep and leaving the money will probably be regarded as dishonest under this section whereas a person removing a pint from an unattended milk float and leaving the money probably will not.]

S. 2 THEFT ACT 1968

Q Define what is and what is not an Appropriation

An appropriation **is**	An appropriation **is not**
any assumption of the rights of the owner, including even if the property was come by innocently, a later assumption by keeping it or dealing with it as an owner.	where property is transferred **for value** to a person **acting in good faith,** who later assumes the rights of the owner.

S. 3 THEFT ACT 1968

Q Define property

A Property includes money [current notes and coins] and all other property, real [land (including soil and cultivated plants), buildings and fixtures] or personal [chattels, moveables] together with things in action and other intangibles.

S. 4 THEFT ACT 1968

Things in action. Means a personal right of property which can only be claimed or enforced by legal action and not by taking physical possession, e.g. copyrights, trade marks, debts, bank accounts in credit.

Other intangible property. Gas, patents.

Q Can land be stolen?

A No, except by the following:

[a] **Trustees & Personal Representatives.** Where a person is in a position of trust or is empowered to dispose of the land he can steal the land if he does something *in breach of trust* or confidence.

[b] **Persons who do not possess the land [strangers].** They steal land if they *sever* it e.g. dig gravel, cut turf, dig up cultivated plants, chop down trees etc.

[c] **Tenants.** They steal land only by taking *fixtures* [wall sockets etc] or *structures* let for use with the land, e.g. garden sheds, coal bunkers. So, a tenant who removes topsoil does not steal land as he is not a stranger to it.

Q   When can things growing wild (i.e. uncultivated plants) be stolen?

A

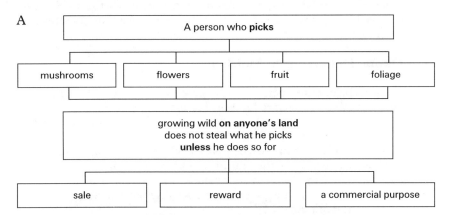

Digging up. Would amount to an offence as this section is limited to **picking.**

Q   When can Wild Creatures be stolen?

A

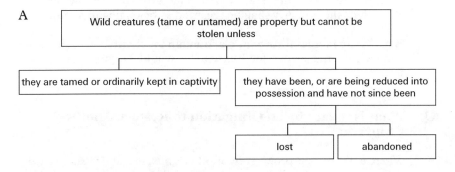

Ordinarily kept in captivity means that a zoo creature can be stolen, and **reduction into possession** means that a person who has, for example, snared a rabbit, is its new owner and that rabbit can be stolen from him. If however he forgets where the snare is or simply abandons the snare [and rabbit], it then reverts to its wild state and cannot be stolen.

S. 4 Theft Act 1968

Q   What is NOT property?

A   Electricity, confidential information and human corpses. (However human body parts which have undergone a process of alteration eg. embalming, *are* capable of being property).

Q   Define Belonging to Another

A   Property belongs to a person having **possession** or **control** of it, or any non-equitable proprietary right or interest.

S. 5(1) THEFT ACT 1968

Can you steal your own property? Yes, where another has possession or control at the time of your appropriation, e.g. say a garage has completed an MOT on your vehicle and you sneak in and remove the vehicle then you are guilty of theft because the vehicle 'belonged to another' at that time.

Q   What is the meaning of Obligations Regarding Another's Property?

A   Where a person receives property or its proceeds and is under a *legal* obligation to deal with it in a particular way (not simply a moral obligation) the property shall be regarded as belonging to another.

E.g. Where monies thrown into a fountain for charitable purposes are removed by the owner for himself, he would be guilty under this section.

S. 5(3) THEFT ACT 1968

Q   What is meant by an Obligation to Restore Another's Property?

A   Where a person gets property by another's mistake, and is under a legal obligation to restore it (or its proceeds), then that property shall be regarded as belonging to that other, and an intention not to restore it shall be regarded as an intention to deprive.

E.g. Money mistakenly credited to an account must be returned.

S. 5(4) THEFT ACT 1968

Q **According to S. 6 which two circumstances may amount to an Intention to Permanently Deprive?**

A [i] If a person treats property as his own to dispose of, regardless of the owner's rights, and a borrowing or lending amounts to a permanent deprivation if done for a period or under circumstances that make it an outright taking. S. 6(1) THEFT ACT 1968

E.g. Borrowing property and then 'lending' it to a total stranger in the 'hope' that he will return the goods! Or borrowing a season ticket and using it for more than the permitted number of times.

[ii] Where a person parts with property [of another] **under a condition for its return** which he may not be able to perform, this amounts to treating the property as his own regardless of the other's rights. S. 6(2) THEFT ACT 1968

E.g. Pawning another's property without his consent. If there is a likelihood he may not be able to redeem it, then S. 6(2) will help to prove an intention to permanently deprive.

Q **Define Robbery**

A

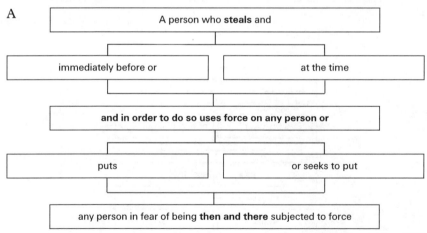

A person who **steals** and

immediately before or | at the time

and in order to do so uses force on any person or

puts | or seeks to put

any person in fear of being **then and there** subjected to force

S. 8 THEFT ACT 1968

Arrest. Arrestable offence.

Steals. Means contrary to SS. 1-6 Theft Act 1968. No theft, no robbery.

Force. Robbery is simply stealing aggravated by the use of force or the threat of force. The **force** may be indirectly applied (e.g. pulling a handbag from someone's grasp) but must be applied **in order to steal**. Where the defendant has used force on another (or put another in fear of immediate force) in order to steal but has not achieved the appropriation of any property (and is therefore not guilty of robbery) he can be convicted of assault with intent to rob.

S. 8(2) THEFT ACT 1968

Q Define Burglary

A

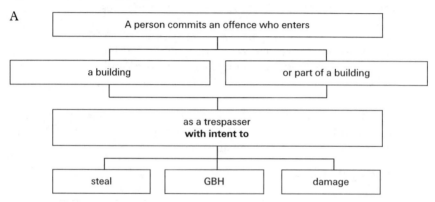

A person commits an offence who enters

| a building | or part of a building |

as a trespasser
with intent to

| steal | GBH | damage |

S. 9(1)(A) THEFT ACT 1968

or

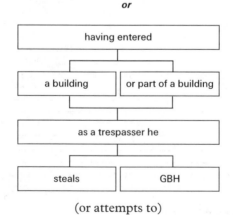

having entered

| a building | or part of a building |

as a trespasser he

| steals | GBH |

(or attempts to)

S. 9(1)(B) THEFT ACT 1968

Arrest. Arrestable offence.

Building. Includes inhabited vehicle or vessel [whether occupant there or not].

Steal. Theft contrary to SS. 1-6 Theft Act 1968. This does not include abstracting electricity (S. 13) or taking a conveyance (S. 12), or pedal cycle (S. 12(5)).

Q When does Burglary become Aggravated?

A   If he commits any burglary and **at the time** has with him any:

W	weapon of offence;
I	imitation firearm;
F	firearm; or
E	explosive.

S. 10 THEFT ACT 1968

Arrest. Arrestable offence.

At the time. For the S. 9(1)(a) offence (entering **with intent**) it must be shown that he had his **wife** with him at the **point of entry.** The S. 9(1)(b) offence (**having entered**) requires him to have his **wife** at the time of stealing or causing GBH.

Has with him. Means readily at hand.

Weapon of offence. Means any article made or adapted or intended for causing injury to or for incapacitating a *person* and would therefore include rope, binding tape, sticking plaster etc [used for tying up victims], but not poisoned meat intended for incapacitating a guard dog.

Q Outline the offence of Removal of Articles from Places Open to the Public

A
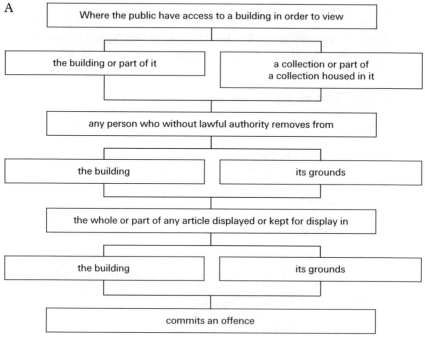

Where the public have access to a building in order to view

| the building or part of it | a collection or part of a collection housed in it |

any person who without lawful authority removes from

| the building | its grounds |

the whole or part of any article displayed or kept for display in

| the building | its grounds |

commits an offence

S. 11 THEFT ACT 1968

Arrest. Arrestable offence.

Collection. Includes a temporary collection. But such collections are only protected *on a day* (ie. from midnight to midnight) when the public has access.

What is not protected. A collection for sale or commercial purpose.

Removes. Merely moving an article to another part of the building is not sufficient.

Public access. Someone entering as a trespasser after the building has closed still commits this offence so long as the building was open to the public on that day. Where the building is usually open to the public but temporarily closed, the offence is still committed.

Defence. If he believes he has lawful authority to remove the item, or would have if the person entitled to give it knew of the removal and its circumstances.

Purpose. This offence was introduced to cover people who removed works of art from display so they could 'live' with the work for a while and then return it! (There was no intention to permanently deprive, so no theft.)

Q Define the offence of Taking a Conveyance Without Authority

A

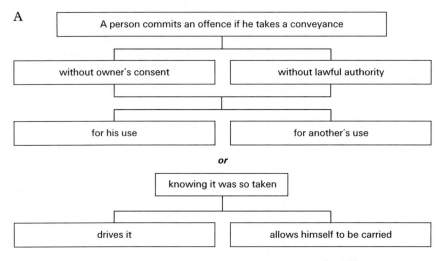

S. 12 THEFT ACT 1968

Arrest. Arrestable offence.

Conveyance. Means any conveyance constructed or adapted for carriage of persons by land, water or air. Not animals used for carriage, or pedestrian-controlled handcarts etc. used only for goods.

Taking for use as a conveyance. Both elements must be satisfied so if, for example, a person 'takes' a vehicle simply by pushing it elsewhere for a practical joke on its owner, the offence is not committed: it has not been taken *for use as a conveyance.*

Q   **When does this offence become Aggravated?**

A

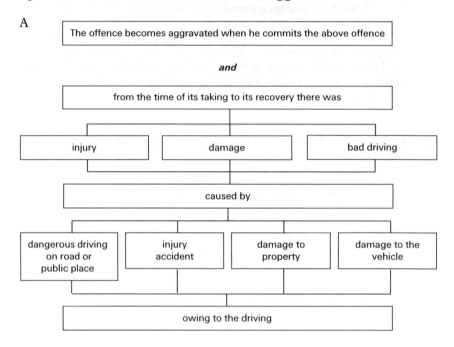

| The offence becomes aggravated when he commits the above offence |

and

| from the time of its taking to its recovery there was |

| injury | damage | bad driving |

| caused by |

| dangerous driving on road or public place | injury accident | damage to property | damage to the vehicle |

| owing to the driving |

S. 12A THEFT ACT 1968

Arrest. Arrestable offence.

Defence. The driving, accident or damage occurred:

[a]   **before** the taking; or
[b]   when the driving, accident or damage occurred, he was **not in or in the immediate vicinity** of the vehicle.

Q   **Define Taking a Pedal Cycle without authority**

A   It is an offence for a person, without having the consent of the owner or other lawful authority, to take a pedal cycle for his/her own or another's use, or to ride a pedal cycle knowing it to have been taken without such authority.

S. 12(5) THEFT ACT 1968

Q Define Abstracting Electricity

A A person who dishonestly *uses* without due authority, or dishonestly causes to be *wasted* or *diverted* any electricity, commits an offence.

S. 13 THEFT ACT 1968

Arrest. Arrestable offence.

Q Define Handling Stolen Goods

A

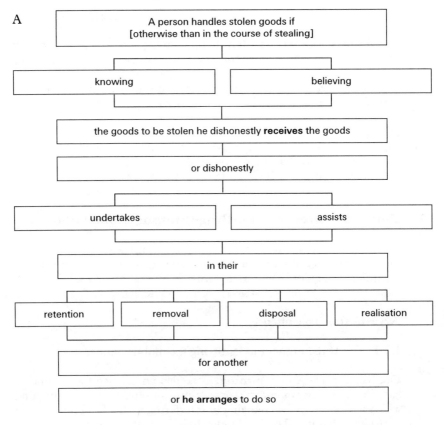

A person handles stolen goods if
[otherwise than in the course of stealing]

knowing — believing

the goods to be stolen he dishonestly **receives** the goods

or dishonestly

undertakes — assists

in their

retention — removal — disposal — realisation

for another

or **he arranges** to do so

S. 22 THEFT ACT 1968

Arrest. Arrestable offence.

Stolen goods:

[a]　a person can be convicted of handling if the goods were stolen **anywhere in the world** so long as the stealing (if not an offence under the Theft Act) was an offence in that other country;

[b]　goods are classed as stolen if they are the original goods or now represent **the proceeds** of the goods;

[c]　goods cease to be stolen when they are restored to lawful possession.

S. 24 THEFT ACT 1968

Proof that goods were stolen. In relation to proceedings for the theft of anything in the course of transmission (whether by post or otherwise), a statutory declaration that a person despatched, received, or failed to receive any goods, or they were in a particular state or condition shall be evidence of the fact providing:

[a]　oral evidence of the fact would be admissible; and

[b]　**7 days' notice** has been given to the person charged, and he has not, **within 3 days** of the trial, given the prosecutor written notice requiring the attendance of the witness.

S. 27(4) THEFT ACT 1968

Q　Define the offence of Re-Programming Mobile Phones

A　A person (not being the manufacturer, or having the written consent of the manufacturer) commits an offence if he (a) changes a unique device identifier (UDI), or (b) interferes with the operation of a UDI.

S. 1 MOBILE TELEPHONES (RE-PROGRAMMING) ACT 2002

Arrest. Arrestable offence.

UDI. The IMEI number indentifying the mobile phone.

Facilitating re-programming. It is also an offence for anyone to have in his custody or control, or to supply or offer to supply, anything which may be used for changing or interfering with a UDI if he knows or believes that it will be used unlawfully for that purpose.

S. 2 2002 ACT.

Q **Define the offence of Dealing in Tainted Cultural Objects**

A It is an offence to dishonestly deal in a tainted cultural object, knowing or believing that it is tainted.

S. 1 DEALING IN CULTURAL OBJECTS (OFFENCES) ACT 2003

Cultural object. Any object of historical, architectural or archaeological interest.

Tainted. Excavated or detached from a building or structure anywhere in the world of historical, architectural or archaeological interest or removed from a monument of such interest, where removal/excavation amounted to an offence (whether in the UK or that other country).

Dealing. Includes acquiring, disposing of, importing, exporting or agreeing/arranging to do so.

Q Define the offence of Advertising a Reward

A

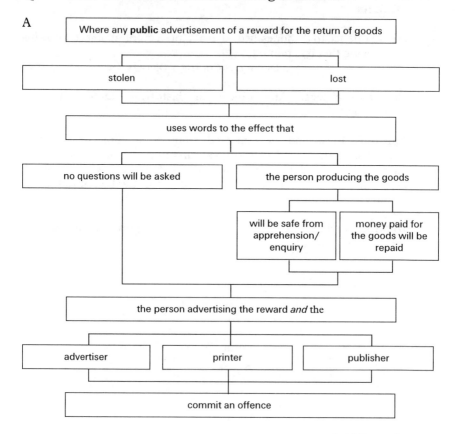

Where any **public** advertisement of a reward for the return of goods

| stolen | lost |

uses words to the effect that

| no questions will be asked | the person producing the goods |

| will be safe from apprehension/ enquiry | money paid for the goods will be repaid |

the person advertising the reward *and* the

| advertiser | printer | publisher |

commit an offence

S. 23 THEFT ACT 1968

Q   Define Going Equipped for Stealing

A

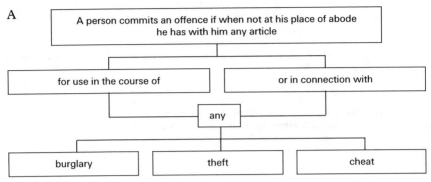

S. 25 THEFT ACT 1968

Arrest. Arrestable offence.

Has with him. Means readily to hand.

Cheat. Means a S. 15 Deception offence.

Place of abode. Does not include business address.

Article. Does not include animate objects such as a trained monkey: *Daly v. Cannon (1954).*

Theft. Includes a S. 12 taking a conveyance offence.

Q   Define the offence of Making Off Without Payment

A

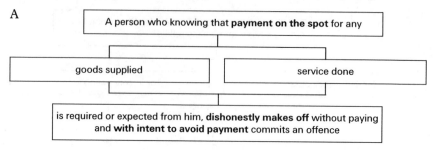

A person who knowing that **payment on the spot** for any

| goods supplied | service done |

is required or expected from him, **dishonestly makes off** without paying and **with intent to avoid payment** commits an offence

S. 3 THEFT ACT 1978

Arrest. Arrestable offence.

Contrary to law. This section does not apply to anything which is contrary to law, eg. prostitution, drugs, unlawful gaming etc.

Makes off. Refers to making off from the spot where payment is required or expected, then and there.

Mens rea. Knowledge that payment is required then and there coupled with dishonest making off with intent to permanently avoid payment.

Q   Define Blackmail

A

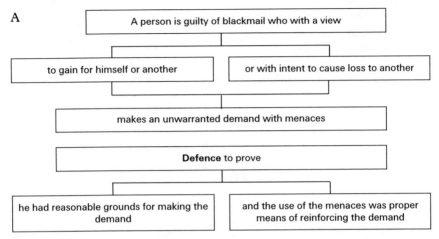

to gain for himself or another   or with intent to cause loss to another

makes an unwarranted demand with menaces

Defence to prove

he had reasonable grounds for making the demand   and the use of the menaces was proper means of reinforcing the demand

S. 21 THEFT ACT 1968

Arrest. Arrestable offence.

Blackmail letters. The offence is complete at the time of posting.

Gain. Includes keeping what one has and getting what one has not.

Loss. Includes parting with what one has and not getting what one might get.

Unwarranted/Menaces. The standard 'red' bill of a last demand from say the Gas Board, threatening to cut you off unless you pay up, is a 'proper' menace attached to a 'reasonable' demand (i.e. the defence would apply).

Q   Define the offence of Retaining a Wrongful Credit

A   A person is guilty of an offence if:

[a]   a **wrongful credit** has been **paid into his account** [or in which he has an interest];

[b]   **he knows** it is wrongful; and

[c]   he dishonestly **fails to cancel** that credit.

It is also an offence to receive a credit deriving from:

[a]   theft;
[b]   obtaining a money transfer;
[c]   blackmail; or
[d]   stolen goods.

Arrest. Arrestable offence.

S. 24A Theft Act 1968

DECEPTION

Q   Define Deception

A   A deception is something which deceives, i.e. an inducement to believe a thing is true which is false. It may be committed in the following ways:

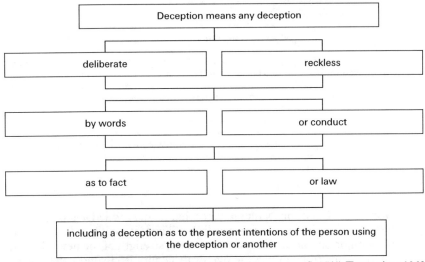

Deception means any deception

deliberate | reckless

by words | or conduct

as to fact | or law

including a deception as to the present intentions of the person using the deception or another

S. 15(4) THEFT ACT 1968

Words or conduct. E.g. dressing up as someone else.

Machines. A machine cannot be deceived, because deception has to act on a human mind, therefore putting a false coin into a vending machine is not an offence of deception (though it may be theft).

Q   Define Obtaining Property by Deception

A   A person who by any deception dishonestly obtains property belonging to another, with intention of permanently depriving the other of it, commits an offence.

S. 15 THEFT ACT 1968

Arrest. Arrestable offence.

Obtain. Means obtaining ownership, possession or control, for self or another, and also enabling another to obtain or retain.

DECEPTION

Q Outline the offence of Obtaining a Pecuniary Advantage by Deception

A

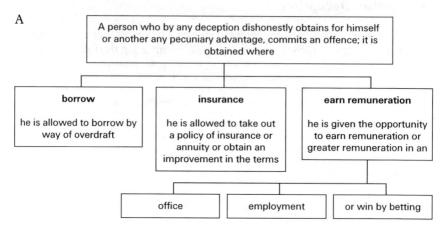

S. 16 THEFT ACT 1968

Arrest. Arrestable offence.

Borrow. 'X' tells his bank manager that he has landed a good job and needs an overdraft for a new wardrobe. There is no job in fact, but the bank manager allows the overdraft on the strength of the new job. The offence is complete once the overdraft facility is created - there is no need for it to be utilised.

Insurance. 'Y' deceives an insurer into issuing insurance in the belief that he holds a clean driving licence and has never been disqualified. His licence is in fact endorsed and he has been disqualified in the past. The offence is complete.

Opportunity to earn. 'Z' applies for a job requiring two 'A' levels which he pretends to possess and is appointed to the job. The offence is complete.

www.janes.com

Q   Define the offence of Obtaining Services by Deception

A

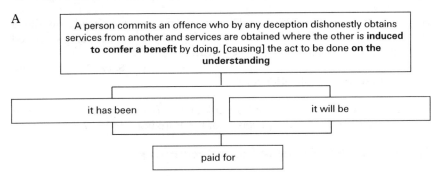

A person commits an offence who by any deception dishonestly obtains services from another and services are obtained where the other is **induced to confer a benefit** by doing, [causing] the act to be done **on the understanding**

it has been   it will be

paid for

S. 1 THEFT ACT 1978

Arrest. Arrestable offence.

Benefit. Includes a loan. (S. 1(3) as amended).

Note. The 'service' does not have to be a lawful or contractual one.

Q   Define the offence of Evading Liability

A   A person commits an offence where, by any deception:

[a]   he dishonestly secures the remission of the whole or part of any **existing liability to make payment** [his own or another's]; or
[b]   with intent to make permanent default of any **existing liability to make payment** [for self or another] he **dishonestly induces another to wait for payment**; or
[c]   he dishonestly obtains **an exemption from making payment.**

S. 2 THEFT ACT 1978

Arrest. Arrestable offence.

Liability. Means legal liability, therefore the evasion of payment for drugs, prostitution, or unlawful gaming, is not an offence.

DECEPTION

Q   What did the Theft [Amendment] Act 1996 introduce?

A   An offence where, by any deception a person dishonestly obtains a **money transfer** for himself or another where one account is debited and the other credited [or vice versa].

S. 15A THEFT ACT 1968

Arrest. Arrestable offence.

Account. Is one kept with a bank or a person carrying on a deposit taking business for the purposes of the Banking Act 1987.

Q   Define the offence of False Accounting

A

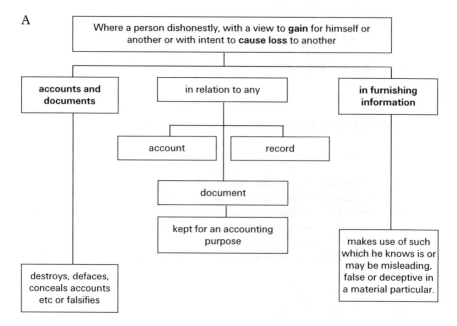

Arrest. Arrestable offence.

S. 17 THEFT ACT 1968

Falsifies. May be by omission as well as by act. Eg. failing to make an entry on a ledger.

A person concurring. In making the account etc, is also guilty.

Q Forgery, what is a False Instrument?

A A document which tells a lie about itself.

Not false, if a constable makes out a claim for overtime he did not work and signs it, the claim is not a forgery because it does not purport to be something it is not.

False, if a constable makes out a claim for overtime and signs his supervisor's signature as having checked the claim to be correct, the document is a lie and therefore forged.

Bank notes. Are not forged, but are *counterfeited.*

Q Define Making a False Instrument With Intent

A A person is guilty of forgery if he makes a false instrument, with intent that he or another use it **to induce someone to accept it as genuine** and as a result someone is prejudiced.

Arrest. Arrestable offence.
S. 1 FORGERY AND COUNTERFEITING ACT 1981

Q Define Using a False Instrument with Intent

A It is an offence for a person to use an instrument which is [and he knows or believes] to be false with the intention **of inducing someone to accept it as genuine** and as a result someone is prejudiced.

Arrest. Arrestable offence.
S. 3 FORGERY AND COUNTERFEITING ACT 1981

Q Define the offence of Copying a False Instrument with Intent

A It is an offence for a person to make a copy of an instrument which is [and he knows or believes] to be false with the intention that he or another shall use it **to induce someone to accept it as a copy of a genuine instrument,** resulting in someone being prejudiced.

Arrest. Arrestable offence.
S. 2 FORGERY AND COUNTERFEITING ACT 1981

Q Define the offence of Using a Copy of a False Instrument with Intent

A   It is an offence for a person to use a copy of an instrument which is [and he knows or believes] to be false with the intention of **inducing someone to accept it as a copy of a genuine instrument** resulting in someone being prejudiced.

Arrest. Arrestable offence.

S. 4 FORGERY AND COUNTERFEITING ACT 1981

Q Define An Instrument

A   [a]   Any document;
[b]   any stamp issued or used by a postal operator;
[c]   any Inland Revenue stamp;
[d]   any disc, tape, sound track or device on which information is stored or recorded by any means (e.g. a tachograph record sheet); and
[e]   a mark used by a postal operator in lieu of a stamp.

S. 8 FORGERY AND COUNTERFEITING ACT 1981

Q Define Having Specific Instruments With Intent

A   [a]   It is an offence for a person to **have in his custody** or under his control an **instrument** which is false [or knows or believes] with the intention that he or another shall use it **to induce someone to accept it as genuine,** resulting in someone being prejudiced; and

[b]   it is an offence for a person **to make** or have in his custody or control a **machine or implement, or paper or material** which is false [or knows or believes] with the intention that he or another shall make an instrument which is false and use it **to induce someone to accept it as genuine** resulting in someone being prejudiced.

S. 5(1), (3) FORGERY AND COUNTERFEITING ACT 1981

Instruments are: Money orders, postal orders, stamps, Inland Revenue stamps, share certificates, passports and documents issued instead of passports, cheques, travellers' cheques, cheque cards, credit cards, copies of certificates of births, adoptions, marriages or deaths.

Arrest. Arrestable offence.

Q Define the offence of Acknowledging Bail in the Name of Another

A Any person, without lawful authority or excuse who acknowledges **bail** by a court or the police, in the name of another person, commits an offence.

S. 34 FORGERY ACT 1861

Arrest. Arrestable offence.

Q What is meant by Counterfeiting?

A [a] It is an offence for a person to make a counterfeit of a **currency note or protected coin** intending that he or another pass it as genuine; and

[b] it is an offence for a person to make a counterfeit **currency note or protected coin** without lawful authority or reasonable excuse.

S. 14(1), (2) FORGERY AND COUNTERFEITING ACT 1981

Arrest. Arrestable offence.

Q Define the offence of Passing or Tendering Counterfeit Coins and Notes with Intent

A It is an offence for a person:

[a] **to pass or tender** as genuine any thing which is [or he knows or believes] to be a counterfeit note or protected coin; or

[b] to deliver to another any thing which is [or he knows or believes]

to be counterfeit intending that **that person pass or tender it as genuine.**

S. 15(1)(A), (B) FORGERY AND COUNTERFEITING ACT 1981

Arrest. Arrestable offence.

Protected coin. Any coin customarily used as money in any country, or otherwise specified as such by the Treasury.

Q   Define the offence of Reproducing a British Currency Note

A   It is an offence for a person, without the written consent of the relevant authority, to reproduce on any substance whatsoever, and whether or not on the correct scale, any British currency note or any part of a British currency note.

S. 18 FORGERY AND COUNTERFEITING ACT 1981

Relevant authority. The authority empowered by law to issue notes of that description (e.g. Bank of England).

CRIMINAL DAMAGE

Q Define simple Damage

A

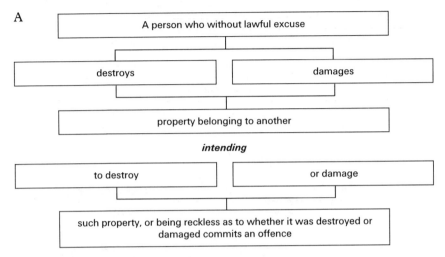

Arrest. Arrestable offence.

S. 1(1) CRIMINAL DAMAGE ACT 1971

Arson. Where the damage or destruction is caused by fire it shall be arson.

Which court? Triable either way, but if value of property damaged or destroyed is less than £5,000 the offence is to be tried summarily (S. 22 Magistrates' Court Act 1980) [unless damaged by fire or racially or religiously aggravated].

Lawful excuse. S. 5(2): the defendant would have a lawful excuse **if:**

[a] at the time he believed he had or would have the consent of the property's owner (or other person entitled to consent); **or**

[b] he acted to protect property believing that there was an immediate need to do so and the means he adopted to do so were reasonable.

Belief. Only needs to be honestly held, need not be a reasonable belief.

Reckless. Following the decision of the House of Lords in *R v. G & R (2003)* this now means subjective recklessness i.e. the defendant is aware that a particular circumstance or consequence will occur and that it is in the circumstances unreasonable to take the risk.

Q   Define the offence of Aggravated Damage

A

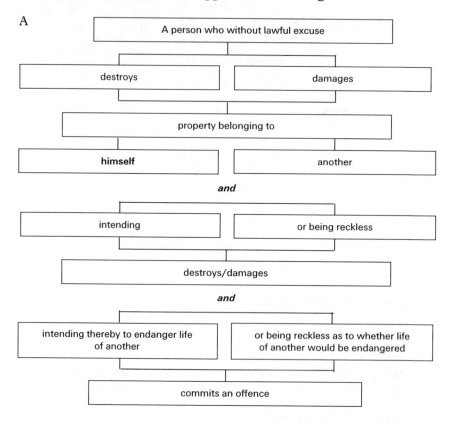

S. 1(2) CRIMINAL DAMAGE ACT 1971

Arrest. Arrestable offence.

Lawful excuse. The lawful excuse defence under S. 5 does not apply to this offence. The 'lawful excuse' referred to here is lawful excuse under the general law, e.g. self-defence or prevention of crime.

Q   Define the offence of Threatening Damage

A

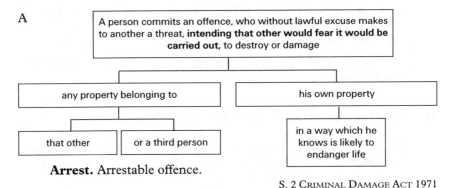

A person commits an offence, who without lawful excuse makes to another a threat, **intending that other would fear it would be carried out,** to destroy or damage

| any property belonging to | his own property |

| that other | or a third person |

in a way which he knows is likely to endanger life

Arrest. Arrestable offence.

S. 2 CRIMINAL DAMAGE ACT 1971

Q   Define the offence of Having Articles with Intent to damage

A.

A person who has anything

| in his custody | or control |

intending
without lawful excuse to use it

| to cause | or permit another to |

destroy or damage

| property belonging to another | his own or the user's property in a way which he knows is likely to **endanger life** |

commits an offence

S. 2 CRIMINAL DAMAGE ACT 1971

Arrest. Arrestable offence.

Articles. These are now 'prohibited' articles for the purpose of PACE stop and search powers. There is also a statutory power to apply to a magistrate for a search warrant.

Lawful excuse. The specific statutory defences of consent/protection under S. 5 *do* apply here.

Q What is a Graffiti Penalty Notice?

A Where an authorised officer of a local authority has reason to believe that a person has committed a relevant offence (which is not racially or religiously aggravated) in that local authority area, s/he may give that person a penalty notice under S. 43 Anti-Social Behaviour Act 2003. Relevant offences include criminal damage involving painting, writing on, soiling or otherwise defacing property; painting or affixing things on structures on the highway; affixing posters; defacing streets with slogans; displaying adverts in contravention of planning regulations.

Q Define the offence of selling aerosol paint to children

A A person commits an offence if he sells an aerosol container to a person under 16.

S. 54 Anti-Social Behaviour Act 2003

Q What are the defences to selling aerosol paint to children?

A To prove that s/he

[a] took all reasonable steps to determine the purchaser's age *and* that he reasonably believed that the purchaser was not under 16, or
[b] where the sale was effected by another person, that he took all reasonable steps to avoid it being committed.

S. 54(4) & (5) Anti-Social Behaviour Act 2003

Q Outline the Contamination/Interference with Goods offence

A

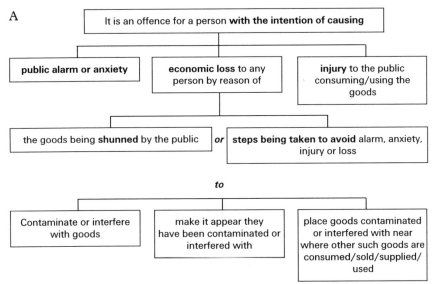

It is an offence for a person **with the intention of causing**

public alarm or anxiety | **economic loss** to any person by reason of | **injury** to the public consuming/using the goods

the goods being **shunned** by the public | *or* | **steps being taken to avoid** alarm, anxiety, injury or loss

to

Contaminate or interfere with goods | make it appear they have been contaminated or interfered with | place goods contaminated or interfered with near where other such goods are consumed/sold/supplied/ used

Arrest. Arrestable offence.

S. 38 PUBLIC ORDER ACT 1986

Threats. It is also an offence for a person to make threats that he or another will do or have done any of the contamination acts with the intention to cause public alarm or economic loss [not injury], although there is a proviso (S. 38(6)) which allows people to communicate warnings in good faith where contamination acts appear to have been committed.

OFFENCES AGAINST THE ADMINISTRATION OF JUSTICE & PUBLIC INTEREST

Q   Define Perjury

A   If any person **lawfully sworn** as a witness or interpreter in a judicial proceeding wilfully makes a statement *material* in that proceeding, which he knows to be false or does not believe to be true, he commits an offence.

S. 1 PERJURY ACT 1911

Arrest. Arrestable offence.

Wilful. Deliberate (not accidental).

Material. The statement must be important to the case. Whether a statement is material is a question of law for the judge.

Q   Define the offence of Aiding and Abetting Perjury

A   Every person who aids, abets, counsels, or procures another to commit an offence of perjury, or incites the offence, commits an offence.

Arrest. Arrestable if principal offence is triable on indictment.

Q   Which other offences are similar to Perjury?

A   1.   If any child wilfully gives false evidence which, had it been given on oath would be perjury, he commits an offence: S. 38(2) Children & Young Persons Act 1933 (False Testimony of Unsworn Child Witness).

   2.   If any person in a **written statement** tendered in criminal proceedings wilfully makes a statement which is material, and which he knows to be false or does not believe to be true, he commits an offence: S. 89 Criminal Justice Act 1967 (False Statements in Criminal Proceedings).

   3.   If any person being required or authorised by law to make any statement on oath and being lawfully sworn **[otherwise than in judicial proceedings]** wilfully makes a statement which is material for that purpose and which he

knows to be false or does not believe to be true, he commits an offence: S. 2 Perjury Act 1911 (False Statements on Oath). This is an arrestable offence.

Q Define the offence of Perverting the Course of Justice

A It is an offence at common law to do an act tending and intended to pervert the course of public justice.

COMMON LAW

Arrest. Arrestable offence.

Note. Requires a positive act and not a mere omission or failure to take steps to prevent an injustice.

Q Outline the offence of Intimidating Witnesses and Jurors in proceedings for criminal offences

A [a] A person who does to another:

    [i] an act which **intimidates,** and is intended to intimidate, another person;

    [ii] knowing or believing that that person is assisting in the investigation of an offence as a witness, or juror; and

    [iii] intending thereby to cause the investigation to be **obstructed, perverted or interfered with,** commits an offence.

  [b] A person who does or threatens to do to another:

    [i] an act which **harms him,** and is intended to harm him; or is intended to make him fear harm;

    [ii] knowing or believing that that person, or another, **has assisted in** an investigation into an offence or has **given evidence** or acted as a **juror;** and

    [iii] does or threatens to do it because of that knowledge or belief.

S. 51 CRIMINAL JUSTICE AND PUBLIC ORDER ACT 1994

Arrest. Arrestable offence.

Q Outline the offence of Intimidation of Witnesses in any proceedings

A

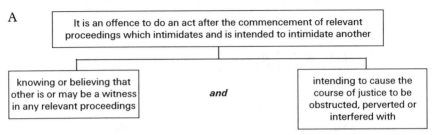

It is an offence to do an act after the commencement of relevant proceedings which intimidates and is intended to intimidate another

| knowing or believing that other is or may be a witness in any relevant proceedings | **and** | intending to cause the course of justice to be obstructed, perverted or interfered with |

S. 39 CRIMINAL JUSTICE AND POLICE ACT 2001

Arrest. Arrestable offence.

Relevant proceedings. Any proceedings in any court save the House of Lords which are not for a criminal offence.

Q Define the offence of Assisting Offenders

A Where a person has committed an **arrestable offence,** any other person who, knowing or believing him to be guilty of the offence, or some other arrestable offence, without lawful authority or reasonable excuse, **does any act with intent to impede** his arrest or prosecution, commits an offence.

S. 4 CRIMINAL LAW ACT 1967

Arrest. Arrestable offence.

Prosecution. DPP's permission is required to prosecute.

Q Define the offence of Concealing Arrestable Offences

A Where a person has committed an **arrestable offence,** any other person, knowing or believing the offence or some other arrestable offence has been committed and **he has information which might be material** in securing the prosecution or conviction of an offender, **accepts** or agrees to accept **for not disclosing that information any consideration** [but not making good loss or injury caused by the offence/compensation] commits an offence.

S. 5 CRIMINAL LAW ACT 1967

Prosecution. DPP's permission is required to prosecute.

Q   Define the offence of Escaping

A   It is an offence at common law to escape from legal custody.

COMMON LAW

Arrest. Arrestable offence.

Assisting escape. A person who aids a prisoner to escape or who conveys anything **inside or outside a prison** with a view to its coming into the possession of a prisoner, commits an arrestable offence.

S. 39 PRISON ACT 1952

Q   Define the offence of Harbouring Offenders

A   Any person who **knowingly harbours** an escapee or person unlawfully at large or **gives assistance with intent to prevent, hinder or interfere** with his arrest commits an arrestable offence.

S. 22 CRIMINAL JUSTICE ACT 1961

Arrest. Arrestable offence.

Q   Outline the offence of Wasting Police Time

A

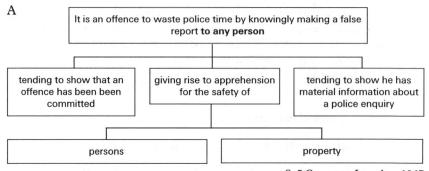

S. 5 CRIMINAL LAW ACT 1967

Prosecution. Consent of DPP is required to prosecute.

Q   Define the offence of Corruption under the Public Bodies Corrupt Practices Act 1889 S. 1.

A   Any person who corruptly solicits, receives, or agrees to receive for himself or another any gift, loan, fee, reward **as an inducement to or reward for** doing or not doing anything in which he, a public body, is concerned commits an offence.

Arrest. Arrestable offence.

Agents. An agent of the public body [official] is also guilty (S. 1 Prevention of Corruption Act 1906).

Prosecution. The consent of the Attorney-General (or Solicitor-General) is required to prosecute.

Q   Define the common law offence of Corruption

A   It is an offence for any public official to misbehave or act corruptly in the discharge of his duties.

Arrest. Arrestable offence.

Taking bribes. This is perhaps the most common form of common law corruption. An offer of a bribe to, or an attempt to bribe, a public official is also a common law offence.

Extraterritorial corruption. The offences can be prosecuted in England and Wales where the person involved is a UK national or company even where the relevant act took place overseas.

IMMIGRATION OFFENCES

Q   Outline the offence of Illegal Entry

A   A non-British citizen commits an offence in any of the following circumstances:

[a]   if he knowingly enters the UK in breach of a deportation order or without leave;

[b]   if, having only a limited permission to enter or remain in the UK, he knowingly either

[i]   remains beyond the time limited by the permission ('overstays') or

[ii]   fails to observe a condition of the permission;

[c]   if, having lawfully entered without leave, he remains beyond any permitted time;

[d]   if, without reasonable excuse, he fails to comply with any requirement to report to a medical officer or attend or submit to any medical test or examination;

[e]   if, without reasonable excuse, he fails to observe any residence, employment, occupation or reporting restrictions imposed on him;

[f]   if he disembarks in the UK from a ship or aircraft after being placed on board with a view to his deportation;

[g]   if he leaves or seeks to leave the UK through the Channel Tunnel in contravention of an imposed restriction.

S. 24 IMMIGRATION ACT 1971

Q **Outline the offence of using Deception to Enter or Remain**

A A person who is not a British citizen is guilty of an offence if, by means which include deception by him

[a] he obtains or seeks to obtain leave to enter or remain in the UK; or

[b] he secures or seeks to secure the avoidance, postponement or revocation of enforcement action against him

S. 24A IMMIGRATION ACT 1971

Q **What is the power of arrest for these immigration offences?**

A A constable (or immigration officer) may arrest without warrant a person

[a] who *has committed or attempted* to commit an offence under S. 24 or S. 24 A; or

[b] whom *he has reasonable grounds for suspecting* has committed or attempted to commit such an offence

except that there is **no power of arrest** for the offence under S. 24(1)(d) [i.e. **failing to comply with a medical requirement**].

Part 3 - Road Traffic

STANDARDS OF DRIVING

Q Define 'Motor Vehicle'

A For most road traffic offences S. 185 Road Traffic Act 1988 defines a motor vehicle as a mechanically propelled vehicle intended or adapted for **use on roads.** Whether it is so adapted is a question of fact in each case, e.g. a 'Go-ped' motorised scooter. (However, for the purposes of powers under S. 59 of the Police Reform Act 2002, a motor vehicle is defined as any mechanically propelled vehicle *whether or not* it is intended or adapted for use on roads.)

Q Define 'Mechanically Propelled Vehicle'

A A wider term than motor vehicle which means a vehicle constructed so it can be propelled mechanically. The test is one of construction rather than use. It must derive its power from an engine which may be powered by internal combustion, steam or battery. It can include a vehicle whose engine has been removed, where there is a possibility that it may soon be replaced, and a vehicle which has broken down because of mechanical failure. Eg. dumper trucks, fork lifts, cranes, quad bikes.

Q Define the offence of Causing Death by Dangerous Driving

A

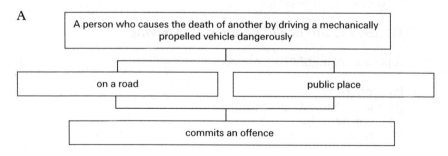

S. 1 RTA 1988

Arrest. Serious arrestable offence.

Death. The driving must be 'a' cause, it need not be the sole or substantial cause. The death must be of *another*, not the defendant himself.

Driving. Must control both **direction and movement** of the vehicle. Pushing a car whilst steering has been held not to be driving (in England and Wales). Straddling a motorcycle and pushing it along using feet is driving. It is also driving to 'free-wheel' down a hill in a car.

Road. Means any highway or road to which the public have access. Vehicles 'half on, half-off' a road, are on the road.

Not a road. If only a restricted section of the public has access [say, members of a club] it is not a road. Equally, it is not a road if members of the public have to overcome physical barriers or defy prohibitions to gain access.

Public place. Includes driving off-road, in places to which the public have access and includes bridleways and footpaths. If the public have access, it is a public place.

How wide is the offence? A man free-wheeling [controlling the brakes and steering wheel] down a multi-storey car park in a dumper truck, whose driving is dangerous and results in the death of another, can be guilty of this offence.

Manslaughter. The offence also amounts to manslaughter, though it is rarely charged as such.

Q Define the offence of Dangerous Driving

A   A person commits an offence who:

[a]   drives;
[b]   a mechanically propelled vehicle;
[c]   dangerously;
[d]   on a road or public place.

S. 2 RTA 1988

Q **What is the test of Dangerous Driving?**

A
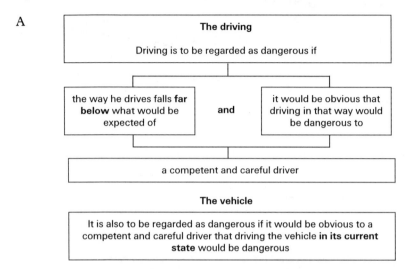

State of the vehicle. Regard may be given to anything attached to, and carried on, the vehicle and to 'how' it is attached or carried.

Q **Define 'Careless and Inconsiderate Driving'**

A
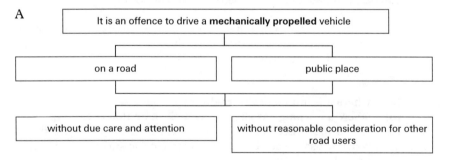

S. 3 RTA 1988

Due care and attention. Is the standard to be expected of a reasonable, prudent and competent driver in all the circumstances.

Inconsiderate driving. e.g. driving through a puddle and splashing a bus queue.

Q   What powers exist to order careless drivers (or unlawful off-roaders) to stop?

A

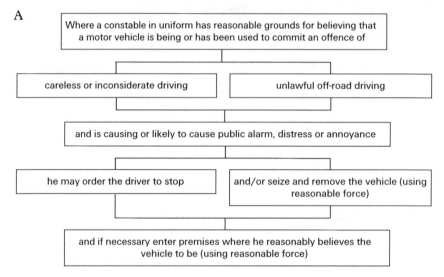

Where a constable in uniform has reasonable grounds for believing that a motor vehicle is being or has been used to commit an offence of

| careless or inconsiderate driving | unlawful off-road driving |

and is causing or likely to cause public alarm, distress or annoyance

| he may order the driver to stop | and/or seize and remove the vehicle (using reasonable force) |

and if necessary enter premises where he reasonably believes the vehicle to be (using reasonable force)

S. 59 POLICE REFORM ACT 2002

Premises. Not private dwelling-houses (though this does not include garages, driveways etc. occupied with the dwelling).

Warnings. In order to exercise the power to seize/remove a vehicle it is necessary in most cases to first warn the driver not to continue the behaviour. However a warning need not be given in the following circumstances:

[a]   where it is impracticable to do so;
[b]   where a warning has already been given on that occasion;
[c]   where the officer has reasonable grounds for believing that a warning has already been given on that occasion by someone else; or
[d]   where the officer has reasonable grounds for believing that a warning has already been given to that person during the previous 12 months.

Q **Outline the defence to bad driving of Automatism**

A Automatism occurs when a driver's movements are beyond his control or his movements are brought about involuntarily, e.g. a driver being attacked by a swarm of bees or losing control as a result of lapsing into a coma. The defence is not available to a person who knows that he is subject to a condition which will result in his losing control, e.g. a diabetic who begins to feel the effects of a hypoglycaemic episode but continues to drive.

Q **Outline the offence of Causing Death by Careless Driving whilst Under the Influence**

A

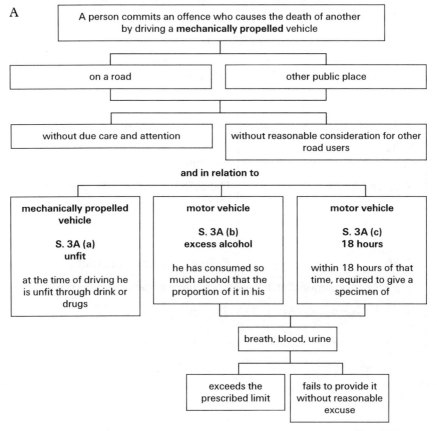

S. 3A RTA 1988

Arrest. Serious arrestable offence.

Power of entry. Unfit - power of entry always. Excess alcohol - injury accident.

S. 3A (a). Relates to a mechanically propelled vehicle. Power of arrest and entry.

S. 3A (b) & (c). Relate to a **motor vehicle** [intended or adapted for use on a road] and the '18 hours' requirement under (c) relates only to police station procedures.

Q   What is a Notice of Intended Prosecution (NIP)?

A   A warning notice which must be served upon offenders before certain offences can be prosecuted.

Q   Which offences are subject to NIP?

Section	Offence
S. 2 RTA 1988	Dangerous driving
S. 3	Careless and inconsiderate driving
S. 22	Leaving vehicle in dangerous position
S. 28 and S. 29	Dangerous, careless and inconsiderate cycling
S. 35	Failure to comply with traffic directions
S. 36	Failure to comply with traffic signs
S. 16 RT Regulation Act 1984	Speeding [temporary restrictions]
S. 17 RT Regulation Act 1984	Speeding [special roads]

NOTICE OF INTENDED PROSECUTION

Q   When is a NIP required?

A

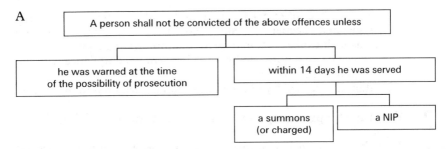

A person shall not be convicted of the above offences unless

| he was warned at the time of the possibility of prosecution | within 14 days he was served |

| | a summons (or charged) | a NIP |

Q   How is Service of a NIP proved?

A

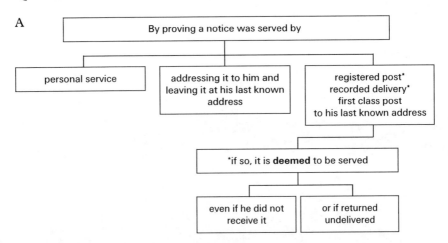

By proving a notice was served by

| personal service | addressing it to him and leaving it at his last known address | registered post* recorded delivery* first class post to his last known address |

*if so, it is **deemed** to be served

| even if he did not receive it | or if returned undelivered |

Q   When is a NIP not required?

A   [a]   In relation to an offence if at the time, or immediately afterwards, and owing to the presence of the vehicle concerned on a road an accident occurred (S. 2(1) RT Amendment Act 1988); or

[b]   when a **fixed penalty** has been issued in respect of the offence (S. 2(2)).

Note. Where the accident is so minor that the driver is unaware of its occurrence then a NIP will have to be served (although if it was so severe that the driver has no recollection of it, there is no need to serve a NIP).

NOTICE OF INTENDED PROSECUTION

Q **What if you are unable to trace the offender?**

A   A lack of a warning notice **will not be a bar to conviction** where:

[a]   neither the offender's name and address, nor that of the registered keeper (if any), could be ascertained, despite reasonable diligence, in time for a summons or a complaint to be served or for a notice to be served or sent in compliance with the requirement to do so; or

[b]   that the accused **by his own conduct** contributed to the failure.

Q **What is the presumption in law in relation to NIPs?**

A   They shall be deemed to have been served unless the contrary is proved by the defence.

ACCIDENTS

Q Define a Reportable Accident

A

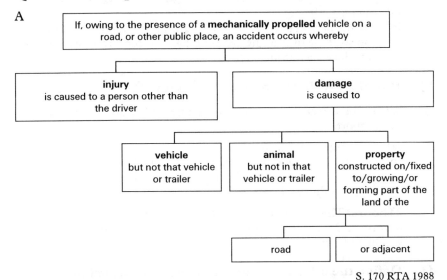

If, owing to the presence of a **mechanically propelled** vehicle on a road, or other public place, an accident occurs whereby

injury is caused to a person other than the driver	**damage** is caused to

vehicle but not that vehicle or trailer	**animal** but not in that vehicle or trailer	**property** constructed on/fixed to/growing/or forming part of the land of the

road	**or adjacent**

S. 170 RTA 1988

Animal. Means horse, cattle, ass, mule, sheep, pig, goat or dog.

Q What are the driver's Duties and Responsibilities in such a case?

A The driver shall:

[a] stop; and
[b] if required to do so by any person having reasonable grounds for doing so, give
   [i] his name and address; and
   [ii] the name and address of the owner; and
   [iii] the identification mark of the vehicle.
[c] if for any reason the driver does not give his name and address, he must **report** the accident.

Note. This is, essentially, a duty 'to exchange details' with any other parties involved (including owners of any property damaged) and as such caselaw states that providing a solicitor's address for further correspondence is sufficient to discharge the duty. The requirement is to **stop** and remain for such a time as to allow interested persons to ask for information from the driver – the driver need not make his own enquiries to find such persons.

Q What about Injury Accidents?

A The driver shall produce his insurance to:

[a] a constable; or
[b] to any person having reasonable grounds. [And if he is unable to do so at the time of the accident, he must report the accident and produce such evidence].

Q How does a Driver Report an Accident?

A Where the driver does not give his name and address at the time he must report:

[a] to a police officer; or
[b] at a police station [personally]; and it must be done
    [i] as soon as reasonably practicable; and in any case
    [ii] within 24 hours.

24 hours. This does not give the driver 24 hours to report the accident, it must be done as soon as is reasonably practicable **and in any case** within 24 hours.

Q Define the offence of Failing to Stop or Report an Accident

A A person who fails to stop or report an accident commits an offence. [two offences].

S. 170(4) RTA 1988

Arrest. Arrestable offence if injury caused to someone other than the driver.

Q Is Failing to Stop or Report also the offence of Perverting the Course of Justice?

A No. In *R v. Clark (2003)* the Court of Appeal held that the failure to report the accident could not amount to perverting the course of justice since that requires an act rather than an omission.

Q What is the defence to not producing Insurance at the time of the Accident?

A To prove that he produced it at a police station specified by him at the time of the accident within **seven days**.

S. 170(7) RTA 1988

Q   **Define the offence of Giving False Details**

A   In the case of an allegation of dangerous or careless driving or cycling, the driver/rider **who refuses,** or **gives a false name and address,** to any person with reasonable grounds for requiring it, commits an offence.

S. 168 RTA 1988

Note. There is no requirement for an accident to have occurred, only for an allegation of such driving to have been made.

DRINK DRIVING

Q   **Outline the offence of being UNFIT to drive through drink or drugs**

A

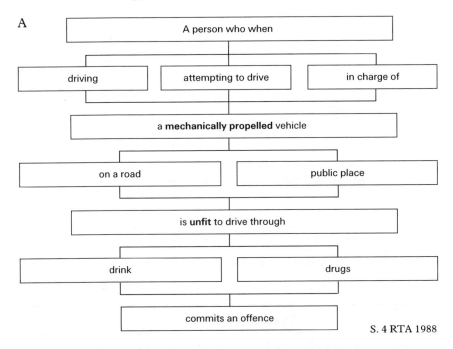

A person who when

driving   attempting to drive   in charge of

a **mechanically propelled** vehicle

on a road   public place

is **unfit** to drive through

drink   drugs

commits an offence

S. 4 RTA 1988

Police Powers. If a constable reasonably suspects that a person **is or has been** committing this offence he may arrest, **and may enter [if need be by force],** the place where he is or the constable reasonably suspects him to be.

Does the constable need to be in uniform? No.

Unfit. Means his ability to drive is for the time being impaired.

When is a driver not in charge? When he can prove that there was no likelihood of his driving so long as he remained unfit.

What if the driver is injured? In determining whether the defendant was likely to drive while unfit the court may disregard any injury to the driver or damage to the vehicle.

Drugs. Means any intoxicant that is not alcohol.

Q   Outline the offences of Driving and Being in Charge whilst OVER PRESCRIBED LIMIT

A

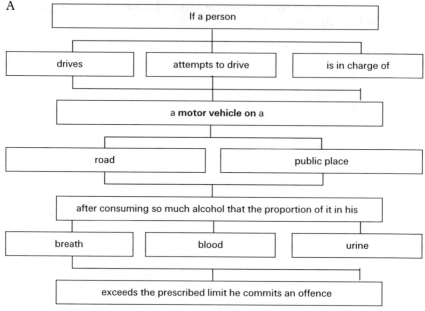

If a person

| drives | attempts to drive | is in charge of |

a **motor vehicle** on a

| road | public place |

after consuming so much alcohol that the proportion of it in his

| breath | blood | urine |

exceeds the prescribed limit he commits an offence

S. 5 RTA 1988

Prescribed limits are		
35 microgrammes of alcohol	in 100 millilitres	of breath
80 milligrammes of alcohol	in 100 millilitres	of blood
107 milligrammes of alcohol	in 100 millilitres	of urine

Arrest. Statutory power.

Defence. For the driver to demonstrate an arguable case that there was no likelihood of his driving whilst he remained over the prescribed limit. The prosecution must then prove beyond reasonable doubt that there was such a likelihood to defeat this defence: *Sheldrake v. DPP (2003).*

What if the driver is injured? In determining whether the driver was likely to drive whilst over the prescribed limit the court may disregard any injury to the driver and damage to the vehicle.

Q   Outline the requirement to Co-operate with a Preliminary Test

A

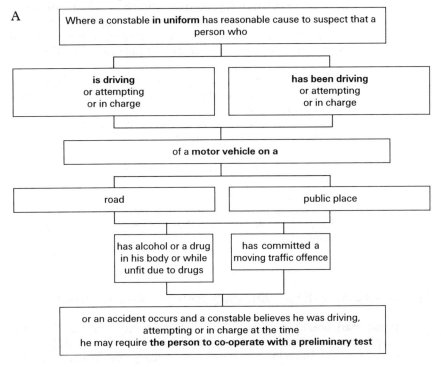

Where a constable **in uniform** has reasonable cause to suspect that a person who

| **is driving** or attempting or in charge | **has been driving** or attempting or in charge |

of a **motor vehicle on a**

| road | public place |

| has alcohol or a drug in his body or while unfit due to drugs | has committed a moving traffic offence |

or an accident occurs and a constable believes he was driving, attempting or in charge at the time he may require **the person to co-operate with a preliminary test**

S. 6 RTA 1988

Uniform. The officer making the requirement need not be in uniform, but the officer administering the test must be.

Q   **Outline the 3 preliminary tests**

A   [1]   Preliminary breath test. A procedure whereby a person provides a specimen of breath for the purpose of obtaining, by means of an approved device, an indication whether the proportion of alcohol in the breath or blood is likely to exceed the prescribed limit.

[2]   Preliminary impairment test. A procedure whereby a constable
(a)   observes the person in his performance of tasks specified by the constable, and
(b)   makes such other observations of the person's physical state as the constable thinks expedient.

[3]   Preliminary drug test. A procedure by which a specimen of sweat or saliva is
(a)   obtained, and
(b)   used for the purpose of obtaining, by means of an approved device, an indication whether the person has a drug in his body.

S. 6A-C RTA 1988

Q   **Where may the preliminary tests be administered?**

A   Preliminary breath tests may only be administered at or near the place where the requirement to co-operate with the test is imposed. (But see below for tests following accidents). Preliminary impairment and drug tests may be administered *either* at that place, *or* if the constable who imposes the requirement thinks it expedient, at a police station specified by him.

Q   **What is the purpose of a preliminary test?**

A   To obtain an indication of the likelihood of an offence having been committed (rather than to prove the offence).

Q   **Who can administer a preliminary test?**

A   In the case of preliminary breath and drug tests, any officer. Impairment tests may only be administered by those approved by their chief officer for this purpose.

Q   What is the procedure following an accident?

A

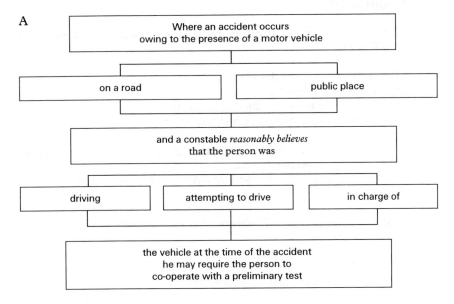

Where an accident occurs
owing to the presence of a motor vehicle

on a road

public place

and a constable *reasonably believes*
that the person was

driving

attempting to drive

in charge of

the vehicle at the time of the accident
he may require the person to
co-operate with a preliminary test

S. 6 RTA 1988

Location of breath test. Note that where an accident has occurred all 3 preliminary tests (including breath tests) may be administered *either* at the place where the requirement is made *or* at a specified police station (where there is no accident breath tests can only be administered at the scene).

Power of entry. S.6E Road Traffic Act 1988 provides a power of entry (using reasonable force) to impose the requirement in case of **injury** accidents.

Q   Outline the offence of failing to co-operate with a preliminary test

A   A person commits an offence if, without reasonable excuse, he fails to co-operate with a preliminary test.

S. 6(6) RTA 1988

Arrest. A constable may arrest if the person fails to co-operate with a preliminary test requirement *and* the constable reasonably suspects that the person has alcohol or a drug in his body or is under the influence of a drug.

Q Outline the Provision of Specimens for Analysis requirement

A In the course of an investigation into whether a person has committed an offence of:

[a] death by careless driving [S. 3A];
[b] drunk in charge [S. 4]; or
[c] being over the prescribed limit [S. 5]
a constable may require him to provide:

[i] two specimens of **breath** for analysis by means of an approved device; or
[ii] a specimen of **blood or urine** for a laboratory test.

S. 7 RTA 1988

Failure. The provision of only one breath specimen is a failure. Failure includes a refusal.

Where? Breath test - at a police station only. Blood or urine - at a police station (but see later) or hospital.

What if no one admits to driving? The requirement can be made of more than one person in respect of the same vehicle.

Q Which are the Approved Devices?

A The CAMIC Datamaster; the Lion Intoxylizer 6000UK and the EC/IR Intoximeter.

Q When can a driver choose to replace a breath test with a specimen of blood/urine?

A Of the 2 breath specimens provided the one with the lower proportion of alcohol shall be used and the other disregarded. If the one used contains no more than 50 mg of alcohol in 100 ml of breath, the provider may request that a blood or urine sample be used, and if he provides such a sample then neither breath specimen may be used.

S. 8(2) RTA 1988

Option. If the driver chooses the option of blood/urine and subsequently fails or refuses he commits no offence - revert to the original breath specimen.

Q   Can you make a request for Blood or Urine at a police station?

A   Only in the following circumstances:

[a]   for medical reasons a breath test cannot be provided or should not be required;

[b]   a breath test device is not available or it is not practicable to use;

[c]   in relation to **causing death by careless driving (S. 3A) or unfit (S. 4)** a doctor has advised that his condition might be due to a drug.

Who decides, blood or urine? The constable, unless a doctor is of the opinion that blood cannot or should not be taken, then it shall be urine.

Doctor's advice. May be given over the telephone if appropriate.

Urine. Two specimens within one hour, the first being discarded.

Blood. Shall be divided into two parts, one being supplied to the defendant.

Q   What is the policy on Prescribed Limits?

A

Between 35 - 39 mg of alcohol in 100 ml of breath	caution
Between 40 - 50 mg of alcohol in 100 ml of breath	driver's option
More than 50 mg of alcohol in 100 ml of breath	charge

Q Define the offence of Failing to Provide Evidential Specimens

A   A person who, without reasonable excuse, fails to provide a specimen when required to do so commits an offence.

S. 7(6) RTA 1988

Reasonable excuse. What amounts to a reasonable excuse is a question of law. Whether the defendant actually had a reasonable excuse is a question of fact for the court. In *DDP v. Falzarano (2001)*, where the defendant was suffering from panic attacks and shortness of breath, it was held that the reasonable excuse had to arise out of a physical or mental inability to provide a specimen or a substantial risk to health in its provision. Being drunk or under stress is not enough in itself to provide a reasonable excuse. It is not reasonable to refuse to provide a specimen until one's legal adviser is present since the public interest requires that specimens be given without delay.

Q Outline the Post Procedure Detention of Subjects

A   [a]   The person may afterwards be detained at a police station until it appears to a constable that, were that person **then driving** he would not be committing an offence;

[b]   he shall not be detained if there is **no likelihood of his driving** whilst he exceeds the prescribed limit;

[c]   in the case of drugs, a doctor's opinion must be sought concerning his fitness to be released.

S. 10 RTA 1988

Q   Outline the Hospital Procedure

A   A breath test or blood/urine specimens cannot be taken from a patient in hospital unless the doctor in immediate charge of his case has been notified of the proposal and:

[a]   if the requirement is made, it shall be for the provision of a specimen at the hospital; but

[b]   if the doctor objects the requirement may not be made. The doctor may object on the grounds that the patient's care and treatment will be adversely affected by any one of:

[i]   the requirement to provide a specimen; or
[ii]   the provision of the specimen itself; or
[iii] the warning [i.e. failure to provide may lead to prosecution].

S. 9 RTA 1988

Patient. A person continues to be a patient until his treatment is finished. (But once a person is discharged he ceases to be a patient even if he has to return later for further treatment).

Q   Outline the Evidence required for offences under Sections 3A, 4 and 5

A   Evidence of the proportion of alcohol or drug in breath, blood or urine **shall in all cases be taken into account** unless the accused proves:

[a]   he consumed alcohol between ceasing to drive; and
[b]   before providing a specimen; **and**
[c]   had he not done so he would have not exceeded the limit or been impaired.

Distinguish between Sections 4 and 5

	Unfit - S. 4	Over prescribed limit - S. 5
Driving	driving, attempting, in charge	driving, attempting, in charge
Vehicle	**mechanically propelled vehicle**	motor vehicle
Where	road or public place	road or public place
Uniform	**No**	**Yes**
Power to arrest or to require a breath test	a constable may arrest [see breath test powers below]	Breath test where a constable suspects: 1. has alcohol in his body or has committed a moving traffic offence 2. has had alcohol in his body and still has alcohol in his body 3. has committed a moving traffic offence
Offence	unfit through drink or drugs	breath, blood, urine, exceeds the prescribed limit
Arrest	is committing or has been committing	1. positive breath test 2. failed breath test **and** the constable suspects alcohol in his body
Entry	Yes where he is or suspected to be	conditional 1. to require breath test 2. to arrest following an injury accident
Defence	no likelihood of him driving whilst he remained unfit	no likelihood of him driving whilst he remained over the limit

A constable [in uniform *or out of uniform*]

1. May arrest a person following a positive breath test or where he has failed to supply a breath test **and** the constable suspects he has alcohol in his body.
2. May **enter** [if need be by force] any place where he is or the constable suspects him to be to:

   [a] require him to provide a breath test following an **injury accident**; or
   [b] to arrest under S. 5 following an **injury accident**.

INSURANCE

Q   Define the offence of Having No Insurance

A   It is an offence to use, [cause/permit] a motor vehicle on a road or
public place without insurance.

S. 143(2) RTA 1988

Q   What is the defence to Having No Insurance?

A   [a]   The vehicle did not belong to him and was not in his possession
under contract of hire or loan;

[b]   he was using the vehicle in the course of his employment; and

[c]   that he neither knew nor had reason to believe that there was no
insurance.

S. 143(3) RTA 1988

Q   What restrictions in a Policy of Insurance are Void?

A   Breach of the following restrictions does not make the policy void for
the purposes of S. 143:

[a]   the age or physical or mental condition of the driver;

[b]   the condition of the vehicle;

[c]   the number of persons carried;

[d]   the weight or physical characteristics of the goods carried;

[e]   the times or areas in which the vehicle is used;

[f]   the horsepower or cc or value of the vehicle;

[g]   carrying any particular apparatus; or

[h]   carrying any particular means of identification of the vehicle.

**Q   Outline police powers to Demand the Production of
Insurance**

A   [a]   A person driving a motor vehicle **on a road** [not an invalid
carriage];

[b]   a person whom a constable [or vehicle examiner] reasonably
believes to have been the driver when an **accident** occurred
owing to its presence on a road or public place; or

[c]   a person whom a constable [or vehicle examiner] reasonably
believes to have **committed an offence** in relation to the use of
the vehicle on a road,

shall, on being required by a Constable or vehicle examiner:

[i] give his name and address; and

[ii] the name and address of the owner; and

[ii] produce the certificate of insurance of that vehicle (and any required test certificate).

Not produced at time. In proceedings for an offence, it is a defence to prove that the insurance was produced within **seven days** at a police station specified by him, or it was produced as soon as was reasonably practicable, or it was not practicable to produce it before the proceedings began.

TRAFFIC SAFETY MEASURES

Q Define the law relating to Seat Belts

A Where a person is aged **14 years old** and over, it is an offence to:

[a] **drive** a motor vehicle; or
[b] ride as a **front seat passenger;** or
[c] ride in the **rear seat** of a motor car or passenger car

without wearing an adult seat belt.   S. 14(3) RTA 1988

Aiding and abetting. There is no offence of aiding and abetting adult offenders. Only the person actually committing the contravention is guilty.

Q Define the law in relation to children under 14 years of age and Seat Belts

A [a] Where a child aged under 14 years is in the front seat, he must wear a seat belt;

[b] he must wear a seat belt in the **rear seat** if it is fitted, except

[i] **aged under 12 years** and is a **small child,** [under 150 cm];
[ii] no seat belt is fitted in the rear; and
[iii] a seat in the front has a seat belt but it is unoccupied.

S. 15(1) RTA 1988

Who commits the offence? The driver [not the child], if he drives without reasonable excuse.

Q Outline the law on Motor Cycle Helmets

A A motor cycle means a two-wheeled motor cycle [with or without sidecar] and it is an offence to ride a motor cycle without protective headgear, except

[a] mowing machines;
[b] it is being pushed [not straddled]; or
[c] a Sikh wearing a turban.   S. 16 RTA 1988

Who commits the offence? Only the person actually failing to wear a helmet i.e. helmeted drivers are not responsible for bare-headed passengers, except in the case of persons under 16, in which case both driver and passenger commit the offence.

Q   What is the law in relation to Passengers on Motor Cycles?

A   [a]   Only one passenger may be carried
    [b]   sitting astride, on a secure seat, behind the driver.

S. 23 RTA 1988

Who commits the offence? The driver. The passenger can be convicted of aiding and abetting.

Q   Who is exempt from Speed Restrictions?

A   Drivers of the under-mentioned vehicles are exempt if the observance of the speed limit would be **likely to hinder** its use on that occasion:

Fire Brigade, Ambulance Service, Police

S. 87 RT REGULATION ACT 1984

Q   How do you prove someone's speed?

A   A person prosecuted for speeding shall not be convicted only on the evidence of one witness to the effect that, in his opinion, the defendant was exceeding the speed limit. Corroboration may be provided by
    [a]   equipment in a police vehicle or other speed measuring equipment; or
    [b]   evidence of 2 police officers (although the court will decide how much weight to place on such evidence).

Q   Define the Obstruction Offences

A   **Highway.** A person who without lawful authority or excuse, wilfully obstructs the highway commits an offence.

S. 137 HIGHWAYS ACT 1980

Arrest. S. 25 PACE Act 1984.

Road. A person in charge of a motor vehicle or trailer who causes or permits it to stand on a road so as to cause an unnecessary obstruction of the road commits an offence.

REG. 103 ROAD VEHICLES (CONSTRUCTION AND USE) REGS 1986

Street. Any person in any street who, to the obstruction, annoyance, danger of residents or passengers, wilfully interrupts any public crossing, or causes any wilful obstruction in any public footpath commits an offence.

S. 28 TOWN POLICE CLAUSES ACT 1847

Q   Define the offence of Parking Heavy Vehicles on Verges

A

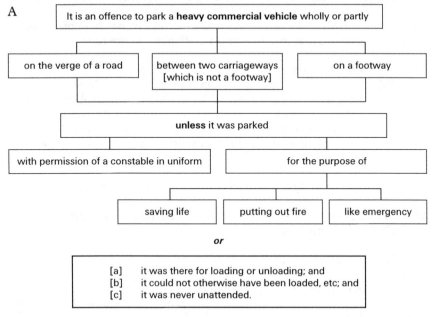

It is an offence to park a **heavy commercial vehicle** wholly or partly

| on the verge of a road | between two carriageways [which is not a footway] | on a footway |

unless it was parked

| with permission of a constable in uniform | for the purpose of |

| saving life | putting out fire | like emergency |

or

[a]   it was there for loading or unloading; and
[b]   it could not otherwise have been loaded, etc; and
[c]   it was never unattended.

S. 19 RTA 1988

Heavy commercial vehicle. Means its operating weight exceeds 7.5 tonnes.

Q   Define the offence of Leaving a Vehicle in a Dangerous Position

A   A person in charge of a vehicle/trailer, who causes or permits it to remain at rest in a road in such a position or in such condition or in such circumstances as to involve a **danger of injury** to other road users commits an offence.

S. 22 RTA 1988

Moving vehicle. This offence applies to moving as well as stationary vehicles e.g. failing to set a handbrake properly so that the vehicle rolls down a hill.

Q   **Define the offence of Wrongful Use of Disabled Person's Badge under S. 117 Road Traffic Regulation Act 1984**

A   A person who fails to comply with, or contravenes, any provision in relation to parking also commits an offence if at the time:

[a]   a disabled badge sticker was displayed; and
[b]   he was using the vehicle in circumstances where a disabled person's concession would be available to a disabled person's vehicle, **unless** the badge was issued and displayed lawfully. [So a driver who commits a parking offence and misuses a disabled badge at the same time commits both the parking offence **and** an offence under S. 117].

Removal of badge. On third conviction, it may be removed.

Q   **What is the law on Removal and Immobilisation of Parked Vehicles?**

A   Where a vehicle is permitted to remain at rest on a road:

[a]   in contravention of a prohibition or restriction; or
[b]   in a position or under circumstances as to obstruct or cause danger;
[c]   or any **land in the open air** so as to appear to have been **abandoned/broken down**,

then a constable may arrange for it to be moved from that road to another position on that road or another road.

REG. 4 REMOVAL AND DISPOSAL OF VEHICLES REGS 1986

Q   **Outline the offence of Causing Danger to Road Users**

A   It is an offence if a person, intentionally and without lawful authority or reasonable cause:

[a]   causes anything to be on or over a road; or
[b]   interferes with a motor vehicle, trailer or cycle; or
[c]   interferes with traffic equipment,

in such circumstances that it would be obvious to a reasonable person **that to do so would be dangerous.**

S. 22A RTA 1988

Traffic equipment. Means anything placed on or near a road by the highway authority, a traffic sign lawfully placed on or near a road by any person and any fence, barrier or light lawfully placed on or near a road, or by a constable or anyone acting under his instructions.

Arrest. Arrestable offence.

Dangerous. Refers to danger either of injury to a person on or near a road or serious damage to property on or near a road and regard will be given to the circumstances of which he could be expected to be aware, but also to circumstances within the accused's knowledge.

Q   Define the offence of Tampering with and Getting on to Vehicles

A

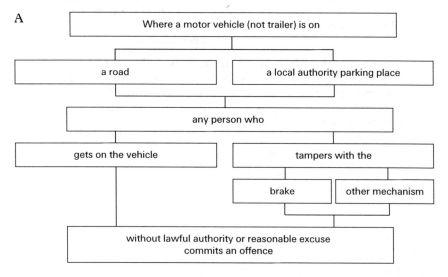

S. 25 RTA 1988

Q   Define the offence of Holding/Getting on to a Vehicle in Motion

A   If, for the purposes of being carried, a person without lawful authority or reasonable excuse, takes hold of, or gets on to a motor vehicle or trailer in motion on a road, or for the purposes of being drawn, he takes hold of, he commits an offence.

S. 26 RTA 1998

Q Define the offence of Abandoning Motor Vehicles

A A person is guilty of an offence who, without lawful authority:

[a] abandons **on any land in the open air,** or on a highway, a motor vehicle or anything which formed part of a motor vehicle and was removed from it whilst dismantling the vehicle on land; or

[b] abandons on such land anything [not a motor vehicle] brought there for the purpose of abandoning it.

S. 2(1) REFUSE DISPOSAL (AMENITY) ACT 1978

Q What is the duty of the local authority to Remove Abandoned Vehicles?

A Where it appears to a local authority that a motor vehicle is abandoned without lawful authority **on any land in the open air,** or on a highway, it is their duty to remove it.

S. 3 REFUSE DISPOSAL (AMENITY) ACT 1978

Motor vehicle. Means a mechanically propelled vehicle intended or adapted for use on roads, whether or not it is in a fit state for such use, and includes trailers, any chassis or body, with or without wheels, appearing to have formed part of the vehicle or trailer, and anything attached to such a vehicle or trailer.

Q Outline police powers to Remove Vehicles from Roads

A

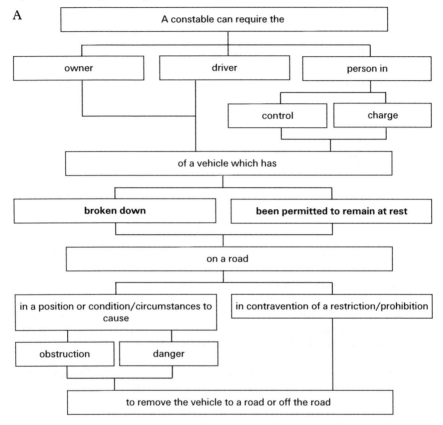

REG. 3 REMOVAL AND DISPOSAL OF VEHICLES REGS 1986

Q Define the offence of Off-road Driving

A It is an offence to drive a mechanically propelled vehicle without lawful authority on:

[a] common or moorland, or any land (not being part of a road); or
[b] footpath or bridleway;

except, it may be driven on any land within **15 yards** of a road which may lawfully be driven on for parking only.

No offence. If done for saving life, extinguishing fire, or like emergency.

S. 34(1) RTA 1988

Q Outline the law on Builders' Skips

A A skip can only be deposited with the written permission of the Highway Authority.

Offences:

[a] placing on a highway without permission;
[b] not properly lit during the hours of darkness;
[c] it does not bear the owner's name and address **or** telephone number
[d] it is not removed as soon as possible after it has been filled;
[e] there is a failure to comply with a condition of the Highway Authority.

S. 139 HIGHWAYS ACT 1980

Who is liable? Both the owner of the skip and the offender.

Defence for owner. To prove that the offence arose due to the action or default of another **and** he had taken all reasonable precautions and exercised due diligence to prevent the offence.

Police powers. A constable **in uniform** may require the removal of the skip and failure to do so is an offence. The requirement must be made **in person.**

Q Outline the law in relation to School Crossings

A Where a vehicle is approaching a place on a road where a person is crossing or seeking to cross the road, a school crossing patrol wearing an approved uniform shall have power by exhibiting a prescribed sign to require a driver to stop. Thereafter he shall stop so as not to stop or impede the person(s) crossing and remain stopped until the sign is not exhibited.

S. 28 RT REGULATION ACT 1984

Offence. To fail to conform.

Presumptions. Unless the contrary is proven, it is presumed that he was in uniform, the prescribed sign was exhibited and that people were crossing or seeking to cross.

Traffic wardens. May exercise this function and they do not have to wear the uniform but they must exhibit the sign.

Q   Outline the law on 'street playgrounds'.

A   The local traffic authority may prohibit or restrict vehicular access to certain roads so that they may be used as street playgrounds. A person who uses a vehicle, or causes or permits a vehicle to be used, in contravention of any such prohibition shall be guilty of an offence.

S. 29(3) RTA 1984

Crown servants. Vehicles or drivers in the public service of the Crown are exempt from this provision.

CONSTRUCTION AND USE

Q Outline the law in relation to Maintaining BRAKES

A Every part of every braking system and of the means of operation fitted to a vehicle shall be maintained in a good and efficient working order.

REGS. 15-18 ROAD VEHICLES (CONSTRUCTION AND USE) REGS 1986

Can a Constable check brakes? Yes, he may be able to give evidence that when the handbrake was applied he could push the vehicle along.

Q Outline the law in relation to Defective TYRES

A A tyre is defective when:

[a] it is unsuitable for use;
[b] it is under or over inflated;
[c] it has a cut in excess of **25 mm** or **10%** of its section width [whichever is greater] and deep enough to reach the ply or cord;
[d] it has any lump, bulge or tear caused by failure of the structure;
[e] ply or cord is exposed;
[f] the base of a groove in a tread is not visible; either:

[i] the tread does not have **1 mm depth at least three-quarters of its breadth** of its tread round the entire outer circumference; or
[ii] if the groove did not extend beyond three-quarters of the breadth of the tread any tread which does not have at least **1 mm;**

[g] it is not maintained in a condition fit for its use; or
[h] it has a defect which might cause damage to the road or to persons.

REG. 27

Q Outline the law in relation to MIRRORS

A With certain exceptions every passenger vehicle, goods vehicle or dual purpose vehicle first used on or after 1 June 1978, must be equipped with:

[a] an interior rear view mirror; and
[b] at least one exterior mirror fitted to the off-side.

If the interior rear view mirror is obscured the driver must have an exterior rear view mirror attached to the near-side of the vehicle.

REG. 33

Q Outline the law in relation to SILENCERS

A Every vehicle propelled by an internal combustion engine must be fitted with an exhaust system including a silencer and the exhaust gases from the engine must not escape without passing through the silencer.

REGS. 54, 57

Q Define the offence of QUITTING

A It is an offence to leave a motor vehicle unattended on a road unless **both** the engine has been stopped **and** the brake set.

REG. 107

Unattended. If there is a person with the vehicle, he must be licensed to drive it.

Q Outline the offence of DANGEROUS VEHICLE

A Every **motor vehicle,** trailer, parts and accessories must at all times be in such a condition that no danger is caused to any person in or on the vehicle or trailer or on a road. The number of **passengers** carried, or the manner of their carriage, must be such that no danger is caused or likely to be caused to any person in or on the vehicle or trailer or on a road. The **load** carried by a motor vehicle or trailer must at all times be so secure and be in such a position, that neither danger nor nuisance is likely to be caused to any person or property by reason of the load or part of it falling or being blown from, or by reason of any other movement of the load or part. It is an offence to use, cause or permit another to use any vehicle contravening the above.

S. 40A RTA 1988

Q   Define the offence of Breach of Brake, Steering Gear, Tyres requirements

A   A person commits an offence who:

[a]   fails to comply with regulations as to brakes, steering gear or tyres; or

[b]   uses on a road a motor vehicle or trailer [or causes or permits], which does not comply with the regulations.

S. 41A RTA 1988

Q   Define the offence of Breach of Weight requirements for Goods and Passenger Vehicles

A   A person commits an offence who:

[a]   fails to comply with regulations in relation to weights applicable to:

[i]   a goods vehicle; or

[ii]   a motor vehicle or trailer adapted to carry **more than eight passengers;** or

[b]   uses on a road a vehicle [or causes or permits] which does not comply with the regulations.

S. 41B RTA 1988

Defence. It is a defence to prove:

[a]   that at the time the vehicle was being used on a road

[i]   it was proceeding to the nearest weighbridge to be weighed, or

[ii]   it was proceeding from a weighbridge to the nearest point at which it was reasonably practicable to reduce the weight to the relevant limit, without causing an obstruction on any road, or

[b]   in a case where it was not more than 5% overweight, that limit was not exceeded at the time of original loading and no person has subsequently added to the weight.

DRIVER LICENSING

Q **What are police powers in relation to Driving Licences?**

A Any person:

[a] **driving** a motor vehicle on a road;

[b] whom a Constable or vehicle examiner has reasonable cause to believe has been the driver of a motor vehicle at the time when an **accident** occurred owing to its presence on a road;

[c] whom a Constable or vehicle examiner has reasonable cause to believe **committed an offence** in relation to the use of the motor vehicle on a road; or

[d] **a supervisor** of a provisional licence holder driving a motor vehicle on a road or a person whom a Constable or vehicle examiner reasonably believes was supervising such a driver at the time of an accident or offence relating to that vehicle:

must, on being required to do so by a Constable or vehicle examiner:

[i] produce his licence;

[ii] and its counterpart so as to enable the Constable or vehicle examiner to examine it and ascertain:

1. name and address of the holder;
2. date of issue; and
3. the authority by which issued.

S. 164 RTA 1988

Defence. It is a defence for him to show that:

[a] he produced the licence and counterpart at a police station specified by him at the time the production was required **within 7 days;**

[b] he produced them in person there as soon as was reasonably practicable; or

[c] it was not reasonably practicable for him to produce them there before the day the proceedings were commenced.

In person. Driving licences must be produced in person by the holder.

Q What are the Grounds for Demanding Date of Birth?

A [a] The person **fails** to produce his licence forthwith; **or**
[b] the driver number has been altered, removed or defaced; or
[c] the person is a supervisor for a provisional licence holder and the constable has reason to suspect he is under 21; or
[d] the Constable has reason to suspect that the licence was not granted to him, was granted in error or contains an alteration made with intent to deceive.

S. 164(2) RTA 1988

Q Define the offence of Failing to Produce and State Date of Birth

A A person who fails, when required, to produce his licence or state his date of birth (or produce his certificate of completion of a training course for motor cyclists) commits an offence.

S. 164(6) RTA 1988

Q Define the offence of Disqualified Driving

A A person is guilty of an offence if, while disqualified from holding or obtaining a licence, he drives a motor vehicle on a road.

S. 103(1)(B) RTA 1988

Arrest. Arrestable offence. (But note that if the reason for the disqualification is age, the offence is under S.87(1) rather than S.103 and there is no power of arrest).

Licence obtained by person disqualified. Has no effect.

Q   **Outline the law in relation to Provisional Licences and Motor Bicycles**

A   The granting of provisional licences is governed by S. 97(3) RTA 1988, which states:

[a]   a provisional licence shall not authorise a **person aged under 21 years:**

[i]   to ride a solo motor cycle unless it is a 'learner motor cycle', or it was first used before 1 January 1982 and does not exceed 125 cc; or

[ii]   to ride a motor cycle with a sidecar unless its power to weight ratio is less than or equal to 0.16 kilowatts per kilogram;

[b]   or authorise a person to ride a motor cycle or moped on a road unless he has successfully completed an approved training course, or is driving while undergoing training on such a course.

How long does the licence last? Two years. No licence will then be issued for one year.

Q   **What are the General Conditions for a Provisional Licence Holder?**

A   **Supervision.** A provisional licence holder shall not drive a motor vehicle [nor a motor cycle] otherwise than under the supervision of a qualified driver who is present with him in or on the vehicle, who is:

[a]   **aged 21 years or over; and**
[b]   **has held a full licence for at least three years.**

'L'& 'D' plates. Plates are required to be clearly visible to other road users within a reasonable distance from the back and front of the vehicle. In Wales there is an option to use 'D' plates.

Towing trailers. The licence holder must not draw a trailer.

Note. If a provisional licence holder fails to observe these conditions he commits an offence under S. 91 RT Offenders Act 1988. If the person has no provisional licence the offence is under S. 87 (driving otherwise than in accordance with a licence).

Q Define the offence of Supervisors Failing to Give Details

A A person who:

[a] supervises the holder of a provisional licence who is driving a motor vehicle (other than an invalid carriage) on a road; or

[b] whom a constable or vehicle examiner has reasonable cause to believe was supervising a provisional licence holder:

[i] when an **accident** occurred; or

[ii] when **an offence** is suspected to have been committed by the holder of the provisional licence,

must, on being so required by a constable or vehicle examiner:

1. give his name and address; and
2. the name and address of the owner.

Q What is the law in relation to Driving Instruction?

A It is an offence to give motor car driving lessons **for money** or money's worth unless the tutor is a registered approved instructor. (Registered in accordance with the provisions of Part V RTA 1988). [Police driving instructors are exempt from this regulation].

S. 123 RTA 1988

'Free' driving lessons. Offered by a person in the business of buying and selling cars will be deemed to be given for payment if the lessons are a condition of buying the vehicle.

S. 132(3) RTA 1988

Q How long can Foreign Nationals Drive in this Country under their own Licence?

A 12 months.

Q Define the offence of Driving with Uncorrected Defective Eyesight

A If a person drives a motor vehicle on a road with uncorrected defective eyesight he commits an offence.

S. 96(1) RTA 1988

Test. A Constable, having reasonable cause to suspect that a person driving a motor vehicle may be guilty of this offence, may require him to submit to an eyesight test. Refusal to do so is an offence.

Defective eyesight. The requirements as to eyesight are contained in Regs. 72-73 and Sch. 8 to the Motor Vehicles (Driving Licences) Regs 1999, which *generally* require a potential driver to be able to read:

[a] letters and figures 79.4 mm high;
[b] on a registration plate;
[c] fixed to a vehicle;
[d] at 20.5 m;
[e] in good light.

(Spectacles may be worn at the time).

Q What is the law in relation to New Drivers?

A A newly qualified driver is a new driver for a probationary period of **two years** and if he sustains **six or more penalty points** the full entitlement to drive is lost until they pass a further test of competence.

FIXED PENALTY SYSTEMS

Q   What is a Fixed Penalty?

A   A fixed penalty notice means a notice offering the opportunity of the discharge of any liability to conviction of the offence to which the notice relates by payment of a fixed penalty.   S. 52(1) RT OFFENDERS ACT 1988

Q   When can a fixed penalty NOT be issued?

A   [a]   Where the penalty points would involve disqualification; or
     [b]   where the driver does not consent to surrendering his licence.

Q   Outline the procedure where the driver is PRESENT

A

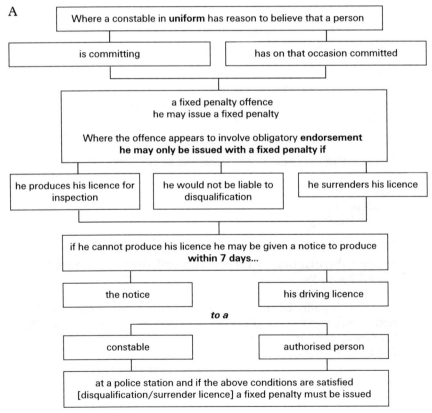

Where a constable in **uniform** has reason to believe that a person

is committing

has on that occasion committed

a fixed penalty offence
he may issue a fixed penalty

Where the offence appears to involve obligatory **endorsement he may only be issued with a fixed penalty if**

he produces his licence for inspection

he would not be liable to disqualification

he surrenders his licence

if he cannot produce his licence he may be given a notice to produce **within 7 days...**

the notice

his driving licence

to a

constable

authorised person

at a police station and if the above conditions are satisfied [disqualification/surrender licence] a fixed penalty must be issued

S. 54 RT OFFENDERS ACT 1988

Q   What is the procedure if the person does not pay the penalty?

A   If a person has not paid the fixed penalty, or given notice requesting a court hearing, the police can register a sum equal to 1.5 times the amount of the penalty for enforcement against that person. Where this happens the justices' clerk will notify him. Where a person receives such a notice he can serve a statutory declaration to the effect that either:

[a]   he was not the person who was given the fixed penalty; or
[b]   he has given notice requesting a court hearing.

He must serve this notice on the clerk **within 21 days** of receiving his notification.

Q   What is the procedure when the driver is NOT PRESENT?

A   Where on any occasion a constable has reason to believe in the case of any stationary vehicle that a fixed penalty offence is being or has on that occasion been committed, he may issue a fixed penalty notice unless the offence appears to him to involve obligatory endorsement.

S. 62 RT OFFENDERS ACT 1988

Q   Define the offence of Making False Statements etc

A   A person who, in response to a notice to owner, provides a statement which is false in a material particular and does so recklessly or knowing it to be false is guilty of an offence.

S. 67 RT OFFENDERS ACT 1988

Q   Define the offence of Removing or Interfering with a Fixed Penalty

A   A person is guilty of an offence if he removes or interferes with any notice fixed to a vehicle, unless he does so by or under the authority of the driver or person in charge of the vehicle, or the person liable for the fixed penalty offence in question.

S. 62(2) RT OFFENDERS ACT 1988

Q What is a CONDITIONAL OFFER?

A   Where a constable has reason to believe that a fixed penalty offence has been committed and no notice has been issued, then a notice can be sent to the alleged offender. A conditional offer must:

[a]   outline the offence;
[b]   state the amount payable; and
[c]   state that no proceedings will take place before **28 days.**

The conditional offer must indicate that if:

[a]   **within 28 days** the alleged offender:

[i]   makes payment to the fixed penalty clerk; and
[ii]   where the offence involves obligatory endorsement, at the same time delivers his licence, and its counterpart to the clerk, and

[b]   where his licence and its counterpart are so delivered, that clerk is satisfied on inspecting them that, if the alleged offender were convicted of the offence, he would not be liable to disqualification, any liability to conviction of the offence shall be discharged.

Failure to pay. If the defendant fails to pay the fixed penalty and/or surrender his licence, the police will be notified. The police will also be notified in any case where the defendant does pay (and surrender his licence) but it turns out that he is in fact liable to disqualification. The defendant's licence and payment should then be returned to him.

S. 75 RT Offenders Act 1988

FORGERY AND FALSIFICATION OF DOCUMENTS

Q Define the offence of Forgery of Documents

A A person who, with intent to deceive:

[a] forges, alters or uses a relevant document or other thing, or

[b] lends, or allows to be used by another a relevant document or thing, or

[c] makes or has in his possession any document or thing so closely resembling a relevant document or thing as to be calculated to deceive, commits an offence.

S. 173 RTA 1988

Relevant Documents or 'things'. Include: licences, test certificates, insurance, certificates of exemption from seat belts, haulage permits and goods vehicle plates.

Arrest. No specific power of arrest (although the *general* offence of forgery is arrestable).

Q Outline the offence of False Statements and Withholding Information

A [a] A person who knowingly makes a **false statement** for the purpose of:

[i] obtaining a licence;

[ii] preventing the grant of a licence;

[iii] procuring a provision or condition on a licence;

[iv] obtaining the grant of an international road haulage permit; or

[b] **in supplying information** or producing documents:

[i] makes a statement which he knows to be false or is reckless in so doing;

[ii] makes use of a document he knows to be false or is reckless in so doing

[c] knowingly produces false evidence or statement in a declaration; or

[d] wilfully makes a false entry in a record required to be kept or with intent to deceive makes use of such an entry; or

[e]   makes a false statement or withholds any information for the purpose of the issue:

[i]   of insurance; or

[ii]   any document issued under the Act commits an offence.

S. 174 RTA 1988

Issue of documents. It is also an offence to knowingly issue such documents (S. 175).

Q   Outline police powers in relation to False Documents/ Forgery

A   If a constable has reasonable cause to believe that a document produced to him is a document in relation to which an offence has been committed, he may seize the document.

S. 176 RTA 1988

Q   Define the offence of Forging/Altering Registration Documents

A   A person is guilty of an offence if he forges, fraudulently alters, fraudulently uses, lends or allows to be used a registration document.

SS. 44-45 VEHICLE EXCISE AND REGISTRATION ACT 1994

Q   Define the offence of Forgery of certain Documents relating to PSVs

A   A person who, with intent to deceive:

[a]   forges or alters, or uses or lends to, or allows to be used; or
[b]   makes or has in his possession any document or other thing so closely resembling a document or other thing as to be calculated to deceive,

commits an offence.

Which documents? Licences, certificates of fitness, certificates of type, operator's disc certificates of competence of any person.

Q   Define the offence of Forgery relating to Goods Vehicles

A   A person is guilty of an offence if, with intent to deceive, he forges, alters or uses a document or thing, lends to or allows to be used, or has in his possession a document or thing so closely resembling a document or other things as to be calculated to deceive.

S. 38 GOODS VEHICLES (LICENSING OF OPERATORS) ACT 1995

Q **Define the offence of Misuse of Parking Documents and Apparatus**

A   A person shall be guilty of an offence if, with intent to deceive:

[a]   he uses, lends or allows to be used:

[i]   any parking device or apparatus designed to be used in connection with parking devices;

[ii]   any ticket issued by a parking meter, parking device or apparatus;

[iii]   any authorisation by a certificate or other means of identification; or

[iv]   any permit or token.

[b]   makes or has in his possession anything so closely resembling any such thing as to be calculated to deceive.

[c]   a person who knowingly makes a false statement for the purposes of procuring the grant or issue of any such authorisation commits an offence.

S. 115 RT REGULATION ACT 1984

Part 4 - Evidence and Procedure

SUMMONSES AND WARRANTS

Q   **Before a summons or warrant can be issued what must be Laid?**

A   An information.

Q   **What is an Information?**

A   A written or verbal allegation made to a magistrate ("laying an information") that a person has committed, or is suspected of having committed, an offence. This must be done before a summons or warrant can be issued.

Q   **What must the Information Contain?**

A   [a]   The name and address of the informant;
    [b]   particulars of the offence suspected;
    [c]   the law which has been contravened.

S. 4 MAGISTRATES' COURTS RULES 1981

Q   **What is a Summons?**

A   A written order issued by a magistrate [or his clerk], ordering the person named to appear at a court at a specified time and date to answer an allegation of an offence.

Witness summons. Requires a witness to give evidence/produce exhibits.

Q   **When and Where can a Summons be Issued?**

A   A summons can be issued if:

    [a]   the offence relates to the justices' area; or
    [b]   where the justices feel that the accused should be tried jointly with or in the same place as another who is charged with an offence and who is either:

        [i]   in custody in their jurisdiction; or
        [ii]   is being proceeded against in their jurisdiction; or

[c] the accused resides in their area; or

[d] a court in the area, by virtue of a statutory provision, has jurisdiction to try the alleged offence; or

[e] the offence was committed outside England and Wales but if the accused were before the court, it would have jurisdiction to try the offence.

Q Before issue of a Summons, what must the Justices' Clerk ensure?

A [a] That the information alleges an offence known to law;

[b] it was laid within any applicable time limit;

[c] any required consents to bring the prosecution have been obtained; and

[d] there is jurisdiction to issue the summons.

When can a summons be refused? In exceptional circumstances, if the Justices' Clerk concludes that it is frivolous or vexatious or amounts to an abuse of the process of the court.

Q What must appear on the face of the Summons?

A The summons must bear the name and signature [rubber stamp] of the clerk issuing it and state:

[a] the substance of the information laid; and

[b] the time and place where the accused must attend to answer the charge.

R. 98(1) Magistrates' Courts Rules 1981

Q How may a Summons be Served?

A

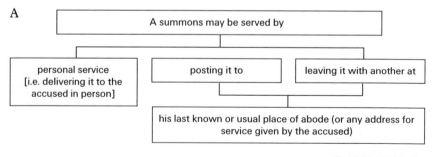

R. 99(1) 1981 Rules

What if by posting/leaving he does not receive it? Provided the offence is summary and it can be proved that the summons was either left at the last known/usual address or sent by registered letter or recorded delivery to that address, then it will be treated as having been sufficiently served and it is not necessary to prove that it came to the accused's knowledge. The court can proceed whether or not he received it.

Q **Can Summonses be served in Scotland and Northern Ireland?**

A Yes, but the rules as to service are different. Summonses issued in England and Wales may be served by post anywhere, but NI summonses may only be personally served. Scottish 'citations' (summonses) may be 'effected' (served) by post.

S. 39 CRIMINAL LAW ACT 1977

Q **Define the five types of Warrant**

A [1] **Arrest warrant.** Where a magistrate can issue a summons they may issue a warrant instead if:

[a] the information is in writing and on oath; and *either*
[b] the offence is indictable or imprisonable, *or*
[c] the accused's address is insufficient to serve a summons.

Can the clerk issue a warrant? No. The information must be on oath and made to a magistrate.

[2] **Warrant to arrest a witness.** Where a magistrate is satisfied that a person who could give material evidence would not voluntarily attend court he may issue a warrant.

[3] **Warrant to arrest in default.** Issued for non-payment of fine etc.

[4] **Warrant to commit to prison.** This warrant authorises a constable to take a person directly to prison [and obtain a receipt].

[5] **Warrant to distrain property.** This warrant is issued to collect money in the form of goods to be seized and sold.

Q **Which warrants do not need to be in the Possession of a constable at the time of their Execution?**

A Warrants:
[a] to arrest for an offence;
[b] Army/Air Force and Naval Discipline Act;
[c] distress;
[d] for the protection of a party to a marriage or child of the family;
[e] non-appearance of a defendant;
[f] committal; and
[g] witness arrest warrants.

What about a fine defaulter? Such warrants are not treated as being warrants of arrest for an offence, therefore the constable must possess the warrant.

What if the warrant is in a police car 'nearby'? The constable has possession, but this is unlikely to be the case if the warrant is in a police station half a mile away (caselaw).

What about entry? A constable may enter and search if he has reasonable grounds for believing the person is on the premises in order to execute the warrant. Reasonable force may be used if necessary, but the search must only be to the extent required and is restricted to those parts of the premises where the constable genuinely has reason to believe the suspect to be.

Q **Outline the law on the Execution of Warrants throughout the UK**

Warrant issued in	Can be executed in	By
Scotland or Northern Ireland	England or Wales	a constable
England, Wales or Northern Ireland	Scotland	a constable
England, Wales or Scotland	Northern Ireland	RUC constable or reserve RUC

S. 38 CRIMINAL LAW ACT 1977

Q **Which warrants may be executed by Civilian Enforcement Officers?**

A In England and Wales CEOs may execute any warrant of arrest, commitment, detention or distress issued by a magistrate. The arrested/committed person is entitled to demand a written statement from the officer which must state (a) the officer's name; (b) the authority by which s/he is employed (c) the fact s/he is authorised to execute warrants.

S. 125A MAGISTRATES' COURTS ACT 1980

BAIL

Q   What is 'bail'?

A   A process whereby an accused person may be temporarily released from custody (whether conditionally or otherwise).

Q   What is 'street bail'?

A   A discretionary power introduced by S.4 Criminal Justice Act 2003 (S.30A-30D PACE Act 1984) whereby constables may grant an arrested person immediate bail at the scene of arrest.

Q   Outline the street bail procedure

A   A constable may, at his/her discretion, release on bail any person arrested or taken into custody, at any time before he arrives at a police station. The bailed person must be required to attend at a police station at a subsequent date, but no other requirement may be imposed as a condition of bail. The bailed person must be given a written notice before he is released stating (a) the offence for which he was arrested (b) the grounds on which he was arrested (c) that he is required to attend a specified police station at a specified time (if this time/place information is not given in the notice at the time it must be given subsequently in a further notice in writing). Any later change to the specified venue/time must be notified in writing to the bailed person. A verbal explanation of the procedure should also be given at the time of bail.

Q   To which offences does street bail apply?

A   Any offence, but it is not recommended that street bail be used in cases of serious arrestable offences.

Q   Once a person is given street bail, can he be rearrested?

A   Yes. Officers can rearrest a person released on bail anytime before he is due to attend a police station if new evidence justifying arrest comes to light.

Q   What if the bailed person fails to attend at the required time?

A   A constable may arrest anyone bailed under S.30A if they fail to answer their bail. They should be taken to a police station as soon as practicable.

Q   What if s/he is no longer required to attend?

A   S/he must be given a notice in writing that his attendance is no longer required.

Q   What are the criteria for granting street bail?

A   In addition to being satisfied that a correct name and address have been provided, the bailing officer should consider:

[a]   the severity or nature of the offence committed
[b]   the need to preserve vital evidence
[c]   the person's fitness to be released back on to the streets
[d]   the person's ability to understand what is being said/happening
[e]   the likelihood that the person may continue to commit the offence or a further offence.

Q   At a police station, when should bail be given without charge?

A   The custody officer must release a detainee either unconditionally or on bail in the following circumstances:

[a]   there is insufficient evidence to charge and the officer is unwilling to authorise detention (S.37 PACE);
[b]   the review officer decides that detention without charge can no longer be justified (S.40(8) PACE);
[c]   following 24 hours' detention without charge (unless the detained person is suspected of a serious arrestable offence and continued detention up to 36 hours is authorised by a superintendent (S.41(7) PACE).

Q What happens after charge?

A Once a person is charged at a police station the custody officer must decide whether to detain that person in custody pending attendance at a magistrates' court, or to release that person, and if so, whether unconditionally or on bail (S.38 PACE). The general presumption is in favour of bail.

Q In which circumstances should bail usually NOT be granted?

A Under S.25 Criminal Justice and Public Order Act 1984 bail should only exceptionally be granted in cases where the charge is

[a] murder
[b] attempted murder
[c] manslaughter
[d] rape
[e] attempted rape

and the charged person has **previously been convicted** of any such offence.

Q Outline the general grounds for refusing bail

A [a] Name and address are doubted or cannot be ascertained;
[b] there is a risk of absconding;
[c] there is a risk of interference with witnesses/evidence;
[d] in the case of imprisonable offences, there is a risk of commission of further offences;
[e] in the case of non-imprisonable offences, there is a risk of injury to others or damage to property;
[f] the detainee's own protection requires it;
[g] detention is necessary for the welfare of a juvenile (S.38 PACE).

Q What conditions may be attached to bail?

A Where it appears necessary to prevent the person

[a] failing to surrender to custody; or
[b] committing an offence while on bail; or
[c] interfering with witnesses/evidence; or
[d] in the interests of his own protection/welfare

then any of the following conditions may be imposed:

[i] live and sleep at a specified address
[ii] notify any changes of address
[iii] report periodically at his local police station
[iv] geographical restrictions
[v] contact restrictions
[vi] surrender passport
[vii] curfews
[viii] provision of surety/security.

Any conditions imposed must be noted in the custody record and a copy given to the bailed person. An application to vary/remove conditions may be made at any time to the custody officer who imposed them or to any custody officer at the same station. The custody officer must consider the application on the merits and may either remove the conditions, vary them (to make them more/less onerous, whichever is justified) or leave them unchanged. This must be noted in the custody record. Applications may also be made to a magistrates' court.

Q What is a 'surety'?

A   A person who is prepared to offer financial security for the bailed person's promise to surrender to custody.

Q What is 'security'?

A   A sum of money or other valuable item given by the accused person or someone on their behalf to secure their promise to surrender to custody.

Q What happens when a Juvenile is refused bail?

A   The custody officer must try to make arrangements for them to be taken into local authority care for detention pending their appearance in court. The only exceptions are where the custody officer certifies that is impracticable to obtain such accommodation or (in the case of a 12 year old or over) where no secure accommodation is available and there is a risk of serious harm to the public from that juvenile.

Q When must detention be reviewed?

A Detention of a person refused bail must be reviewed by the custody officer within 9 hours of the last decision to refuse bail. This may only be delayed when the custody officer is unavailable to carry it out and in such a case the review must be carried out as soon as practicable thereafter. If detention can no longer be justified, the person must be released: S.40 PACE.

Q When must such a person be brought before the court?

A A person charged but refused bail must be brought before a magistrates' court at the next available session: S.46 PACE.

Q Outline the offences of Failing to Surrender

A It is an offence for any person released on bail to fail, without reasonable cause, to surrender to custody.

S. 6 Bail Act 1976

A person **with** reasonable cause for failing to surrender at the appointed time must still surrender as soon as practicable after the appointed time. Failure to do so is an offence.

S. 6(2) Bail Act 1976

COURT PROCEDURE AND WITNESSES

Q **Who is Competent and Compellable to give Evidence?**

A 'Competence' relates to whether a person is legally able to provide testimony. 'Compellability' relates to whether competent persons can be made to provide testimony. In short, all people are competent and all competent witnesses are compellable but there are special rules relating to accused persons, their spouses, children, persons of impaired intellect and certain other groups.

Q **What is the law in relation to Accused Persons?**

A **On behalf of the prosecution:** the accused is not competent to give evidence on behalf of the prosecution unless:

[a]   he pleads guilty;
[b]   he is convicted;
[c]   the charges against him are dropped.

Therefore, if the prosecution wish an accused to give evidence against a co-accused (i.e. a person charged with him at the same trial) they must make him competent to give evidence, either by dropping the charges against him, or by obtaining a conviction or a guilty plea. [The admission of the guilty plea of a co-defendant has been found not to violate the accused's rights to a fair trial under Art. 6 ECHR].

On behalf of the defence. Every person charged with an offence shall be a competent witness for the defence at every stage of the proceedings, whether charged solely or jointly, but shall not be called except on his own application.

Q When is a Spouse Competent and Compellable to give Evidence?

Competent	Compellable
A spouse (other than when husband and wife are jointly charged) is competent to give evidence **FOR THE PROSECUTION**	and is compellable (unless jointly charged) when the offence charged: [a] involves assault on, or injury or threat of injury to, the other spouse; [b] involves assault on, or injury or threat of injury to, a person under 16; [c] involves a sexual offence against a person under 16; [d] involves aiding, abetting, conspiring to commit etc. any of the above
A spouse (other than when jointly charged) is competent to give evidence **FOR THE DEFENCE**	Yes
A spouse is competent to give evidence **FOR ANY CO-ACCUSED**	Yes

Q Outline the position of Children as Witnesses in Criminal Proceedings

A The evidence of any child **under 14** shall be unsworn. A deposition of a child's unsworn evidence may be taken for criminal proceedings as though it had been given on oath. Witnesses over 14 are to be sworn provided they have a sufficient appreciation of the solemnity of the occasion and of the particular responsibility to tell the truth when on oath.

S. 55 YOUTH JUSTICE AND CRIMINAL EVIDENCE ACT 1999

Q   How is a Child's Age Determined?

A   By all the evidence available to the court at the time, usually by the production of a birth certificate.

Q   Outline the position of People with Impaired Intellect

A   Expert evidence can be received as to the person's competence, i.e. whether they can give 'intelligible testimony' and understand questions put to them and give answers which can be understood.

Q   Outline the law in relation to Hostile Witnesses

A   A hostile witness is a witness who does not give evidence fairly or shows no regard for the truth **as against the side calling him to give evidence.** [Not simply a witness who happens to give unfavourable evidence]. In such cases the Judge may deem the witness to be hostile whereupon the party calling him can:

[a]   ask leading questions;
[b]   contradict him with other evidence;
[c]   prove that on another occasion he made a statement inconsistent with the present testimony.

Q   When can Live Television Links be used for giving evidence?

A   They may be used [other than for the accused] for witnesses who:

[a]   are outside the UK; or
[b]   a child; or

in the case of trials on indictment, appeals to the Court of Appeal, proceedings in youth courts and appeals to the Crown Court arising from offences of:

[a]   assault on, or injury or threat of injury, to a person;
[b]   cruelty to a person under 16;
[c]   certain sexual offences;
[d]   offences under the Protection of Children Act 1978; and
[e]   aiding and abetting the above.

S. 32 Criminal Justice Act 1988

It may also be used at preliminary court hearings where an accused is being detained in custody in prison or other institution (S. 57 Crime and Disorder Act 1998).

Q   When can a witness Refresh his Memory?

A   A person giving oral evidence in criminal proceedings may, at any stage, refresh his memory of it from a document made or verified by him at an earlier time if

[a]   he states in his oral evidence that the document records his recollection of the matter at that earlier time, and

[b]   his recollection of the matter is likely to have been significantly better at that time than it is at the time of his oral evidence.

Transcripts of tape recordings of previously given oral accounts may also be used in the same way.

S. 139 CRIMINAL JUSTICE ACT 2003

Q   Can a constable give oral evidence of conversations held via an interpreter?

A   No. The only valid evidence of such a conversation is that of the interpreter.

YOUTH CRIME AND DISORDER

Q   **Under the Crime and Disorder Act 1998 summarise a Parenting Order**

A   The order requires a parent to:

[a]   comply with the requirements of the order for **not more than 12 months**; and

[b]   to attend counselling and guidance sessions specified by the responsible officer. These shall **not exceed three months** and **not be more than one a week.**

The order shall not infringe on the parents':

[i]   religious beliefs, or

[ii]   times of work, or

[iii]   attendance at an educational establishment.

SS. 8-9 CRIME AND DISORDER ACT 1998

Q   **Who can the order be made against?**

A   [a]   One or both biological parents, and

[b]   a guardian, (being any person who, in the opinion of the court, was for the time being the carer of a child or young person).

Q   **Which court can discharge or vary the order?**

A   The original court making the order.

Q   **When SHALL an order be made?**

A   Where a person **under 16** is convicted of **an offence.**

Q   **Who is the Responsible Officer?**

A   [a]   A probation officer;

[b]   a social worker, or

[c]   a person nominated by the chief education officer;

[d]   a member of a youth offending team.

S. 8(8) CRIME AND DISORDER ACT 1998

Q   What is the position if the terms of the order are breached?

A   The parent who breaches the order without reasonable excuse commits an offence.

S. 9(7) 1998 ACT

Q   What is the purpose of a Child Safety Order?

A   To help prevent children **under 10** from turning to crime.

Q   When can a Child Safety Order be made?

A   If a magistrates' court, on the application of a local authority, is satisfied that a **child under 10**:

[a]   has committed an offence; or
[b]   that an order is necessary to stop him committing offences; or
[c]   that the child has breached a curfew notice; or
[d]   the child has caused harassment, alarm or distress, to someone other than a person in his own household.

S. 11 1998 ACT

Q   Which magistrates' court makes the order?

A   The family proceedings court. This is to ensure that the order is not seen to be 'criminal' in nature.

Q   What if the child breaches the Order?

A   The court can:

[a]   vary the order, or
[b]   cancel the order and make a care order.

S. 12(6) 1998 ACT

Q   What is a Child Curfew Scheme?

A   These are designed to tackle unsupervised young children engaging in anti-social and offending behaviour. Where the scheme is in force, a local authority or a chief officer of police (having consulted with each other) may:

[a]   ban children **under 16,**
[b]   for up to **90 days,**
[c]   from being in specified areas:

    [i]   **between 9 pm and 6 am,** and
    [ii]   without a responsible person **aged 18 or over.**

S. 14 1998 ACT

Q   When does such a Scheme become effective?

A   Generally one month after confirmation by the Home Secretary.

Q   What if the child breaches the ban?

A   A constable with reasonable cause to believe that a child is in contravention of a ban shall:

[a]   inform the local authority ASAP, and
[b]   take the child home [unless he is likely to suffer significant harm].

Q   What are Police Powers to deal with Truants?

A   If following a direction by a superintendent (or above) that the powers contained in S. 16 Crime & Disorder Act 1988 are to apply, a constable has reasonable cause to believe that a child he finds in a public place in a specified area is:

[a]   of school age, and
[b]   is absent from school without lawful authority,
    the constable can remove him to:

    [i]   a designated place, or
    [ii]   back to his school.

S. 16 CDA 1988

Lawful authority. Means leave, sickness, unavoidable cause or day set apart for religious observance.

Designated place. Any premises designated by a local authority as premises to which children of school age may be taken by a constable following a superintendent's direction to deal with truants.

Specified area. Any area specified in the superintendent's direction.

Q   What is a Truancy Penalty Notice?

A   The Anti-Social Behaviour Act 2003 provides for a penalty notice scheme under the Education Act 1996 whereby parents or guardians of persistent truants may be issued with a penalty notice by a constable, senior teacher (head, deputy or assistant head, or other authorised staff member) or local education officer. The amount of the penalty is currently £50 if paid within 28 days (or £100 if paid between 28-42 days).

SENTENCING

Q Outline the procedure for Release of Short-term Prisoners on Licence

A The Secretary of State may order the release of a prisoner on licence when s/he has served the 'requisite period' of their sentence. For those imprisoned for between 4-18 months this period is one quarter of their term, for those with sentences of 18 months or more the period is 135 days less than one half of their term. Release may be subject to conditions such as electronic monitoring. Certain categories of prisoner are excluded from this provision (e.g. those covered by sex offender notification requirements).

S. 246 CRIMINAL JUSTICE ACT 2003

Q Outline the procedure for Release of Short-term Prisoners on Home Curfew

A Some prisoners may be permitted to complete part of their sentence under the home curfew scheme. This runs for between 14-60 days, and will only apply where the prisoner agrees to the curfew conditions (which are to be determined by the prison govenor). Generally the curfew will be from 7pm – 7am, with a minimum curfew duration of 9 hours. The Parole Service is responsible for monitoring the scheme. The police must be notified of curfews at least 14 days prior to release, and may subsequently request, *with a superintendent's authority*, information as to the prisoner's compliance with his curfew. Such requests for information must be answered within 24 hours.

Q What happens if a curfew is broken?

A If it appears to the Secretary of State that a person released on licence has broken his curfew conditions, or his whereabouts can no longer be electronically monitored, or that it is necessary to do so in order to protect the public from serious harm, the Secretary of State may revoke the licence and recall the person to prison. Following revocation of the licence the person shall be liable to be detained and, if at large shall be deemed to be unlawfully at large.

Q What types of detention are applicable to young offenders?

A [a] Detention at Her Majesty's Pleasure (murder sentences for under 18s);
  [b] life sentences (murder sentences for those aged 18 – 21 years old);
  [c] detention for specific periods (certain serious offences, where the court may sentence the offender to detention for a term not exceeding the maximum available when it is of the opinion that there is no other way of dealing with the case);
  [d] detention in young offenders institutions (for those aged 18 – 21 years old);
  [e] detention and training orders (under 18s).

Q Outline the Community Order requirements

A [a] **unpaid work** requirement (of between 40 – 300 hours within a 12 month period);
  [b] **activity** requirement (for a specific number of days not exceeding 60 in total);
  [c] **programme** requirement (such as anger management or substance abuse courses);
  [d] **prohibited activity** requirement (refrain from certain activities during a specified period);
  [e] **curfew** requirement (remain at a specified place for a specified time, which must be between 2 – 12 hours a day);
  [f] **exclusion** requirement (not to enter a specified place for a specified time, up to 2 years);
  [g] **residence** requirement (to reside at a specified place for a specfied period);
  [h] **mental health treatment** requirement (to submit to treatment);
  [i] **drug rehabilitation** requirement (to submit to treatment for at least 6 months);
  [j] **alcohol treatment** requirement (to submit to treatment for at least 6 months);
  [k] **supervision** requirement (to attend appointments with the responsible officer for the promotion of rehabilitation);
  [l] **attendance centre** requirement (to attend an attendance centre for between 12 – 36 hours in total).

EVIDENCE

Q   What two Questions are applied to any Evidence?

A   [a]   Admissibility (i.e. is the evidence relevant to a fact in issue?); and
[b]   weight (i.e. what weight should be attached to the evidence – how far does it prove or disprove the case?).

Q   What Reasons exist for Excluding Admissible Evidence?

A   A trial judge may exclude evidence if he believes its prejudicial effect outweighs its probative value, and in cases of admissions and confessions they may be excluded if obtained by improper or unfair means [inducements and oppression]. Evidence may also be excluded for the following reasons:

[a]   the incompetence of the witness;
[b]   it relates to previous convictions or character of the accused;
[c]   it is hearsay;
[d]   it is non-expert opinion evidence;
[e]   it is privileged information; or
[f]   as a matter of public policy.

Q   What is meant by the Facts in Issue?

A   The facts which must be proved to establish guilt, e.g.:

[a]   the identity of the defendant;
[b]   the *actus reus* [the physical act or criminal conduct]; and
[c]   the *mens rea* [the state of mind - knowingly, wilfully etc].

Q   On whom lies the Burden of Proof?

A   Generally the prosecution, to a standard of *beyond all reasonable doubt.* Exceptionally the defence, e.g. when raising a Defence such as Diminished Responsiblity or proving a lawful excuse. This standard is known *as the balance of probabilities, i.e. more probable than not.*

Q   What is a Formal Admission?

A   A formal admission dispenses with the need to prove a fact because it is admitted. Any fact may be admitted by the prosecutor or defendant, and admissions:

[a]   may be made before or at the proceedings;
[b]   if not made in court, shall be in writing;
[c]   if made by an individual:

[i]   shall be signed; and
[ii]   shall be made by his counsel or solicitor (or approved by them, if made before trial).
S. 10 Criminal Justice Act 1967

Q   What is meant by Drawing Inferences?

A   The courts are permitted to draw 'such inferences as appear proper' against the accused in circumstances relating to the accused's silence. They relate to:

[a]   silence when questioned or charged by a constable;
[b]   silence when questioned by a person charged with a duty to investigate offences;
[c]   silence in court; and
[d]   failure to give evidence in his defence.
SS. 34-38 Criminal Justice and Public Order Act 1994

Q   When can a court draw Such Inferences as Appear Proper?

A   Where in proceedings against a person for an offence evidence is given that he:

[a]   on being questioned under caution by a constable; or
[b]   on being charged or reported; he

failed to mention any fact relied on in his defence then:

a court or jury may draw such inferences as appear proper.

This does not prejudice:

[a]   the admissibility in evidence of the silence of the accused in the face of anything **said in his presence** in so far as evidence would in any case be admissible; or
[b]   the drawing of any inference from such silence.

Q   When can an Inference be Drawn at Court?

A   At a trial of a person who has attained 14 years and the court is satisfied that the accused is aware that the stage has been reached at which evidence can be given for the defence

[a]   if he refuses to answer questions; or
[b]   does not give evidence;

the court or jury may draw such inferences as appear proper from his refusal without good cause, to answer questions.

This does not prejudice:

[a]   the admissibility in evidence of the silence of the accused in the face of anything **said in his presence** in so far as evidence would in any case be admissible; or
[b]   the drawing of any inference from such silence.

Q   When must a Special Warning be given?

A

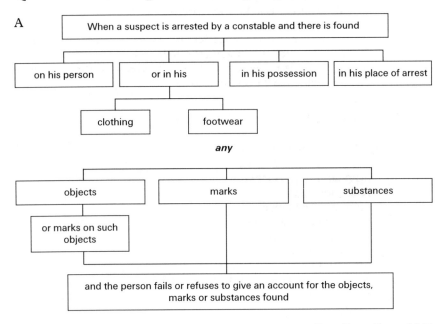

PACE CODE C PARA 10.10

or

an arrested person was **found** by a constable

at the place	at, or about the time

the offence for which he was arrested, or is alleged to have been committed and he fails or refuses to account for his presence at that place

then

for an inference to be drawn from the suspect's failure or refusal to answer a question about one of the matters, or to answer in a satisfactory manner, the investigating officer must tell the suspect in ordinary language:

[a] what offence he is investigating;
[b] what fact he is asking the suspect to account for;
[c] that he believes this fact may be due to his taking part in the crime;
[d] that a court may draw inferences if he fails or refuses to account for the fact which is being questioned; and
[e] that a record is being made of the interview and that it may be given in evidence if brought to trial.

S. 36 - 37 PACE ACT 1984

Q What are the Sources of Evidence?

A Evidence is classified as follows:

[a] original [oral] evidence;
[b] real evidence;
[c] secondary evidence;
[d] documentary evidence;
[e] hearsay evidence;
[f] circumstantial evidence;
[g] presumptions;
[h] evidence of character and convictions;
[i] evidence of opinion;
[j] corroboration; and
[k] judicial notice.

A. **Original or primary [oral] evidence.** Is evidence given to a court from the witness box which is evidence of the first-hand knowledge of the witness about a fact or facts, and which is subject to cross-examination.

B. **Real evidence.** Usually takes the form of a material object, e.g. exhibits. Also evidence about a person's behaviour, appearance or demeanour.

C. **Secondary evidence.** Is evidence which is not the best evidence, e.g. copy of a document.

It may be produced when:

[a] a party fails to produce evidence in court when required to do so;
[b] where a stranger to the case lawfully refuses to produce a document, eg. where he could claim privilege;
[c] where a document has been lost or destroyed;
[d] where the production of the original document is impossible, e.g. painting on a wall;
[e] where a public document is concerned, where its production would be illegal or inconvenient.

D. **Documentary evidence.** E.g. documents, maps, plans, graphs, drawings, photographs, discs, tapes, video tapes and films. They include CCTV video.

Evidence by Certificate of Plan or Drawing. In criminal proceedings, a plan or drawing signed by a constable or person with prescribed qualifications [architect, engineer etc], as a plan or drawing made by him which is drawn to a scale specified shall be evidence of the things shown on the plan or drawing. Before this can be adduced in evidence a copy must be served on the defendant **not less than seven days** before the hearing and the defendant may serve notice **not less than three days** before the hearing that he wishes the witness to attend the trial to give evidence. Otherwise the evidence may be adduced without the witness appearing. (S. 41 Criminal Justice Act 1948).

Admissibility of S. 9 CJ Act 1967 written statements. Written statements shall be admissible as evidence to the same extent as oral evidence if:

[a] signed by the maker;
[b] it contains a declaration that it is true to the best of his knowledge and belief and that he made it knowing that, if it were tendered in evidence, he would be liable to prosecution if he wilfully stated in it anything which he knew to be false or did not believe to be true;

[c] before the hearing copies are served on the other parties; and

[d] none of the other parties **within seven days** from the service, serves a notice requiring attendance of the witness. (Parties may agree to waive this provision before or during the hearing);

[e] if under 18, it shall give his age;

[f] if he cannot read, it shall be read to him before he signs it and contain a declaration by the person who read it to him to that effect;

[g] exhibits shall be served on the other parties;

Service of S. 9 statements. S. 9 Statements may be served:

[a] by delivering it to him or his solicitor;

[b] by addressing it to him and by leaving it at his usual or last known place of abode or place of business or by addressing it to his solicitor and leaving it at his office;

[c] by sending it by registered letter or recorded delivery addressed to him at his usual or last known place of abode, or addressed to his solicitor at his office; or

[d] in the case of a company, addressed to the secretary at their registered office or by registered letter or recorded delivery

Documentary records. A statement made by a person in a document shall be admissible if:

[a] he is dead or by reason of bodily or mental condition is unfit to attend as a witness; or

[b] the person is outside the UK and it is not practicable to secure his attendance; or

[c] that all reasonable steps have been taken to find him without success; or

[d] the statement was made to a police officer or person charged with the duty of investigating offences or charging offenders, and that the person does not give evidence through fear or because he is kept out of the way.

Business documents. A statement in a document shall be admissible in criminal proceedings of any fact of which oral evidence would be admissible if:

[a] the document was created or received by a person in the course of a trade, business, profession or other occupation, or as the holder of a paid or unpaid office, and

[b] the information contained in the document was supplied by a person who had personal knowledge of the matter dealt with, but it will only be admissible if:

[i] the information was supplied directly or indirectly, but if indirectly only if each person through whom it was supplied received it in the course of a trade, business, profession or other occupation or is the holder of a paid or unpaid office, or

[ii] a confession which would be inadmissible is not rendered admissible by virtue of the above.

Computer records. In any proceedings a statement in a document produced by a computer shall not be admissible as evidence unless it is shown:

[a] that there are no reasonable grounds for believing that the statements are inaccurate because of improper use of the computer;

[b] that at all material times the computer was operating properly, or if not that any aspect in which it was not operating properly, or was out of operation, was not such as to affect the production of the documents or accuracy of the contents; and

[c] the relevant conditions in the rules of the court are satisfied.

E. **Hearsay evidence.** The hearsay rule is that any statement, other than one made by a witness while giving evidence, is inadmissible as evidence of the *facts* stated. Any statement made out of court is hearsay. Exceptions to the hearsay rule are:

[a] **statements by the accused.** Are admissible as to their factual contents;

[b] **statements made in the presence and hearing of the accused.** To prove the reaction of the accused. The statements do not prove what the author of the statement has said;

[c] **dying declarations.** Are admissible in trials for murder or manslaughter providing that:

[i] the declarant was in 'hopeless expectation of death';

[ii] the death was the subject of the charge; and

[iii] the circumstances of the death were the subject of the declaration. [e.g. identifying who had killed him].

[d] **statements made by deceased.** Where the deceased was under a duty to make declarations contemporaneously in the course of his business, written or oral, e.g. a statement by a constable to an inspector that he was going to keep an eye on the prisoner who later killed him. Also declarations against one's own pecuniary interest.

[e] **entries in public documents.** Are exempted from the hearsay rule, providing:

[i] the statements and entries have been made by the authorised agents of the public in the course of official duties; and

[ii] the facts recorded are of public interest, or required to be recorded for the benefit of the public.

Res gestae. Is evidence which would ordinarily be hearsay but is so *closely connected with a specific event that it ought to be admitted in evidence under the res gestae rule.*

The trial judge must be satisfied that:

[a] the event was so unusual or startling or dramatic as to dominate the thoughts of the victim; and

[b] that very effect on the thoughts of the victim exclude the possibility of their lying or being mistaken; and

[c] the statement was made at approximately the same time as the event.

e.g. Suppose that A and B are standing drinking at a bar when the door opens. A shouts 'don't shoot Bob' whereupon a shot rings out and A falls to the floor mortally wounded. From B's position he could not see who fired the shot and the assassin has now made off. Whilst B is comforting A who is dying A says, 'I can't believe it, Bob Russell shot me'. Although hearsay, these facts would fit the *res gestae* rule and be admitted as evidence.

F. Circumstantial evidence. Is evidence not of the fact to be proved, but of other facts from which that fact may be proved with more or less certainty.

G. Presumptions. Fall into three categories:

[a] **irrebuttable presumption of law.** E.g. A child under 10 cannot be guilty of an offence.

[b]   **Rebuttable presumption of law.**

> **E.g. presumption of regularity.** Until it is rebutted, it is assumed that officials have been properly appointed, police officers are acting in the execution of their duty, etc.

[c]   **Presumption of facts.** A court *may* presume, in the absence of evidence to the contrary, a fact from the evidence of other facts. Where evidence that a person was alive on a certain date is given to the court, it may be presumed that the person was still alive on a subsequent date.

H.   Character. A defendant shall not be asked any questions concerning any offence other than the offence for which he is charged, unless:

[a]   the proof that he has committed an offence is admissible to show that he is guilty of the offence charged [e.g. disqualified driving];

[b]   he has put his own or the defence character in issue; or

[c]   he has given evidence against any person charged in the same proceedings.

Previous offences as a juvenile. When a person reaches 21 years any offences he was convicted for when under 14 years shall be disregarded.

I.   Opinion. May be given by non-expert and expert witnesses.

Non-expert evidence. May be given in relation to such matters as the time of day, temperature, the value of an item, whether a person was drunk etc;

Expert evidence. Usually arises in relation to such issues as:

> [i]   medical;
> [ii]   science;
> [iii]   determining mental illness;
> [iv]   handwriting samples;
> [v]   facial mapping.

Full disclosure requires any party intending to produce an expert to furnish the other party with written statements of the expert's findings.

J. **Corroboration.** Must be independent testimony which affects the accused by connecting him with the crime. *"In other words, it must be evidence which implicates him, that is, which confirms in some material particular not only the evidence that the crime has been committed, but also that the prisoner committed it. "* per Lord Reid in *R v Baskerville (1916)*.

Corroboration required as a matter of law. For the offences of treason, perjury and speeding (corroboration as to the speed the vehicle was travelling).

Identification evidence. In *R v Turnbull (1976)* it was held that the factors that should be considered in identification evidence include:

[a]   how long did the witness have the accused under observation?
[b]   at what distance;
[c]   in what light;
[d]   was the observation impeded [e.g. passing traffic?];
[e]   had the witness seen the accused before;
[f]   how often;
[g]   if only occasionally, had he any special reason for remembering him;
[h]   how long elapsed between the original observation and subsequent identification;
[j]   was there a material discrepancy between first description and the accused's actual appearance.

K. **Judicial notice.** The courts may take notice of facts that are so well known that they need no further proof, e.g. night follows day, the grass is green, Glasgow is in Scotland.

SIMILAR FACT EVIDENCE

Q Outline the Similar Fact Principle

A Evidence may be admitted if it goes beyond mere evidence of a propensity to commit crime and has a crucial bearing upon the question whether the crime was committed by the defendant. *"If you find an 'accident' which benefits a person and you find that the person has been fortunate to have that accident happen to him a number of times, benefiting each time, you draw a very strong, frequently irresistible inference that the occurrence of so many accidents benefiting him is such a coincidence that it cannot have happened unless it was designed".* per Lord Reading in *R v Smith (1915)*.

Q What were the facts of *R v Smith (1915)*?

A A man was charged with the murder of his wife who was found dead in the bath. There was evidence of two previous marriages where the former wives had been found dead in a bath, along with other similarities including the defendant profiting financially from the death on each occasion.

Q When is Similar Fact Evidence Admissible?

A [a] **Striking similarity.** This is where the court looks for something *striking* about an offence, e.g. a particular *modus operandi* of a burglar, who uses black masking tape to break windows without noise being caused or glass falling to the ground.

[b] **Multiple offence cases.** This was considered in *R v Sims (1946)* where it was observed that the evidence of a number of accusations taken together is much greater than one alone. Where a jury might think one man might be telling an untruth, three or four are hardly likely to tell the same untruth unless they were conspiring together.

[c] **Possession of Objects by the Accused.** Where objects are found belonging to the defendant which provide evidence that is more than coincidence, the objects may be admitted under the rule, e.g. an assault occurred whereby an injury was caused by a green beer bottle bearing a French name, allegedly wielded by the defendant. A search of his home reveals a number of green beer bottles all bearing a French name.

[d] **Association with an event.** This 'association' may not be directly involved with the offence charged but will go to show a background to the offence, e.g. a man whose height is 6 feet 6 inches was seen leaving a number of burgled houses for which there is no real evidence to implicate him, but he is arrested nearby at the scene of another unlawful entry to a house [no offence yet having been committed] on suspicion of burglary.

[e] **Previous sexual conduct and the 'Same Transaction' Rule.** Evidence of sexual behaviour which is not the subject of the charge may also be admissible to show the true nature of the relationship between the defendant and victim. In *DPP v Boardman (1975)* evidence of the accused's *previous* approaches to a boy was admitted. Similar evidence was given by another boy of indecent conduct leading over a period of time to incitement to buggery. Preliminary behaviour is all part of the 'same transaction' and therefore admissible.

Q What is the special evidential rule regarding proof of Handling Stolen Goods?

A Where a person is being proceeded against for handling stolen goods (but for no other offence), if evidence has been given during the proceedings of his having, or having arranged to have, those goods in his possession, or of his undertaking or assisting or arranging their retention, removal, realisation or disposal, then the following evidence is admissable *in order to prove that he knew or believed the goods to be stolen:*

[a] evidence that he had in his possession (or had undertaken or assisted in the retention, removal, realisation or disposal of) stolen goods from any theft taking place not earlier than **12 months before the date of the offence charged; and**

[b] (provided he has been given 7 days notice) evidence that he has within **5 years preceding the date of the offence charged** been convicted of theft or of handling.

S. 27(3) THEFT ACT 1968

EXCLUSION OF ADMISSIBLE EVIDENCE

Q When should Confessions be Excluded in Evidence?

A When they are:

[a] obtained by oppression; or
[b] considered unreliable.

S. 76 PACE ACT 1984

Oppression. In any proceedings where the prosecution proposes to give in evidence a confession made by an accused, if it is represented to the court that it may have been obtained by oppression, the court may exclude the evidence. **Oppression is** *'the exercise of authority or power in a burdensome, harsh or wrongful manner; unjust or cruel treatment...the imposition of unreasonable or unjust burdens'. R v Fulling (1987).*

Unreliable. Means the confession was obtained in consequence of anything said or done which was likely to render it unreliable and the court shall not allow the confession to be given. In *R v Fulling (1987)* it was suggested that *"...questioning which by its nature, duration, or other attendant circumstances (including the fact of custody) excites hopes (such as the hope of release) or fears, or so affects the mind of the subject that his will crumbles and he speaks when otherwise he would have stayed silent".* Courts have held the following confessions to be unreliable:

[a] no caution was given, the suspect was not asked if he wanted his solicitor present and he was not shown the notes of the interview;
[b] flagrant breach of the Codes of Practice;
[c] interviewing a suspect who had just vomited [should have been seen by a doctor];
[d] where the appropriate adult had a low IQ and was unable to assist the detained person;
[e] suggested to a suspect of a sexual assault that it would be better for them to receive treatment than go to prison;
[f] where a person had been kept in custody for 14 hours, had been interviewed four times before confessing and had been refused any visits from his family;
[g] where the officers had a 'warm-up chat' with the suspect before the interview and the 'chat' lasted over two hours;
[h] an offer of bail if the suspect admits the offence or conversely telling the suspect that he will be kept in custody until he admits the offence.

EXCLUSION OF ADMISSIBLE EVIDENCE

Q **What is the effect of Excluding Confessions?**

A While additional evidence obtained after a confession may be admissible, its value may be lost as S. 76 of the PACE Act 1984 prevents the prosecution from linking the discovery of the additional evidence to any confession which has been excluded.

Q **What is the law in relation to the Exclusion of Evidence Generally?**

A In any proceedings the court may refuse to allow evidence on which the prosecution rely to be given if it appears to the court that, having regard to all the circumstances, the admission of the evidence would have such an adverse effect on the fairness of the proceedings that the court ought not to admit it.

S. 78 PACE ACT 1984

Evidence that has been excluded includes:

[a] informing the suspect [wrongly] that his fingerprints had been found at the scene;
[b] undercover operations where the police failed to record conversations in accordance with PACE;
[c] failure by custody officer to inform a detained person of his rights;
[d] interviewing without informing the detained person of his rights;
[e] failing to provide the detained person with adequate meals;
[f] 'off the record' interviews which were not recorded;
[g] failing to make contemporaneous notes of conversations;
[h] failing to get an interpreter or appropriate adult.

DISCLOSURE OF EVIDENCE

Q   Define a Criminal Investigation

A   Is an investigation which police officers or other persons have a duty to conduct with a view to it being ascertained:

[a]   whether a person should be charged with an offence; or
[b]   whether a person charged with an offence is guilty of it.

S. 1(4) CRIMINAL PROCEDURE AND INVESTIGATIONS ACT 1996

Q   To whom do the Disclosure Provisions apply?

A   All not guilty pleas.

Q   What is meant by Primary Disclosure?

A   Relates to the duty of the prosecutor to disclose material which is in his possession or which he has inspected and which in his opinion **might undermine the case** against the accused, i.e. which might be helpful to the defence. Material is material of any kind, including information and objects which are obtained in the course of a criminal investigation and which may be relevant to the investigation.

S. 3 1996 ACT

Q   What is Disclosure by the Defence?

A   This duty only arises **after** the prosecution's primary disclosure and may be:

[a]   compulsory; or
[b]   voluntary.

Compulsory. [This does not apply to cases being tried at magistrates' court.] The statement would outline the defence in general terms. It should include those issues which the accused disputes with the prosecution and any alibi evidence. This must be done **within 14 days of primary disclosure.**

S. 5 1996 Act

Voluntary. This applies to cases being tried at magistrates' court. This happens where:

[a] the defence is not satisfied with the material disclosed at the primary disclosure;
[b] where they wish to examine items listed in the schedule of non-sensitive material; or
[c] they wish to show the strength of their case in order to persuade the prosecution not to proceed.

S. 6 1996 ACT

Q What is meant by Secondary Disclosure by the Prosecutor?

A Once a defence statement has been provided [compulsory or voluntarily], the prosecution must disclose any material which:

[a] has not already been disclosed; and
[b] might be reasonably expected to **assist the accused's defence.**

S. 7 1996 ACT

Q What if the defence is not satisfied about the Level of prosecution disclosure?

A They may apply to the court for an order requiring the prosecution to disclose material which ought reasonably to be disclosed.

S. 8 1996 ACT

Q What is the Continuing Duty of Prosecution to Disclose?

A The prosecution must continue to review the disclosure of material right up until the case is completed. The duty falls in two stages:

[a] after primary disclosure the prosecutor **must** review material not disclosed in terms of whether it might undermine the prosecution case; and
[b] after secondary prosecution disclosure.

S. 9 1996 ACT

Q Outline those with Roles and Responsibilities under the 1996 Act

A **Prosecutor.** Means any person acting as a prosecutor whether an individual or a body.

Officer in charge of the case. Is the police officer responsible for directing a criminal investigation. He is also responsible for ensuring that proper procedures are in place for the recording of information, and retaining records of information and other material at the request of the prosecutor.

Disclosure officer. Is the link between the investigation team and the CPS. He is the person responsible for examining material retained by the police during the investigation; revealing material to the prosecutor during the investigation and any criminal proceedings resulting from it, and certifying that he has done this, and disclosing material to the accused at the request of the prosecutor.

Supervisor. There must be an officer in charge and a disclosure officer. If either can no longer perform his task his supervisor must assign another person to take over his duties.

Q   What are the duties of the disclosure officer in relation to Primary Disclosure?

A   First, to create a schedule of all *non-sensitive material* and secondly a schedule of *sensitive material.* He must then decide what material might undermine the prosecution case. In addition to the schedules and copies of material which undermine the prosecution case he must provide a copy of material **whether or not it undermines the prosecution case.** This is:

[a]   first description of the alleged offender;
[b]   the alleged offender's explanation for the offence;
[c]   material casting doubt on the reliability of a confession; and
[d]   any material casting doubt on the reliability of a witness.

Q   What are the duties of the Disclosure Officer in relation to Secondary Disclosure?

A   After primary disclosure the defence may provide a defence statement setting out their case, together with reasons why they wish to inspect additional items of the schedule which have not been disclosed. Once the defence statement has been provided, the disclosure officer must:

[a]   review the material contained in the schedules; and
[b]   inform the prosecutor of any material which might reasonably be expected **to assist the defence** as disclosed by the defence statement.

Secondary disclosure may then be made to the defence.

Q   What is the Continuing Duty of the Disclosure Officer?

A   His continuing duty is to review material for items that should be disclosed to the defence **as undermining the prosecution.**

Q   What are the duties of Investigators?

A   Investigators are required to pursue all reasonable lines of inquiry, *whether they point towards* or *away* from *the suspect.* All material that is relevant to the case must be recorded and retained.

Q   What is Sensitive Material?

A   Material which is not in the public interest to disclose, e.g.:

[a]   material given in confidence;
[b]   observation posts;
[c]   informants;
[d]   police communications, etc. [many such items would be covered by Public Interest Immunity].

Q   What did The JOHNSON ruling state in relation to Observation Posts?

A   In *R v Johnson (1988)* the following guidance as to the *minimum evidential requirements* was outlined:

[a]   The police officer in charge of the observations (not lower than the rank of **sergeant**) must be able to give evidence that beforehand he visited all OPs to be used to ascertain the attitude of the occupiers of premises, not only as to the use to be made of them, but also as to the possible **disclosure of their use** and other facts which could lead to the identification of the premises and occupiers.

[b]   A police officer (of no lower rank than **chief inspector**) must be able to testify that, immediately before the trial he visited the places used for observations and ascertained whether the occupiers are the same as when the observations took place and what attitude the current occupiers have as to the **possible disclosure** of the use made of the premises and of other facts which could lead to the identification of the premises and occupiers.

Q   What are the Retention Periods for material?

A   Material must be retained until a decision is taken whether to prosecute and then until the case has been dealt with. In the event of a conviction it must be retained at least until:

[a]   the person is released from custody; otherwise
[b]   6 months from the date of conviction.

In the case of an appeal, until:

[a]   the appeal is concluded; or
[b]   the appeal does not go ahead.

CUSTODY OFFICER DUTIES

Q Which prisoners must be taken to a Designated Police Station?

A Persons who are to be detained [or likely to be] for **more than six hours** must be taken to a designated police station, otherwise they may be taken to a non-designated police station.

S. 35 PACE Act 1984

Designated. One that has enough facilities for detaining arrested people. Stations are 'designated' by the Chief Officer.

Q Who shall act as a Custody Officer?

Designated police station
Sergeant - designated custody officer; or, where the custody officer is not available
any officer

Non-designated police station
Any officer who is not involved in the investigation of the offence, if readily available; or
by the arresting officer who took him to the police station; or
any officer
and in all cases
If he is the officer who took him to the station, inform an inspector at a designated police station.

S. 36 PACE Act 1984

Q What is meant by Police Detention?

A A person is in police detention when:

[a] he has been taken to a police station after being arrested for an offence; or

[b] he is arrested at a police station; or

[c]   he has been taken to a police station after being arrested under the Terrorism Act 2000.

and is detained there [or elsewhere] in the charge of a Constable.

S. 118 PACE ACT 1984

Not in detention. A person charged and who is at court is not in police detention. Nor is a person who has been removed to a police station as a place of safety under the Mental Health Act 1983.

Being transferred. Under the Police Reform Act 2002, where persons are being transferred into the custody of investigating officers, or where designated escort officers are taking an arrested person to a police station or transferring a detainee between stations, such persons are deemed to be in police detention.

Q   What is the Right to Have Someone Informed of Arrest?

A   Any person arrested and held in custody may on request have:

[a]   one person known to him; or
[b]   who is likely to take an interest in his welfare, informed at public expense of his whereabouts.

S. 56 PACE ACT 1984

Alternatives. If the requested person cannot be contacted two alternatives may be chosen, thereafter the custody officer or officer in charge of the investigation has discretion to allow further attempts.

Change of police station. The above rights apply to every move to another police station, even if someone was already informed at the former station.

Q   Who can Delay this Right?

A   An inspector or above, but only in relation to serious arrestable offences. The delay can be for a maximum of 36 hours (48 in terrorism cases) calculated from the 'relevant time'.

Q   What about Juveniles?

A   In the case of juveniles the person responsible for their welfare MUST be informed that the juvenile is in detention, but should the juvenile wish any other person to be informed, this right may be delayed in the same circumstances as it may for adults.

Q What other Rights of Communication does a Detainee have?

A   The right to speak to a person on the telephone for a reasonable time, or be supplied [on request] with writing materials for sending letters. Interpreters may do this on the detainee's behalf.

Q When can an Inspector delay this additional Right to Communicate?

A   Where he is detained for an arrestable offence or serious arrestable offence the right can be denied or delayed if an **Inspector** [or above] considers that it would result in:

[a]   **interference with or harm** to evidence connected with a serious arrestable offence or interference with, or physical injury to, other people; or

[b]   will lead to the **alerting of other people** suspected of having committed such an offence but not yet arrested for it; or

[c]   will **hinder the recovery** of property obtained as a result of such an offence.

They may also be delayed where the serious arrestable offence is either:

[a]   **a drug trafficking offence** and the officer has reasonable grounds for believing that the detained person has benefited from it and that the recovery of the value of that person's proceeds will be hindered; or

[b]   an offence covering **confiscation orders** applies and the officer has reasonable grounds for believing that the detained person has benefited from the offence and that the recovery of the value of the property or anything connected with it will be hindered.

S. 56 PACE ACT 1984

Q What is the right to legal advice?

A   A person arrested and held in custody at a police station or other premises has the right to consult privately with a solicitor free of charge if he requests it and must be informed of the right when he first arrives at the police station.

S. 58 PACE ACT 1984

What if he declines? The custody officer shall ask the reasons.

What if he changes his mind? Where a suspect first requires a solicitor then changes his mind the interview may proceed providing he has given his agreement in writing or on tape to being interviewed without legal advice and an **Inspector** or above has inquired into his reasons and given authority to proceed.

Superintendents. May delay access to legal advice in cases of serious arrestable offence, for a maximum of 36 hours (from the 'relevant time'), or until the time the person will first appear at court, whichever is sooner. Authorisation to delay may be made orally at first, but must be recorded in writing as soon as practicable. Note that any such delay will restrict the drawing of adverse inferences from silence.

Terrorism cases. The right may also be delayed under the Terrorism Act 2000, for a maximum of 48 hours from the time of arrest.

Q   What is meant by a Solicitor?

A   This means a solicitor who holds a current practising certificate, a trainee, a duty solicitor representative or an accredited representative.

Q   Who can refuse to admit a Non-accredited or Probationary representative?

A   Both may give advice unless an officer of **Inspector** or above considers that such a visit will hinder the investigation of crime and directs otherwise. If admitted he should be treated as any other legal adviser.

Q   What should the Inspector have regard to in deciding whether to Admit a non-accredited person?

A   [a]   That his identity and status has been established;
    [b]   is he a suitable character to give legal advice [a person with a criminal record is unlikely to be suitable, unless minor and not recent]; and
    [c]   any other matters in a letter of authorisation provided by the solicitor on whose behalf he is acting.

Q   Can a person be interviewed in the Absence of a Solicitor who has been Requested?

A   A **Superintendent** (or above) may authorise an interview to continue without a solicitor being present if he has reasonable grounds for believing that to wait for a solicitor might:

[a]   lead to interference with, or harm to, evidence connected with an offence;

[b]   lead to interference with, or physical harm to, other persons;

[c]   lead to serious loss of, or damage to, property;

[d]   lead to alerting others suspected of having committed an offence but who are not yet arrested for it;

[e]   hinder the recovery of property obtained in consequence of an offence.

An **inspector** (or above) may authorise an interview to continue without a solicitor being present in the following cases:

[a]   the solictor nominated by the detainee cannot be contacted; or

[b]   the nominated solicitor has previously indicated that he/she does not wish to be contacted; or

[c]   the nominated solicitor declines to attend after having been contacted; **and**

[d]   the detainee has been advised of the Duty Solicitor Scheme but has declined to ask for a duty solicitor.

Q   What should not be delayed until a Solicitor arrives?

A   It is not necessary to delay taking breath, blood or urine samples.

Q   Distinguish Relevant Time from Review Time

A

Relevant time	Review time
Calculates the 24 hours that the detainee is permitted to be kept in police custody and runs from the **time of arrival at the police station**	Calculates the times when reviews of detention must be carried out and runs from the **time detention is authorised**
Note: Invariably the relevant time runs before the review time. This has the effect of having two clocks ticking at the same time!	

CUSTODY OFFICER DUTIES

The Relevant time		
Prisoner's status	**Conditions**	**Relevant time begins**
Attends police station voluntarily or accompanies a constable there voluntarily	is arrested at the police station	on arrest
Brought to police station under arrest		on arrival at police station
Arrested outside England and Wales		*the earlier of* time of arrival at the first police station in the police area where the offence is being investigated OR 24 hours **after entry** into England and Wales
Arrested by Force 1 for Force 2	he is not wanted by Force 1 and not questioned about the Force 2 offence	*the earlier of* time of arrival at the police station in the area where he is wanted by Force 2 OR 24 hours **after arrest** by Force 1
Arrested by Force 1 for their offence and is also wanted by Force 2	he is dealt with by Force 1 for their offence and not questioned about the offence in Force 2	*the earlier of* time of arrival at the first police station in the area where he is wanted by Force 2 OR 24 hours **after leaving** the police station where he is detained by Force 1
Hospitals. The relevant time clock stops when he is on his way to, whilst at, and on his way back from hospital so long as he is **not questioned** to obtain evidence of the offence.		

Suppose that Smith is arrested by Thames Valley Police for an offence and he is being dealt with for that offence by Thames Valley. Before release a PNC check reveals he is also wanted for an offence by Devon & Cornwall Constabulary. He is not questioned by Thames Valley about the Devon & Cornwall offence. The relevant time clock for Devon & Cornwall will start at the

earlier time of

| His arrival at the first police station where he is wanted in Devon & Cornwall | 24 hours **after leaving** the police station in Thames Valley |

Q   Who is responsible for conducting Reviews of Detention?

A

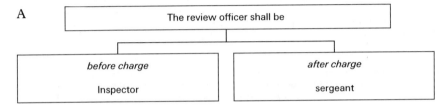

Q   When does the Review Time begin?

A   From the time the custody officer authorises detention.

Q   When shall Review be carried out?

A

Reviews			
1st	not more than	6 hours	from first authorisation
2nd	not more than	9 hours	after the first
3rd	not more than	9 hours	intervals

S. 40 PACE ACT 1984

Note. Terrorism Act 2000 reviews: First, as soon as reasonably practicable after arrest, then at least every 12 hours; after 24 hours it must be conducted by a superintendent (or above).

CUSTODY OFFICER DUTIES

Q   When can a review be Delayed?

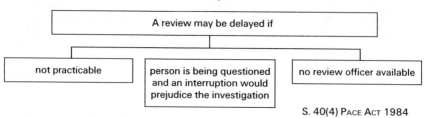

A review may be delayed if

| not practicable | person is being questioned and an interruption would prejudice the investigation | no review officer available |

S. 40(4) Pace Act 1984

Q   Who can make Representations to the review officer?

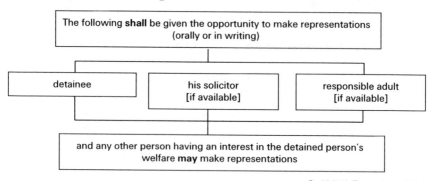

The following **shall** be given the opportunity to make representations (orally or in writing)

| detainee | his solicitor [if available] | responsible adult [if available] |

| and any other person having an interest in the detained person's welfare **may** make representations |

S. 40(12) Pace Act 1984

Q   Can a review be conducted over the Telephone?

A   Where a review is due and the detainee *has not been charged,* the review may be conducted by telephone if:

[a] the use of video conferencing facilities is not applicable, or not reasonably practicable **and**

[b] it is not reasonably practicable for the review officer to attend the station.

Q   What if a review falls at the time when a person is likely to be asleep?

A   Bring the review forward, so the detainee can be present: Code C, note 15C.

Q   When can detention be authorised beyond 24 hours?

A   Detention may be authorised for up to **36 hours** where the offence is a **serious arrestable offence** and a **superintendent** or above responsible for the station is satisfied:

[a]   there is not sufficient evidence to charge; and
[b]   the investigation is being conducted diligently and expeditiously; and
[c]   the person's detention is necessary to secure or preserve evidence relating to the offence or to obtain evidence by questioning him.

S. 42(1) PACE ACT 1984

Q   When can the decision to keep a person in detention for over 24 hours be made?

A   [a]   Within 24 hours of the relevant time; and
[b]   not before the 2nd review.

S. 42(2) PACE ACT 1984

Q   Who is the Review Officer during the 24 - 36 hour period?

A   The superintendent.

Q   What about Terrorism cases?

A   Where a person has been arrested under S.41 Terrorism Act 2000 s/he can be kept in police detention for up to 48 hours without court authorisation.

Q   How long can a Court Authorise Further detention?

A   A total of 96 hours. (Once the 36 hour limit is reached, further detention must be authorised by a court through the issue of a Warrant of Further Detention).

Q Outline the Procedure for applying for a Warrant of Further Detention

A The application is made under oath in court by the police. The detainee must be present. The information must set out:

[a] the nature of the offence;
[b] the general evidence on which the person was arrested;
[c] what inquiries have been made;
[d] what further inquiries are proposed; and
[e] why it is believed that continuing detention is necessary for the enquiries.

S. 43 Pace Act 1984

Q When should the application be made?

A Within 36 hours [may be extended by six hours if there is no court sitting]. An application for a warrant or its extension should be made between 10 am and 9 pm, and if possible during normal court hours.

Q When can a person be Cautioned?

A [a] Where there is evidence of guilt with a realistic prospect of conviction; and
[b] he admits the offence; and
[c] he agrees to be cautioned.

Who administers the caution? A uniformed inspector.

Q Outline the custody officer's duties on Arrival of arrested persons

A [a] Open custody record;
[b] inform him of his rights;
[c] provide a written notice of rights;
[d] ask for signature on custody record of receipt of rights;
[e] undertake a risk assessment of detainee.

Q **What must be noted about the author of Entries in the custody record?**

A All entries must have the person's name and rank except for officers dealing with Terrorism Act 2000 offences.

Q **What other duties are there in relation to Special Groups?**

A [a] If the person is deaf or has difficulty with English, use an interpreter;
[b] if blind or seriously visually impaired, he should have help from his representative;
[c] if a juvenile, obtain an appropriate adult;
[d] if mentally impaired, obtain an appropriate adult.

Q **What must be done when Deciding to authorise detention?**

A [a] The arresting officer gives the reason for arrest;
[b] record any comment made by that person in response to the officer;
[c] decide whether to authorise detention or release with or without bail;
[d] record any comment made by that person.

If detention is authorised inform the detained person unless he is:

[i] violent [or likely to become so];
[ii] incapable of understanding what is being said; or
[iii] in need of urgent medical treatment.

Relevant time. If the person is surrendering to S. 47(3) bail the relevant time began at the time of his first arrest. So that if he spent 22 hours in custody before being bailed to re-appear at the police station, then on surrender to bail there are only two hours left.

CUSTODY OFFICER DUTIES

Q Who can authorise a search at the Police Station?

A   The custody officer. He shall:

[a]   ascertain what property he has on his arrival at the police station;
[b]   ascertain what property he might have for a **harmful or unlawful purpose;**
[c]   decide what property to keep and what to let the detained person keep;
[d]   inform him of the reasons why any property is being retained;
[e]   record all property in the custody record and have him sign the record.

Sex. The search must be carried out by a person of the same sex.

Force. Reasonable force may be used.

Q What Property cannot be seized?

A   Items subject to legal privilege.

Q When does a search become a Strip Search?

A   Where the custody officer authorised removal of more than the outer clothing.

Q When may a strip search take place?

A   Only if the custody officer reasonably believes that the detainee might have concealed an article which might be used to:

[a]   harm himself or others;
[b]   damage property;
[c]   effect an escape; or
[d]   which might be evidence of an offence **and** it is necessary to remove such an article.

Q What is an Intimate Search?

A   A search consisting of the physical examination of a person's body orifices other than the mouth.

Q   When can an Intimate Search take place?

A   Only if authorised by an inspector (or above) who has reasonable grounds for believing:

[a]   that an article which could cause physical injury to the detainee or others has been concealed; or

[b]   the detainee has concealed a Class A drug which he intends to supply to another or to export.

The authorising officer must also believe that an intimate search is the only practicable means of removing the item.

Q   What about Intimate Searches of Juveniles?

A   In the case of juveniles (and mentally vulnerable persons) an appropriate adult should be present during an intimate (or strip) search. The appropriate adult may be of the opposite sex. However, the search may continue without the appropriate adult present where there is a risk of serious harm to the detainee or others, or where the juvenile requests that the appropriate adult should not be present and the appropriate adult agrees.

Q   How often should detainees be Visited in Cells?

A   Every hour and drunks every half hour. Drunks should be roused and spoken to on each visit.

Q   Can Juveniles be placed in Cells?

A   Only if there is no other secure accommodation and the custody officer considers that it is not practicable to supervise him.

Adult/juvenile, same cell? No.

Q   Before Handing Over a detainee, what should the custody officer consider?

A   [a]   Whether he is in need of a rest period;
[b]   whether he is unfit through drink or drugs; and
[c]   whether the right of access to legal advice is being complied with.

Q   What is meant by Rest Period?

A   In any 24 hours he shall have at least **eight hours for rest,** free from questioning, travel or any interruption by police officers in connection with the investigation. His rest may not be interrupted unless there are reasonable grounds for believing that it would:

[a]   involve a risk or harm to people or serious loss of, or damage to property;
[b]   delay unnecessarily the person's release from custody; or
[c]   otherwise prejudice the outcome of the investigation.

CODE C 12.2

Q   When must an Appropriate Adult be informed?

A   In cases where the detained person is:

[a]   a juvenile [under 17];
[b]   mentally handicapped; or
[c]   appears to be suffering from a mental disorder.

Juveniles held incommunicado. Must have an appropriate adult.

Q   What is meant by an Appropriate Adult?

A   **In the case of a juvenile:**

[a]   parent or guardian;
[b]   social worker; or
[c]   failing above, an adult [aged 18 or over].

In the case of the mentally ill:

[a]   a relative, guardian or person responsible for his car;
[b]   a person experienced with the mentally ill;
[c]   failing above, an adult [aged 18 or over].

What about police employees? A police officer or police employee cannot act as an appropriate adult.

Q   Who should Not Act as an appropriate adult?

A   Any person who is suspected of involvement in the offence, is a victim, witness or a **person receiving admissions** prior to attending as an appropriate adult. If a juvenile is estranged from a parent and expressly objects to the parent's presence.

Q **When should an Interpreter be used?**

A Whenever a detainee is unable to speak or understand English effectively.

IDENTIFICATION

Q   Outline identification methods where the Suspect is Known

A

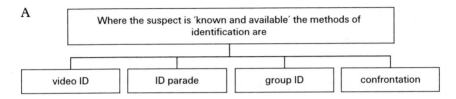

Priority. The revised Code D indicates that a suspect should initially be offered a video ID unless video ID is not practicable or an ID parade is both practicable and more suitable. A group ID may initially be offered if the officer in charge considers it is more suitable than either video or ID parade.

Who is the identification officer? A uniformed inspector.

Known and available. Means available for arrest *(R v Kitchen (1994))*. Do not go to photograph ID if the suspect is known and available.

Q   Who may Not take part in the procedures?

A   Officers involved in the investigation of the offence.

Q   What if the suspect refuses the method offered?

A   The suspect must be asked to state their reasons for refusal and may seek advice from their solicitor and/or appropriate adult. Any of these persons may then make representations about why another method is preferred. This should be recorded. If the officer considers an alternative is suitable and practicable that should be offered. If s/he does not consider an alternative is suitable the reasons must be recorded.

IDENTIFICATION

Q What is meant by First Description?

A The first description provided of a person suspected of a crime must be recorded. It must be disclosed to the defence in the pre-trial procedure in all cases and, in particular, before any identification procedures take place.

Media publicity. Before any procedures take place, witnesses must be asked if they have seen any material previously released to the media.

Q When can Fingerprints be taken Without Consent?

A

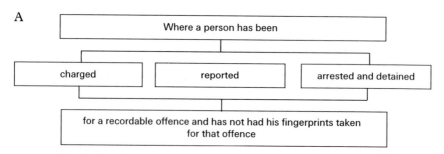

S. 61 PACE ACT 1984

Q When can Fingerprints be taken Following Conviction?

A

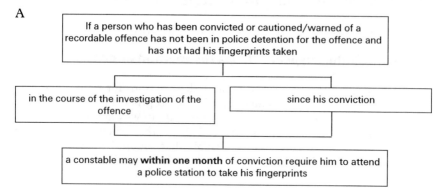

Notice. He must be given **seven days' notice** of the requirement and it may direct that he attends at a specific time of day or between specific times.

Arrest. In the event of failure to comply a constable may arrest.

S. 27 PACE ACT 1984

Why this power? This power fits the position where a person is reported for an offence, e.g. shoplifting, and is not taken to the police station resulting in fingerprints not being taken, but subsequently is convicted for the offence.

Q Define an Intimate Sample

A Intimate sample means:

[a] blood;
[b] semen;
[c] tissue fluid;
[d] urine; or
[e] pubic hair; and
[f] a dental impression;
[g] a swab from a body orifice other than the mouth.

S. 65(2) PACE ACT 1984

Q Define a Non-intimate Sample

A Non-intimate samples include:

[a] hair [not pubic];
[b] nails [from a nail or under a nail];
[c] swabs from any part of the body including the mouth [but not any other orifice];
[d] footprints and other impressions of the body [but not his hand]; and
[e] saliva.

Q Can an intimate sample be taken Without Consent?

A No.

Q **Whose consent is required?**

A **Both** the suspect and an Inspector (or above). The taking of such a sample without consent is a serious matter and may give rise to both criminal (assault) and civil liability. It may also amount to a breach of Art.3 ECHR (inhuman or degrading treatment).

Q **Whose consent is required in the case of Juveniles?**

under 14	14 but under 17
parents or guardian only	**both** the juvenile and the parents or guardian
and the inspector	

Q **What happens where a sample proves 'Insufficient for Analysis'?**

A Retake them [again with both consents].

Q **When can an Inspector Authorise the taking of Intimate Samples?**

A
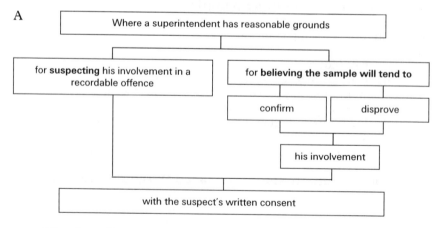

Warning. 'You do not have to provide a sample but if you refuse without good cause your refusal may harm your case if it comes to trial.'

S. 62 PACE ACT 1984

Q   What information has to be Recorded?

A   The inspector's authority may be given orally but if so must be confirmed in writing as soon as practicable. The suspect's authority must be in writing. Also the following:

[a]   the authorisation;
[b]   the grounds;
[c]   the suspect consented;
[d]   at a police station the suspect was informed the sample would be subject to a speculative search; and
[e]   the warning had been given.

Q   Outline the power to take Non-intimate Samples

A

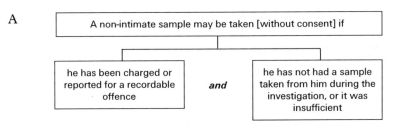

Non-attendance at police station. Where a person is convicted not having attended a police station, e.g. reported, samples may be taken identical to the subsequent taking of fingerprints following conviction.

Q   Can Samples be Retained?

A   Yes, but they can only be used for purposes related to the prevention or detection of crime, the investigation of any offence or the conduct of a prosecution. Where a person has provided a sample voluntarily (eg. for elimination purposes) he must consent to its retention. If he does not, it must be destroyed and information derived from it cannot be used as evidence against him for any offence or for the investigation of any offence.

IDENTIFICATION

Q   When can Photographs be taken of an arrested person?

A   Photographs can be taken if:

[a]   he is arrested at the same time as other people, or at a time when it is likely that other people will be arrested and a photograph is necessary to establish the who, when and where; or

[b]   he has been charged or reported for a recordable offence; or

[c]   he is convicted and his photograph is not on record as a result of [a] or [b]; or

[d]   a superintendent authorises it, having reasonable grounds for suspecting his involvement in a criminal offence and where there is identificational evidence.

Arrest. No power to arrest to take photographs but they may be taken during a fingerprint recall.

Can force be used to take photographs? No.

INTERVIEWS

Q Define an Interview

A An interview is the questioning of a person regarding his involvement or suspected involvement in a criminal offence.

Questions of identification. Do not amount to an interview, e.g. to establish his identity or ownership of a vehicle etc.

Q When should a person be Cautioned?

A A caution should be administered to all people who are:

[a] arrested for an offence;
[b] whom there are grounds to suspect of an offence,

before any questions about it are put to them if their answers or silence may be given in evidence.

CODE C

The caution. 'You do not have to say anything but it may harm your defence if you do not mention, when questioned, something which you later rely on in court. Anything you say may be given in evidence'.

CODE C PARA 10.5

Q What questions may be asked without caution?

A Where the questions are

[a] solely to establish identity or ownership of any vehicle;
[b] to obtain information in accordance with any statutory requirement (e.g. under the Road Traffic Act 1988);
[c] in furtherance of the proper and effective conduct of a search (e.g. to determine the need to search in the exercise of stop and search powers);
[d] to seek verification of a written record; or
[e] in certain Terrorism Act matters.

Q What should be told to a person Cautioned, but not under Arrest?

A That he is not under arrest and is not obliged to remain with the officer.

Q **When can an arrested person be Interviewed NOT at a Police Station?**

A If the delay in taking him to a police station would be likely to:

[a] lead to interference with or **harm** to **evidence** connected with an offence or interference with or physical harm to other **people or serious loss/damage to property;** or

[b] lead to the **alerting of others** suspected of having committed an offence but not yet arrested; or

[c] **hinder the recovery of property** obtained in consequence of the offence.

CODE C PARA 11.1

When must it cease? When the relevant risk has been averted.

Q **When can a person be interviewed AFTER charge?**

A If it is necessary to:

[a] prevent or minimise harm or loss to some other person or the public; or

[b] clear up an ambiguity in a previous answer or statement; or

[c] in the interest of justice to allow him to comment on information that has come to light since he was charged or reported.

Q **When MUST an interview be Taped?**

A [a] Where a person has been cautioned for an indictable offence;

[b] when further questions, after charge, are put in relation to [a] above;

[c] when bringing to the notice of a person at [a] the contents of:

[i] an interview; or

[ii] a statement made by another person.

CODE E

Q   When can a custody officer authorise an interview NOT to be Taped?

A

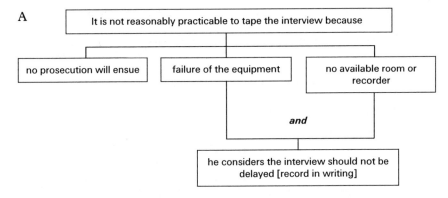

Q   Outline the position of Solicitors and Legal Advice

A   [a]   A suspect must not be dissuaded from obtaining legal advice;
  [b]   if a request for legal advice is made during interview, the interview shall stop and legal advice be sought;
  [c]   if a solicitor arrives at a police station to see a suspect, the suspect must be asked if he wants to see the solicitor, regardless of what legal advice has already been received. The custody officer must be informed and the attendance and suspect's decision recorded.

CODE C PARA 6.15

Excluding a solicitor. If the investigating officer considers that a solicitor is acting in a way that he is unable properly to put questions to the suspect he will stop the interview and consult a **superintendent,** and if not available, an **inspector** who will decide whether or not to exclude the solicitor from the interview.

CODE C PARA 6.10

Unacceptable conduct by solicitor. Includes answering questions on his client's behalf and providing written replies for him to quote.

Q   When should questioning Cease?

A   If it is considered that:

[a]   there is enough evidence to prosecute; and
[b]   there is enough evidence for a prosecution to succeed; and
[c]   that the person **has said all he wishes** about the offence.

Q   When is an Interpreter required?

A   An interpreter is required when:

[a]   the suspect has difficulty in understanding English;
[b]   the interviewer cannot speak the interviewee's language;
[c]   the suspect wishes an interpreter to be present; and
[d]   the suspect appears to have a hearing/speaking difficulty, unless he agrees **in writing** to proceed without an interpreter.

CODE C PARA 13.2

Q   When are Special Warnings required?

A   They are required in relation to questions put to suspects about:

[a]   objects, marks or substances found on them; or
[b]   in or on their clothing or footwear, or
[c]   in their possession; or
[d]   in the place where they were arrested,
and in relation to why
[e]   they were at the scene at or near the time of their arrest; and
[f]   their failure to account for their presence.

CODE C PARA 10.10

Q   What is the procedure when a person makes a statement in a Foreign Language?

A   [a]   The interpreter shall take the statement in the foreign language,
[b]   the person making it shall sign it; and
[c]   a translation shall then be made.

CODE C PARA 13.4

QUICK CHECKLIST

OFFENCES REQUIRING CONSENT FOR PROSECUTION

ATTORNEY-GENERAL (OR SOLICITOR-GENERAL)

1) **Homicide** where victim dies more than 3 years after injury or where D has already been convicted of an offence connected with the death (Law Reform (Year and a Day Rule) Act 1996 S. 22)

2) **Torture** (Criminal Justice Act 1988 S. 134)

3) **Hostage Taking** (Taking of Hostages Act 1982 S. 1)

4) **Conspiracy to Commit Offences Outside the UK** (Criminal Law Act 1977 S. 1A and Criminal Justice (Terrorism and Conspiracy) Act 1998)

5) **Offences under the Explosive Substances Act 1883**

6) **Offences of Racial Hatred** (Public Order Act 1986)

7) **Wearing Political Uniform in Public Places** (Public Order Act 1936 SS. 1 & 2)

8) **Corruption** (Public Bodies Corrupt Practices Act 1889 S. 1)

9) **Corruption of Agents** (Prevention of Corruption Act 1906 S. 1)

10) **Harmful Publications** (Children and Young Persons (Harmful Publications) Act 1955)

DPP

1) **War Crimes** (War Crimes Act 1991)

2) **Aiding and Abetting Suicide** (Suicide Act 1961 S. 2)

3) **Riot** (Public Order Act 1986 S. 7)

4) **Theft or Criminal Damage** where the property in question belongs to D's spouse (Theft Act 1968 S. 30(4))

5) **Concealing Arrestable Offences, Assisting Offenders, Wasting Police Time** (Criminal Law Act 1967 SS. 4(4) and 5(3))

6) **Homosexual Offences** where either party was under 16 (Sexual Offences Acts 1956 and 1967)

7) **Sexual Intercourse with Patients** (Mental Health Act 1959 S. 128)

8) **Incest** (Sexual Offences Act 1956 SS. 10 and 11)

9) **Child Abduction** (Person Connected with Child) and **kidnapping** where victim is under 16 or parent/guardian offender (Child Abduction Act 1984 SS. 4(2) and 5)

10) **Indecent Photographs** (Protection of Children Act 1978)

11) **Unlawful Interception of Public and Private Communications** (Regulation of Investigatory Powers Act 2000 SS. 1(1) and 1(2))

12) **Data Protection Offences** unless prosecuted by Information Commissioner (Data Protection Act 1998)

NOTES

NOTES

NOTES

NOTES